The Chinese Grammar Wiki

BOOK:

Elementary (A1-A2)

The Chinese Grammar Wiki BOOK:

Elementary (A1-A2)

Editor-in-Chief John Pasden

Foreword by Dr. David Moser

SHANGHAI

Published by AllSet Learning, Shanghai, China.

For information about educational or bulk purchases, please contact AllSet Learning at sales@allsetlearning.com.

1st print edition, 2017.

ISBN: 978-1-941875-26-1

For anyone who ever tried
to learn Chinese and thought,
“there has to be an easier way.”

Table of Contents

Foreword

Learning Chinese used to be a frustratingly "front-loaded" endeavor. One had to first learn Pinyin, the four tones, how to write thousands of characters with the correct stroke order, how to use the 214 radicals to look up unfamiliar characters in a dictionary, and, of course, how to limn the mysterious principles of Chinese grammar. This process entailed inordinate sacrifices of eyesight, friends, and years of precious life spent "learning to learn Chinese," before the hapless student could be weaned from a diet of pre-digested pabulum and delve into the messy, glorious world of real texts.

The Chinese Grammar Wiki is on the cutting edge of a growing arsenal of digital and Web resources that have made this front-loaded Sisyphean nightmare a thing of the past. This very cool tool, developed by John Pasden and the folks at AllSet Learning, is in accordance with the new "learning grammar as you go" principle of Chinese study in the digital age. Learners can now boldly embark on the ocean of Chinese very early on, with navigational tools like the Grammar Wiki to reduce the risk of getting lost at sea. For the intrepid, motivated learner, studying Chinese can now be an adventure, instead of a five-year stint in solitary confinement. And from the very outset, students can begin to move toward the goal that was formerly so elusive: the acquisition of 语感 (yǔgǎn), the "feeling for the language."

In my opinion, the Chinese Grammar Wiki has at least three very strong characteristics:

Modularity. This is a long-standing commonsense feature of website design, but it's absolutely crucial for a grammar tool like this. The Wiki has conveniently carved up Chinese grammar into useful modular chunks with the beginner in mind, so that searching for a structure or topic is intuitive, quick, and yields a clear explanation that enables the user to forge ahead, enlightened and empowered. The structure and site map is user-friendly at every level, which means that the Wiki can be easily "plugged in" to existing Chinese syllabi, or simply employed by the student independently to explore texts and materials outside of class.

Interlinking. The Wiki is structured so that alongside the grammar points on most pages there are helpful links to related or similar grammar points within the Wiki. For example, in exploring the grammatical points for 比 (bǐ) involving comparison, you will find explanations of the basic 比 (bǐ) structure, examples, and common errors, but in addition you will also see links to other "comparison" structures using 没有 (méiyǒu). This interlinking feature gives the user a fuller picture of various grammatical structures that serve similar functions in the language.

Universality. One of the strongest points of the Chinese Grammar Wiki is that the grammatical explanations have been tailored so as to contain the right amount of information, at the right level of specificity and complexity for the majority of learners. Designing a grammar resource with such wide applicability is not an easy task, requiring not only technical know-how and careful thinking, but also a strong intuitive sense of what the average student needs to know. Linguist Edward Sapir said "all grammars leak," and this mutable, watery quality of language means that no grammatical framework is going to contain only tidy, airtight rules that cover every situation. In explanations, there is always a tradeoff between succinct simplicity and the real-life complexity, and the wiki does an admirable job of striking a satisfying balance between these two yin-yang poles.

Being digital in nature, the Chinese Grammar Wiki is very much a work in progress, and the designers always welcome input and suggestions. Product development is always an interactive process, and the more people use the resource, the more useful it will become. I encourage Chinese students at all levels – and even Chinese teachers – to check it out and discover what the reference tools of the 21st century will look like.

No matter what well-meaning pedagogical Pollyannas might tell you, Chinese is still "damn hard." Thankfully, there now are digital resources like the Chinese Grammar Wiki, which goes a long way to making the struggle easier.

David Moser
Academic Director, CET Beijing Chinese Studies
Beijing Capital Normal University

Introduction

The **Chinese Grammar Wiki** began life as an Excel spreadsheet full of grammar points organized by difficulty level. This list was needed to track the progress of AllSet Learning's clients and to design personalized grammar practice where it was most needed. But as the lists continued to grow and evolve, it quickly became apparent that it made sense to put the grammar points online, so that the newest version would always be front and center. For ease of editing, what could be better than a wiki? And if AllSet Learning teachers were to have access, why not open up access to *all learners*? The Chinese Grammar Wiki was developed internally for about a year before becoming public in January of 2012. Since then, it has grown tremendously, both in content and in traffic.

Probably the most important feature of the Chinese Grammar Wiki, which has always been kept at the forefront of its development, is its focus on learner level. An absolute beginner can't absorb a multitude of uses for every grammar point she encounters, and she shouldn't be expected to. And she certainly shouldn't be given frustratingly difficult example sentences when trying to grasp the most basic grammar concepts. That's why example sentences on the Chinese Grammar Wiki are plentiful, but relentlessly edited to be level-appropriate. And for the learners that can't get enough, relevant articles of all levels are always just a link away. Although the wiki aims to be 100% comprehensive, it's no coincidence that there are fewer A1 grammar points than A2 grammar points, and fewer A2 grammar points than B1 grammar points. Considerable thought and care has gone into curating and pruning the lists of grammar points.

The Chinese Grammar Wiki is not a Chinese course. Rather, it is a companion resource that can complement any Chinese class. Don't expect to read it from start to finish, or to go through the grammar point lists from top to bottom. But do expect to come back often. And expect to get sucked into the curiously logical world of Chinese grammar.

John Pasden
Editor-in-Chief and CEO
AllSet Learning, Shanghai, China

Beginner Guide to Chinese Grammar

As a beginner, Chinese grammar can be challenging to understand. In this quick overview, we will provide you with some basic information on Chinese grammar as well as some good starting points.

Background

English is classified as an Indo-European language. This language family includes a lot of languages spoken in the western world, including the romance languages (such as Spanish, French, and Portuguese) as well as the Slavic languages (such as Russian, Czech, and Polish), and many others. All of these languages have common grammatical features which include conjugating verbs for different tenses, following specific rules about subject-verb agreement, and adding endings to words to make them plural.

Chinese is not part of the Indo-European family at all. Instead, it is classified as a Sino-Tibetan language, and, unsurprisingly, its grammar is quite different from the grammar of those European languages you may have encountered before. Still, Chinese grammar may surprise you with its pleasing simplicity and consistent logical structure.

As a language, Chinese (quote famously) does not have an alphabet. Instead, characters known as "*hanzi*" (汉字) are used to express the different sounds of the language. These characters can also be written using the roman letters in a system called "pinyin." All beginners should learn pinyin first. Pinyin is provided for all Chinese characters that appear in A1 and A2 grammar points.

The Basics

There are a number of misconceptions about Chinese grammar, the most egregious being that "Chinese has no grammar." If Mandarin Chinese truly had *no grammar*, you could make no grammar mistakes, and no learners would ever struggle with it. We will start this overview by looking at some specific areas of Chinese grammar that can sometimes trip up beginners.

Word Order

For many simple cases, the basic sentence structure[1] of Chinese is the same in Chinese as it is in English. Both languages use a subject-verb[1] or subject-verb-object[1] (SVO) formula for making simple sentences. This familiar pattern means that you shouldn't have much trouble with word order at first.

1. Basic sentence order (A1), page 88

Subject-Verb Examples:

Subject	Verb	Translation
你 Nǐ	吃。 chī.	You eat.
他 Tā	笑。 xiào.	He laughs.
我 Wǒ	去。 qù.	I go.

Subject-Verb-Object Examples:

Subject	Verb	Object	Translation
我 Wǒ	吃 chī.	肉。 ròu.	I eat meat.
你 Nǐ	喝 hē	水。 shuǐ.	You drink water.
他 Tā	说 shuō	中文。 Zhōngwén.	He speaks Chinese.

More examples can be found on our basic word order[1] page.

As sentences get more complex, you'll note that Chinese word order does, in fact, diverge significantly from English word order, even for some relatively simple sentences. For help with those, check out our articles on time words[2], locations of actions[3], using simple adverbs correctly[4], and making simple noun-adjective sentences[5].

Questions

Simple sentences can be turned into yes/no questions by adding 吗 (ma)[6] to the end of simple statements. For each of the following, you could make a simple statement by dropping 吗 (ma).

1. Basic sentence order (A1), page 88
2. Time words and word order (A2), page 211
3. Indicating location with "zai" before verbs (A2), page 288
4. The "also" adverb "ye" (A1), page 17
5. Simple "noun + adjective" sentences (A1), page 96
6. Tag questions with "ma" (A1), page 118

- 他是老师吗？ *question*
  Tā shì lǎoshī ma?
  Is he a teacher?
- 你喜欢咖啡吗？ *question*
  Nǐ xǐhuan kāfēi ma?
  Do you like coffee?
- 他是机器人吗？ *question*
  Tā shì jīqìrén ma?
  Is he a robot?

Another important question particle for beginners to understand is 呢 (ne)[1]. 呢 (Ne) is simply added after a topic to turn it into a "what about...?" question. This is useful in conversations to say things like "what about you?" or "what about my money?" This particle is simply tagged onto a subject to form the question.

- 我吃饭了。你呢？
  Wǒ chīfàn le. Nǐ ne?
  I've eaten. What about you?
- 北京下雨了。上海呢？
  Běijīng xià yǔ le. Shànghǎi ne?
  It's raining in Beijing. How about Shanghai?
- 你说他们可以去。我们呢？
  Nǐ shuō tāmen kěyǐ qù. Wǒmen ne?
  You said they can go. What about us?

There are of course other ways to form questions[2]. In English, we use question words, commonly referred to as the "5 W's and 1 H" (what, where, who, when, why, how), to make questions. These question words[2] also exist in Chinese, but their placement within a sentence in Chinese is different from English. The structure of a question in Chinese follows the same structure as a normal statement.

For example, in English the structure of the question "Who are you?" puts the question word "who" at the beginning of the sentence. If the person answering this question says, "I am Li Li" we can see that the answer to the question comes at the end of the sentence. In Chinese, the structure of the question to learn someone's name is "You are who?" So the question follows the same structure as the answer (subject-verb-object). This works for all kinds of other

1. Questions with "ne" (A1), page 49
2. Placement of question words (A1), page 105

questions too. For example, in Chinese, to ask "What is it?" you literally say, "It is what?"

- 什么

  shénme

  what

- 哪里 / 哪儿

  nǎlǐ / nǎr

  where

- 谁

  shéi

  who

- 什么时候

  shénme shíhou

  when

- 为什么

  wèishénme

  why

- 怎么

  zěnme

  how

Possession

Possession can be shown using the particle 的 (de)[1]. This character functions the same way as an apostrophe-"s" does in English and is added after the "owner," before the "thing owned." One interesting result of this extremely versatile system is that you don't need separate words for "my" or "your" or "his"; you just follow the words for "I" or "you" or "he" with a 的 (de).

- 小李 的 手机

  Xiǎo Lǐ de shǒujī

  Xiao Li's cell phone

- 我 的 手机

  Wǒ de shǒujī

  My cell phone

---

1. Expressing possession with "de" (A1), page 47

- 公司 的 老板
  gōngsī de lǎobǎn
  the company's boss
- 他 的 小狗
  Tā de xiǎogǒu
  His puppy

Possession can also be expressed with 有 (yǒu)[1], the Chinese verb meaning "to have." Just like we can say in English "I have the tickets" or "she has the camera," 有 (yǒu) can indicate this type of possession.

- 我 有 钱。
  Wǒ yǒu qián.
  I have money.
- 他 有 两个女儿。
  Tā yǒu liǎng gè nǚér.
  He has two daughters.
- 你 有 工作吗?
  Nǐ yǒu gōngzuò ma?
  Do you have a job?

Negation

The same basic word order holds true when using the negative. Simply put the word 不 (bù)[2] before verbs[2] and adjectives[2]. This functions much like the word "not" in English.

- 她 不 喝 酒。
  Tā bù hē jiǔ.
  She doesn't drink alcohol.
- 我 不 想工作 。
  Wǒ bù xiǎng gōngzuò .
  I don't want to work.
- 很多人 不 喜欢 热狗。
  Hěn duō rén bù xǐhuan règǒu.
  Many people don't like hot dogs.

---

1. Expressing possession with "you" (A1), page 58
2. Standard negation with "bu" (A1), page 85

When talking about what you do not "have," you use the particle 没 (méi)[1] instead of 不 (bu). It is placed right before the verb 有 (yǒu)[2] to form the "do not have" phrase 没有 (méiyǒu)[1]. This allows you to say sentences like "Walter doesn't have a car" or "Voltron doesn't have the books."

- 我 没 有手机。

  Wǒ méi yǒu shǒujī.

  I don't have a cell phone.

- 我们 没 有房子。

  Wǒmen méi yǒu fángzi.

  We don't have a house.

- 我们公司 没 有电脑。

  Wǒmen gōngsī méi yǒu diànnǎo.

  Our company doesn't have computers.

Aspect

As we mentioned already, there is a silly notion floating around that Chinese has no grammar. While this belief is false, it probably stems from the fact Chinese has no formal tenses to express events that took place in either the past or the future. Instead of tense, the language makes use of time words[3] and puts more emphasis on aspect. You don't need to worry about this in the beginning; just remember to use time words to make clear when something happened, and the aspect thing will come with time. (Hint: aspect involves the particle 了 (le), which you'll be spending more time with later.)

Parts of Speech

All words can be classified into parts of speech to define what roles the words play in sentences. Here, we will briefly recap how these different parts of speech work in English, and explain how the same rules apply to Chinese grammar.

Nouns are commonly referred to as "person, place, or thing" words. As you start learning more Chinese vocabulary, many of the words you will learn will be nouns. These will make up the subjects and the objects of the sentences you study.

Verbs are words that describe actions (sometimes mental or abstract rather than physical). Chinese does not conjugate verbs. Chinese verbs stay the same, regardless of when the action takes place or who performs it.

Here are some good verbs for beginners to start learning:

---

1. Negation of "you" with "mei" (A1), page 12
2. Expressing possession with "you" (A1), page 58
3. Time words and word order (A2), page 211

- 是 (shì) - verb for "to be"[1]
- 在 (zài) - verb for "to be located"[2]
- 有 (yǒu) - verb for "there is / there are"[3]
- 叫 (jiào) - verb for "to be called"[4]
- 去 (qù) - verb for "to go"[5]

Adverbs are words that modify verbs and adjectives. In Chinese, the adverb *always* goes *before* the verb or adjective. Instead of saying "I run also," proper grammar in Chinese would be "I also run." It's very consistent in Chinese.

Here are some good adverbs for beginners to start learning:

- 都 (dōu) - adverb for "all"[6]
- 也 (yě) - adverb for "also"[7]
- 太 (tài) - adverb for "too," as in "excessively"[8]

Adjectives are words that describe nouns. Chinese has some unique rules about how adjectives interact with different nouns and verbs.

Here are some good adjective rules for beginners to start learning:

- Simple sentences with adjectives[9]
- 是 (shì) - the verb for "to be"[1]

Conjunctions are words that join two thoughts together in a sentence. The three most common ones in English are "and," "but," and "or." As you learn more about these conjunctions in Chinese, you will discover that they're each a little different from their English equivalents.

---

1. Connecting nouns with "shi" (A1), page 91
2. Expressing existence in a place with "zai" (A1), page 54
3. Expressing existence with "you" (A1), page 56
4. Using the verb "jiao" (A1), page 60
5. Using the verb "qu" (A1), page 62
6. The "all" adverb "dou" (A1), page 15
7. The "also" adverb "ye" (A1), page 17
8. Expressing "excessively" with "tai" (A1), page 94
9. Simple "noun + adjective" sentences (A1), page 96

Here are some good conjunctions for beginners to start learning:

- 和 (hé) - conjunction for "and"[1]
- 还是 (háishì) - conjunction for "or"[2]

Articles are kind of a confusing concept in English, but the main English articles are "a," "an," and "the." We use them when saying things like "I have a laptop" or "open the door." In Chinese, articles *don't exist*. There is no word for "a" or "the" in Chinese.

Numbers are the words we use to express specific quantities. We use numbers to express value, time, and other important functions in our lives. They can be used for all of these same functions in Chinese.

Here are some good number structures for beginners to start learning.

- Structure of numbers[3]
- Structure of times[4]
- Structure of days of the week[5]
- Structure of dates[6]

Measure words are words that pair up with numbers and help describe the nouns that are being counted (or "measured"). We don't have such a pervasive, complete system for this in English, but we do something similar when we say, "5 pieces of pizza" or "3 sheets of paper."

Here is the only measure word beginners need to start learning the concept:

- Measure word 个 (gè)[7]

Ready for more?

Of course all of this is just the beginning. There are many more interesting grammar patterns that can help you correctly express lots of different things in Chinese. Take a look at the A1 grammar points for more beginner-friendly grammar help. Just keep in mind that these grammar points are not sequential. Start with what you need help with most, and branch out from there.

1. Expressing "and" with "he" (A1), page 22
2. Offering choices with "haishi" (A1), page 24
3. Structure of numbers (A1), page 36
4. Structure of times (basic) (A1), page 42
5. Structure of days of the week (A1), page 33
6. Structure of dates (A1), page 31
7. Measure word "ge" (A1), page 28

Negation of "you" with "mei" (A1)

The verb 有 (yǒu) is negated differently from ordinary verbs. Rather than placing 不 (bù) before it as with other verbs, you must use 没 (méi) to negate the verb 有 (yǒu).

Structure

Nearly all verbs can be negated with 不 (bù)[1]. The verb 有 (yǒu) is an important exception to this rule, and must be negated with 没 (méi).

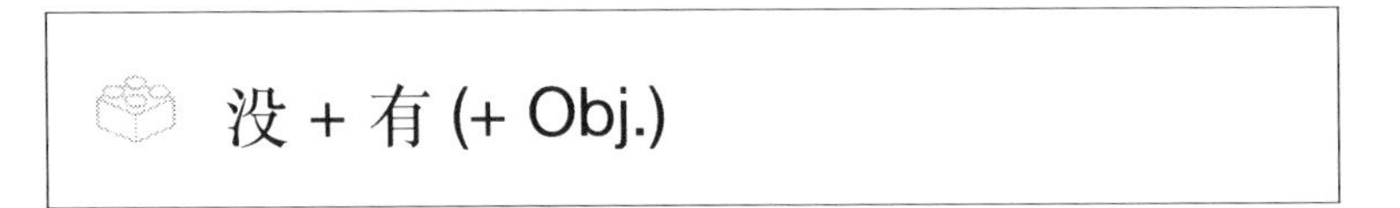

Note: because of the special relationship between 没 (méi) and 有 (yǒu), the pinyin for 没有 is normally written without a space: "méiyǒu."

Examples

- 我 没有 问题。
  Wǒ méiyǒu wèntí.
  I don't have any questions.
- 我们现在 没有 钱。
  Wǒmen xiànzài méiyǒu qián.
  We don't have money now.
- 他 没有 工作吗？
  Tā méiyǒu gōngzuò ma?
  Does he not have a job?
- 他们 没有 爸爸妈妈。
  Tāmen méiyǒu bàba māma.
  They don't have parents.
- 我们在北京 没有 房子。
  Wǒmen zài Běijīng méiyǒu fángzi.
  We don't have a house in Beijing.

---

1. Standard negation with "bu" (A1), page 85

- 你爸爸 没有 手机吗？
  Nǐ bàba méiyǒu shǒujī ma?
  Does your dad not have a cell phone?
- 你们在上海 没有 朋友吗？
  Nǐmen zài Shànghǎi méiyǒu péngyou ma?
  Do you not have friends in Shanghai?
- 我的老师现在 没有 男朋友。
  Wǒ de lǎoshī xiànzài méiyǒu nánpéngyou.
  My teacher doesn't have a boyfriend now.
- 他们都 没有 电脑吗？
  Tāmen dōu méiyǒu diànnǎo ma?
  Do they all not have computers?
- 这个周末你们都 没有 时间吗？
  Zhège zhōumò nǐmen dōu méiyǒu shíjiān ma?
  Do you all not have time this weekend?

Remember that trying to negate 有 (yǒu) with 不 (bù) is a classic mistake that many people make in the early stages of studying Chinese:

✘ 我 不 有 车。
Wǒ bù yǒu chē.

Never use 不 with 有!

✔ 我 没 有 车。
Wǒ méi yǒu chē.
I don't have a car.

Always use 没 with 有.

Never use 不 (bù) with 有 (yǒu).

The Short Form of 没有 (méiyǒu) is 没 (méi)

没有 (méiyǒu) can be shortened to 没 (méi) without altering its meaning.

- 我 没 钱。
  Wǒ méi qián.
  I don't have money.
- 你 没 男朋友吗？
  Nǐ méi nánpéngyou ma?
  Do you not have a boyfriend?

- 你们 没 车吗?
  Nǐmen méi chē ma?
  You don't have a car?
- 老板现在 没 时间。
  Lǎobǎn xiànzài méi shíjiān.
  The boss doesn't have time right now.
- 我 没 工作，我老公也 没 工作。
  Wǒ méi gōngzuò, wǒ lǎogōng yě méi gōngzuò.
  I don't have a job. My husband doesn't have a job either.

Similar to

- Expressing existence with “you” (A1), page 56
- Expressing possession with “you” (A1), page 58
- Negation of past actions with “meiyou” (A1), page 81
- Standard negation with “bu” (A1), page 85
- Basic comparisons with “meiyou” (A2), page 258
- Comparing “bu” and “mei” (A2), page 358

The "all" adverb "dou" (A1)

The adverb 都 (dōu) is used to express "all" in Chinese. It's common to use 都 (dōu) in a variety of sentences where it would seem unnecessary in English.

都 (dōu) for "All"

Structure

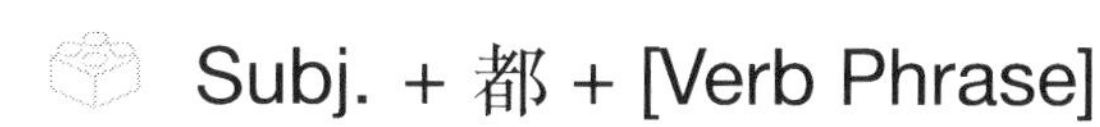

Remember that 都 (dōu) appears *after* the subject. A common mistake learners make is to put 都 (dōu) at the beginning of the sentence (as "all" often appears there in English). This isn't good Chinese - make sure you put 都 (dōu) after the subject and before the verb.

Examples

- 你们 都 认识 John 吗?
  Nǐmen dōu rènshi John ma?
  Do you all know John?
- 他们 都 在上海。
  Tāmen dōu zài Shànghǎi.
  They are all in Shanghai.
- 明天我们 都 可以去。
  Míngtiān wǒmen dōu kěyǐ qù.
  Tomorrow we all can go.
- 你们 都 用 wiki 吗?
  Nǐmen dōu yòng wiki ma?
  Do you all use the wiki?
- 我们 都 要冰水。
  Wǒmen dōu yào bīngshuǐ .
  We all want ice water.

都 (dōu) for "Both"

Chinese doesn't normally use a special word for "both" like English does. It just uses 都 (dōu) as if it were any other number greater than one. Chinese also doesn't have a special pattern like "neither / nor" for the negative case. Just use 都 (dōu) and make the sentence negative.

Structure

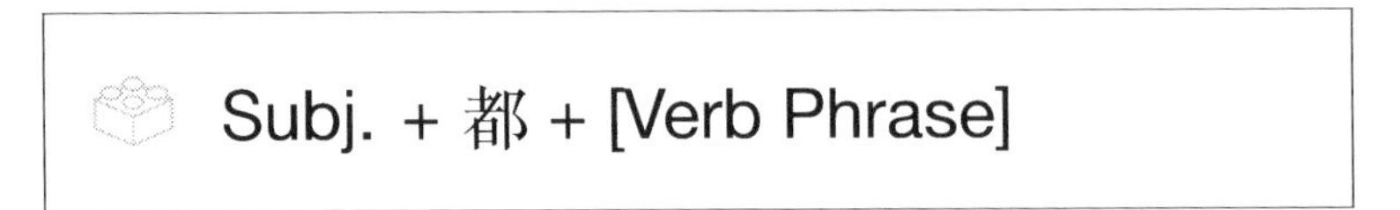

This pattern should look familiar.

Examples

These examples follow exactly the same form in Chinese as the ones above. The only difference is that here we don't translate 都 (dōu) as "all" in English; we translate it as "both," and for negative cases, we translate it as "neither."

- 我们两个 都 爱你。
  Wǒmen liǎng gè dōu ài nǐ.
  The two of us both love you.
- 你爸爸和你妈妈 都 是美国人吗?
  Nǐ bàba hé nǐ māma dōu shì Měiguó rén ma?
  Are your father and your mother both Americans?
- 我和我太太 都 不吃肉。
  Wǒ hé wǒ tàitai dōu bù chī ròu.
  Neither my wife nor I eat meat.
- 你们两个 都 喜欢中国菜吗?
  Nǐmen liǎng gè dōu xǐhuan Zhōngguó cài ma?
  Do you both like Chinese food?
- 她和她老公 都 没有工作。
  Tā hé tā lǎogōng dōu méiyǒu gōngzuò.
  Neither she nor her husband has a job.

Similar to

- Emphasizing quantity with "dou" (A2), page 133
- Using "ye" and "dou" together

The "also" adverb "ye" (A1)

The English adverb "too" or "also" is expressed in Chinese as 也 (yě). In Chinese, it *always* needs to come before the verb (or adjective).

也 (yě) with Verb Phrases

Structure

Since it is an adverb, 也 (yě) is inserted after the subject, before the verb or verb phrase.

 Subj. + 也 + Verb / [Verb Phrase]

Examples

- 我 也 喜欢。
  Wǒ yě xǐhuan.
  I also like it.
- 我 也 是学生。
  Wǒ yě shì xuésheng.
  I am a student too.
- 她 也 有一个儿子。
  Tā yě yǒu yī gè érzi.
  She also has a son.
- 他们 也 是法国人吗?
  Tāmen yě shì Fǎguó rén ma?
  Are they also French?
- 我 也 想学中文。
  Wǒ yě xiǎng xué Zhōngwén.
  I also want to study Chinese.
- 他们 也 会去吗?
  Tāmen yě huì qù ma?
  Are they also going?

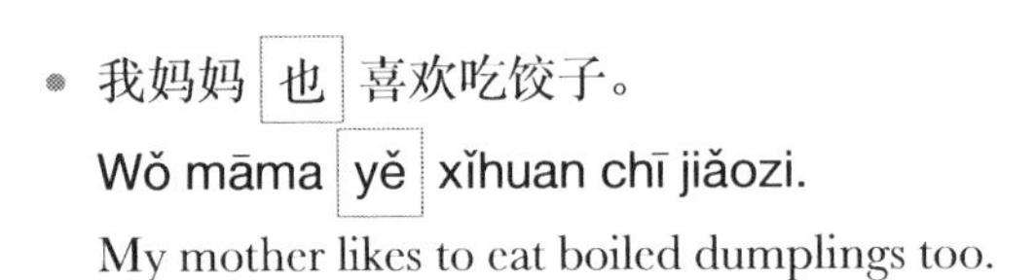

- 孩子 也 可以喝酒吗?
  Háizi yě kěyǐ hējiǔ ma?
  Can kids drink alcohol too?
- 你 也 想来我家吗?
  Nǐ yě xiǎng lái wǒ jiā ma?
  Do you want to come to my house too?
- 她 也 觉得这个老师不好。
  Tā yě juéde zhège lǎoshī bù hǎo.
  She also thinks this teacher isn't good.

Let's take one more look at two different English sentences which mean the same thing, but can result in bad Chinese if you translate word-for-word.

I like it too.

Note that the translation for the first sentence is "I also like it." The translation of the second sentence is "I like it too," which is equally correct in English, but translated word-for-word into Chinese, the 也 (yě) comes at the end of the sentence, which is *100% wrong* in Chinese.

A Note on the Negative Form

Please note that in English, we replace the word "too" with "either" in negative sentences. For example:

A: I like cats.

B: I like cats *too*.

A: I *don't* like cats.

B: I don't like cats *either*.

In Chinese, regardless of whether the sentence is positive ("I like them **too**") or negative ("I **don't** like them **either**"), 也 (yě) is used the same way. Just make sure you put the 也 (yě) *before* the 不 (bù) or other negative part that comes before the verb.

- 我 也 不 喜欢。
  Wǒ yě bù xǐhuan.
  I don't like it either.
- 我 也 不 知道。
  Wǒ yě bù zhīdào.
  I don't know either.
- 他 也 没 有。
  Tā yě méiyǒu.
  He doesn't have it either.
- 你 也 不 想来我家吗?
  Nǐ yě bù xiǎng lái wǒ jiā ma?
  You don't want to come to my house either?

也 (yě) with Adjectives

Structure

也 (yě) can also be used with adjectives. Remember that for simple "noun + adjective" sentences[1] you normally need to include an adverb like 很 (hěn) before the adjective. In that case, just put the 也 (yě) before the adverb.

Subj. + 也 (+ Adv.) + Adj.

Examples

- 你 也 很 高。
  Nǐ yě hěn gāo.
  You are also tall.
- 他 也 很 胖。
  Tā yě hěn pàng.
  He is also fat.
- 我爸爸 也 很 帅。
  Wǒ bàba yě hěn shuài.
  My dad is also handsome.

---

1. Simple "noun + adjective" sentences (A1), page 96

- 湖南菜 也 很 辣。
  Húnán cài yě hěn là.
  Hunan food is very spicy too.
- 这种酒 也 很 好喝。
  Zhè zhǒng jiǔ yě hěn hǎohē.
  This kind of alcohol is also good.
- 这个地方 也 很 漂亮。
  Zhège dìfang yě hěn piàoliang.
  This place is also pretty.
- 昨天很冷，今天 也 很 冷。
  Zuótiān hěn lěng, jīntiān yě hěn lěng.
  Yesterday was cold, and today is also cold.
- 他生气了？我 也 很 生气！
  Tā shēngqì le? Wǒ yě hěn shēngqì!
  He got angry? I'm also angry!
- 这个问题 也 很 麻烦。
  Zhège wèntí yě hěn máfan.
  This problem is also very troublesome.
- 我觉得这个餐厅 也 很 好。
  Wǒ juéde zhège cāntīng yě hěn hǎo.
  I think that this restaurant is also good.

Expressing "Me Too" with 也 (yě)

It can be tricky to know how to say "me too" when you first study 也 (yě), as you can't say "wǒ yě" all by itself. That's not a complete sentence; you can't just leave 也 (yě) hanging there with nothing after it.

The all-purpose correct sentence is "wǒ yě shì," which literally means, "I am too," but can also stand in for "me too."

Structure

The correct structure uses the verb 是 (shì):

✔ 我 也 是 。
Wǒ yě shì .
I am too. / Me too.

The 是 fills in for whatever was just said.

× 

Always put something after 也! It never ends a sentence.

Examples

The "me too" structure works with other subjects, as well. But for these simple examples, we'll stick to the classic 我 (wǒ) subject.

A: 我是美国人。

Wǒ shì Měiguó rén.

I am an American.

B: 我也是。

Wǒ yě shì.

Me too. / I am too.

For this next one, you'll notice that the "me too" reply repeats the original verb 喜欢 (xǐhuan) instead of using 是 (shì). Both ways are possible.

A: 我喜欢看书。

Wǒ xǐhuan kàn shū.

I like to read.

B: 我也喜欢。

Wǒ yě xǐhuan.

Me too. / So do I.

You'll notice that some of those English translations use "so do I." The Chinese works exactly the same; they're just translated that way to produce more natural-sounding English.

Similar to

- Simple "noun + adjective" sentences (A1), page 96
- Expressing "and also" with "hai" (A2), page 144
- Using "ye" and "dou" together

Expressing "and" with "he" (A1)

When listing out multiple nouns, 和 (hé) is there to help you out. Just remember that 和 (hé) isn't a word you can use to translate just *any* usage of the English word "and."

Structure

The most common way to express "and" in Chinese is with 和 (hé). It's important to note that 和 (hé) **is mainly used to link nouns**. This is how you should use it *exclusively* as you get used to it. Don't try to link verbs (or whole sentences) with 和 (hé).

Noun 1 + 和 + Noun 2

Examples

- 你 和 我
  nǐ hé wǒ
  you and I
- 老板喜欢 咖啡 和 茶 。
  Lǎobǎn xǐhuan kāfēi hé chá .
  The boss likes coffee and tea.
- 我的爷爷 和 奶奶 都 70 岁。
  Wǒ de yéye hé nǎinai dōu qīshí suì.
  My grandpa and grandma are both 70 years old.
- 他 和 他女朋友 都喜欢中国菜。
  Tā hé tā nǚpéngyou dōu xǐhuan Zhōngguó cài.
  He and his girlfriend both like Chinese food.
- 你爸爸 和 你妈妈 都是美国人吗?
  Nǐ bàba hé nǐ māma dōu shì Měiguó rén ma?
  Are your father and your mother both Americans?
- 手机 和 电脑 都很贵。
  Shǒujī hé diànnǎo dōu hěn guì.
  Cell phones and computers are both expensive.

- 德语 和 法语 都很难吗?
  Déyǔ hé Fǎyǔ dōu hěn nán ma?
  Are both German and French difficult?
- 今天 和 明天 都可以吗?
  Jīntiān hé míngtiān dōu kěyǐ ma?
  Are today and tomorrow both OK?

(If you're unclear why the 都 (dōu) is used in the sentences above, see our article on the adverb 都 (dōu)[1].)

Just to be absolutely clear what we mean by using 和 (hé) with nouns only, here are two English examples of what you should and shouldn't try to express with 和 (hé):

⚠ I went to the store and bought some gum.

✔ I like to eat cucumbers and cheese.

Similar to

- Expressing "in addition" with "haiyou"
- Combining verbs with "bing"
- Expressing "and" with "he" (advanced)

1. The "all" adverb "dou" (A1), page 15

Offering choices with "haishi" (A1)

还是 (háishì) is used in Chinese to provide options in a **question**. This is equivalent to one of our uses of "or" in English.

Simplest Form

Structure

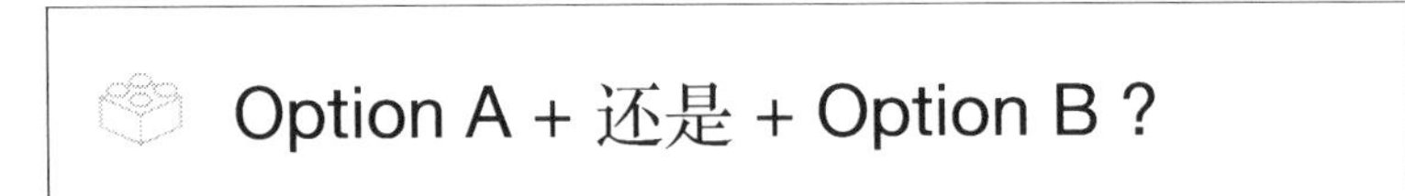

Option A + 还是 + Option B ?

When you're asked a question of this form, there are two ways you're expected to answer: either Option A or Option B. (Pick one, but not both.) It's not that no other answers are possible, it's that usually when you're asked a question this way, the person asking expects you to just choose one. For example, if asked if you'd like to drink coffee or tea, most people are going to choose one or the other, not ask for both. 还是 (háishì) is used to ask people to make that choice between the two.

Examples

- 我还是他？
  Wǒ háishì tā?
  Me or him?
- 一个还是两个？
  Yī gè háishì liǎng gè ?
  One or two?
- 辣的还是不辣的？
  Là de háishì bù là de ?
  Spicy or non-spicy?
- 冰的还是热的？
  Bīng de háishì rè de ?
  Cold or hot?
- 上海还是北京？
  Shànghǎi háishì Běijīng?
  Shanghai or Beijing?

The eternal China expat question! Choose wisely...

Full Sentence Form

Structure

You can take the structure above, add a subject and a verb, and create all kinds of questions with the following structure:

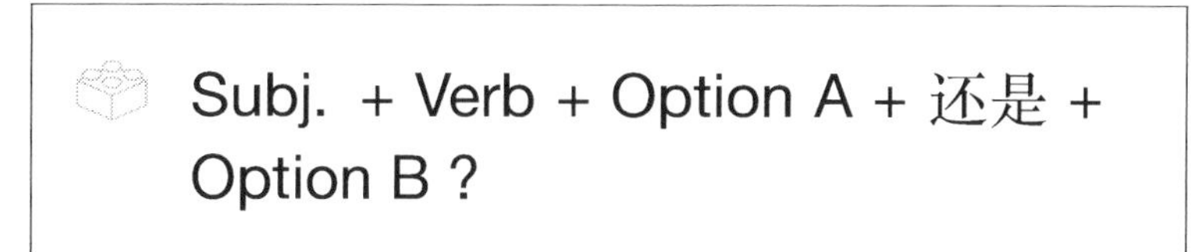

Examples

- 这是 水 还是 酒 ?
  Zhè shì shuǐ háishì jiǔ ?
  Is this water or alcohol?
- 他是 美国人 还是 英国人 ?
  Tā shì Měiguó rén háishì Yīngguó rén ?
  Is he American or British?
- 你喜欢 我 还是 我的钱 ?
  Nǐ xǐhuan wǒ háishì wǒ de qián ?
  Do you like me or my money?
- 你要喝 茶 还是 咖啡 ?
  Nǐ yào hē chá háishì kāfēi ?
  Do you want to drink tea or coffee?
- 你们想吃 中国菜 还是 法国菜 ?
  Nǐmen xiǎng chī Zhōngguó cài háishì Fǎguó cài ?
  Do you want to eat Chinese food or French food?

Please note that 还是 (háishì) is for offering options in a **question**. It should not be used for "or" in statements[1].

Similar to

- Affirmative-negative question (A1), page 99
- Expressing "or" in statements (A2), page 189

1. Expressing "or" in statements (A2), page 189

Age with "sui" (A1)

Use 岁 (suì) to give a person's age, similar to how we say "years old" in English. There are a details that work differently from English, however.

Basic Structure for 岁 (suì)

Structure

The structure for telling someone's age with 岁 (suì) is:

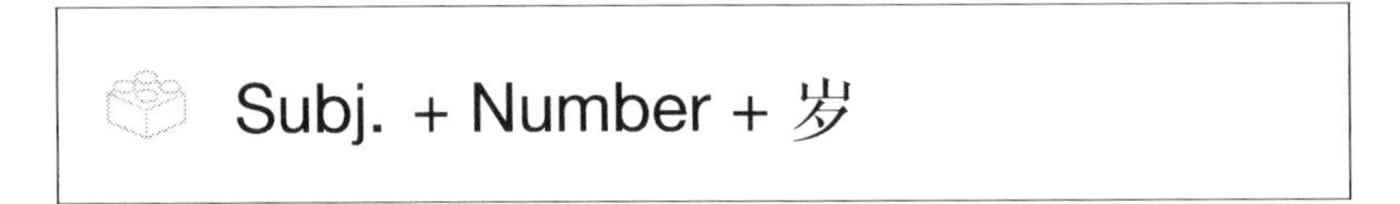

This is equivalent to someone "**is** x years old" in English. Notice that you don't need to include any verb when you use 岁 (suì).

Examples

- 我 20 岁 。

  Wǒ èrshí suì.

  I am 20 years old.

- 我儿子一 岁 。

  Wǒ érzi yī suì.

  My son is one year old.

- 我妈妈今年 45 岁 。

  Wǒ māma jīnnián sìshí-wǔ suì.

  My mother is 45 years old this year.

- 你爷爷今年 80 岁 吗?

  Nǐ yéye jīnnián bāshí suì ma?

  Is your grandpa eighty years old this year?

- 他女朋友也 20 岁 吗?

  Tā nǚpéngyou yě èrshí suì ma?

  Is his girlfriend also twenty years old?

Note that you shouldn't use either the verb 是 (shì) or the measure word like 个 (gè) in any of these sentences.

✘ 我的孩子一 个 岁 。

Wǒ de háizi yī gè suì.

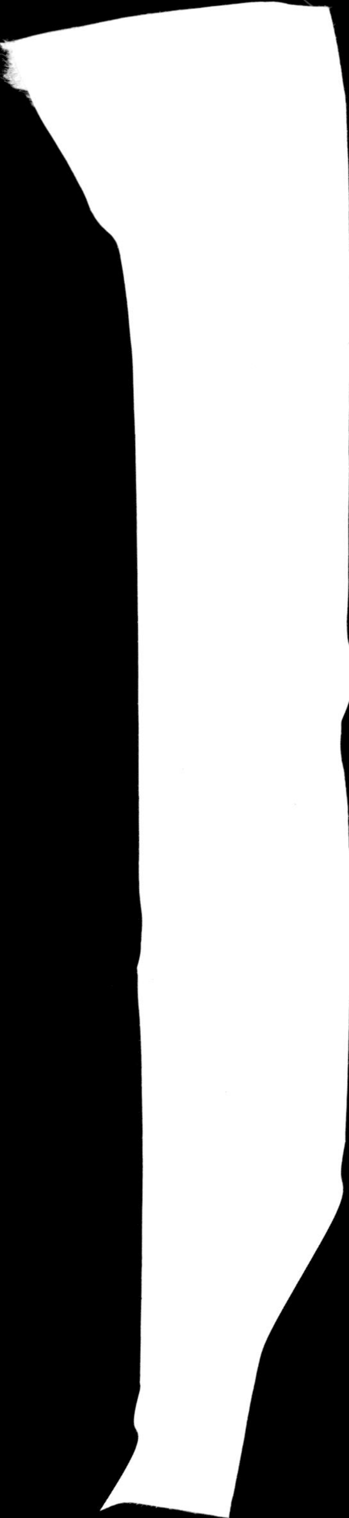

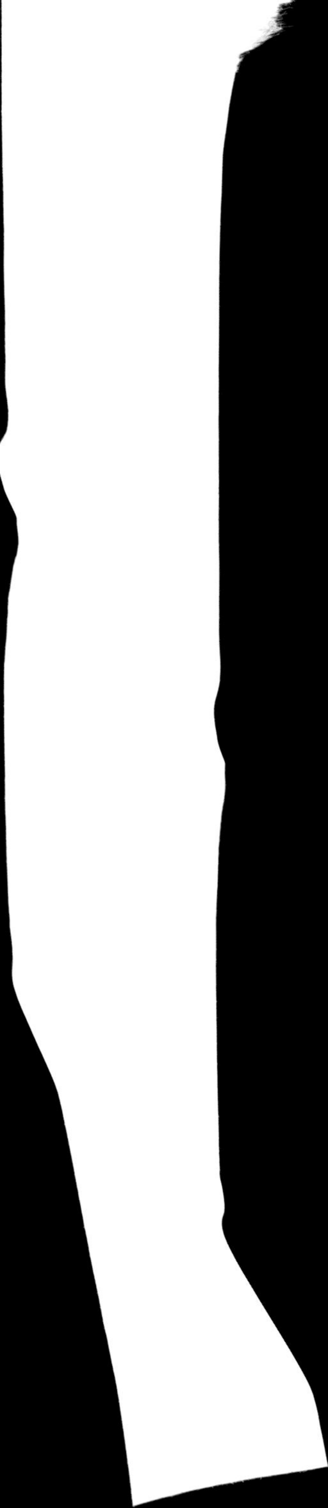

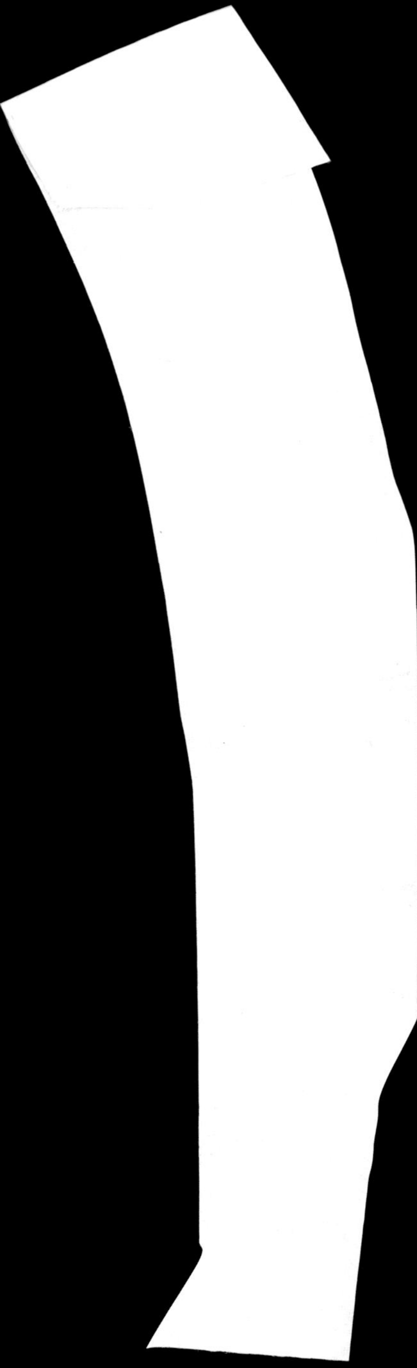

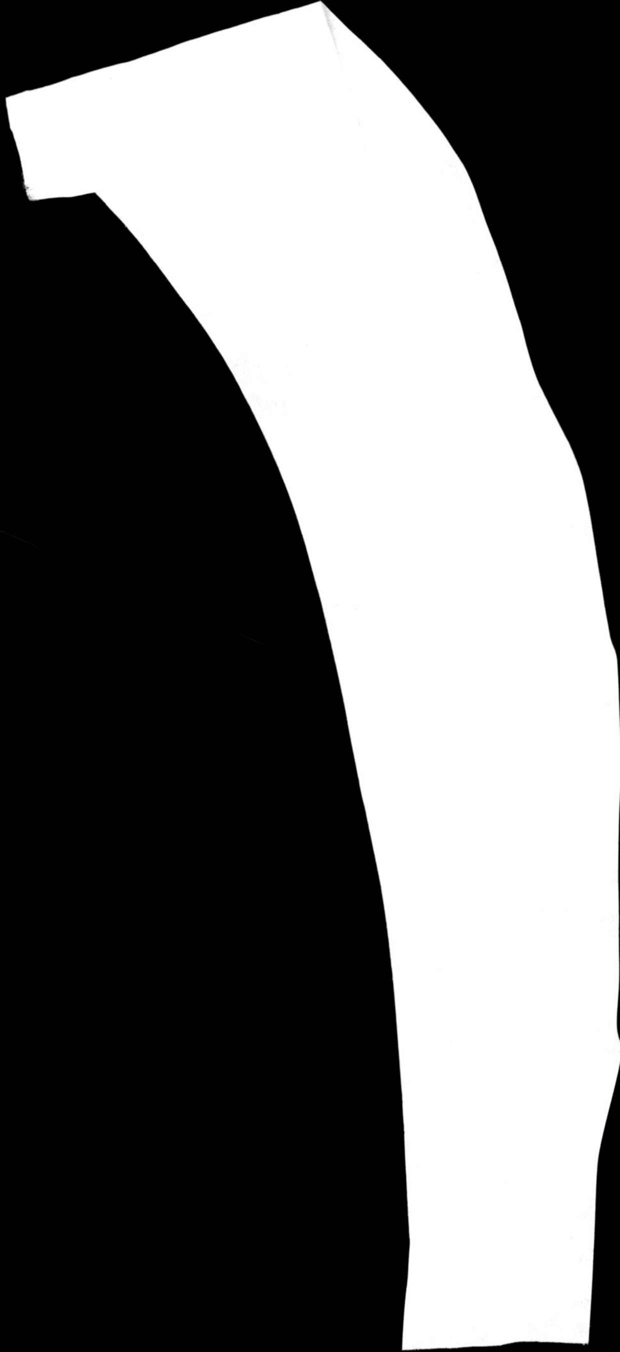

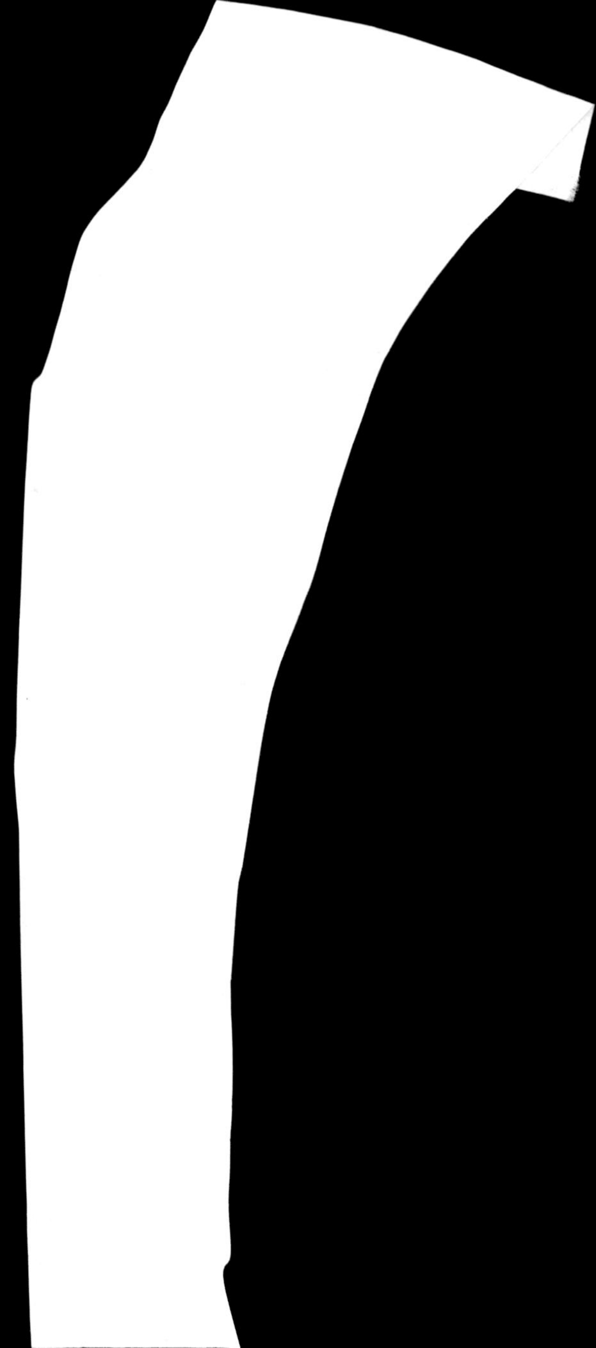

× 我的孩子是一岁。

Wǒ de háizi shì yī suì.

✓ 我的孩子一岁。

Wǒ de háizi yī suì.

My child is one year old.

Adding "And a Half" to an Age

Structure

The word for "half" in Chinese is 半 (bàn), and you simply add this after 岁 (suì).

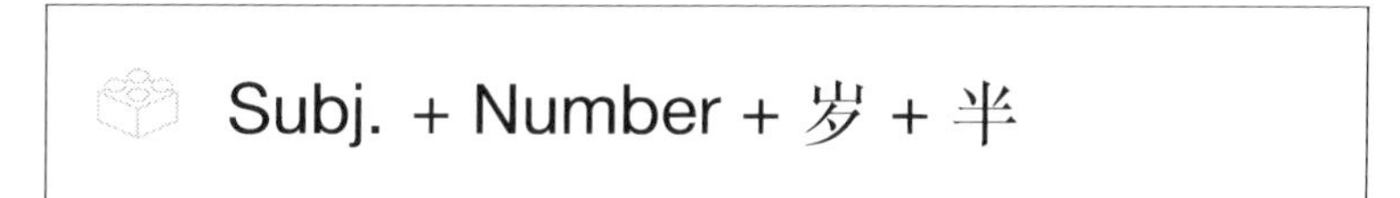

Examples

- 她两岁半。

  Tā liǎng suì bàn.

  She is two and a half years old.

- 我儿子一岁半。

  Wǒ érzi yī suì bàn.

  My son is one and a half years old.

Similar to

- Measure word "ge" (A1), page 28

Measure word "ge" (A1)

个 (gè) is the most commonly used measure word. It can be used in a pinch for any noun if you can't think of a more precise measure word. (Although you might not sound quite as smart, you'll still get your point across). Also, for many nouns, 个 (gè) *is* the only correct measure word.

Counting Nouns

Structure

The general structure for 个 (gè) and measure words in general is:

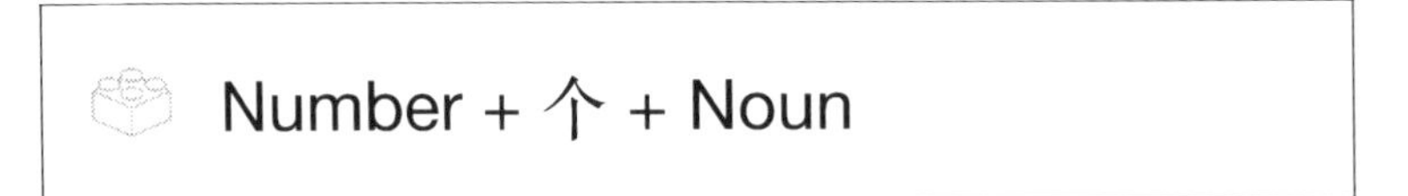

Any time you want to state *how many* of a noun in Chinese, you probably need a measure word. First get used to how they are used with 个 (gè).

Examples

- 一个人
  yī gè rén
  one person
- 四个朋友
  sì gè péngyou
  four friends
- 三个苹果手机
  sān gè Píngguǒ shǒujī
  three iPhones
- 五个星期
  wǔ gè xīngqī
  five weeks
- 六个月
  liù gè yuè
  six months
- 两个老婆
  liǎng gè lǎopo
  two wives

- 十 个 男人，七 个 傻，八 个 坏。 *A line from a song*
  Shí gè nánrén, qī gè shǎ, bā gè huài.
  Ten men: seven are fools, and eight are bad.

Omitting the Number

Structure

If the number is one (1), you can omit it and use 个 (gè) by itself. This is similar to "a" or "an" in English, for example in "a person" or "an idiot." (The tone on 个 (gè) is normally somewhat de-emphasized in this usage, but still written as fourth tone. You don't need to stress about it, though.)

Examples

- 他是 个 老外。
  Tā shì gè lǎowài.
  He is a foreigner.
- 我有 个 儿子。
  Wǒ yǒu gè érzi.
  I have a son.
- 她是 个 好老师。
  Tā shì gè hǎo lǎoshī.
  She is a good teacher.
- 你想吃 个 包子吗?
  Nǐ xiǎng chī gè bāozi ma?
  Would you like to eat a stuffed steamed bun?
- 老师，我有 个 问题。
  Lǎoshī, wǒ yǒu gè wèntí.
  Teacher, I have a question.

Similar to

- Age with "sui" (A1), page 26
- Measure words for counting (A2), page 328

Structure of dates (A1)

Dates in Chinese follow the order "year, month, day." This is in keeping with the "from big to small" trend which pervades many facets of Chinese culture.

Structure

Dates are arranged from largest unit to smallest: *year, month, day*.

x 年 + y 月 + z 日

So April 1st, 2019 is **2019** 年 **4** 月 **1** 日 (**èr-líng-yī-jiǔ** nián **Sì**yuè **yī** rì).

Note that 号 (hào) is commonly used in *spoken* Mandarin instead of 日 (rì):

x 年 + y 月 + z 号

The above example becomes: **2019** 年 **4** 月 **1** 号 (**èr-líng-yī-jiǔ** nián **Sì**yuè **yī** hào). In written Chinese, however, you will see 日 (rì) rather than 号 (hào).

Examples

- 1868 年 1 月 18 号
  Yī-bā-liù-bā nián Yī yuè shíbā hào
  January 18, 1868
- 1910 年 8 月 9 号
  Yī-jiǔ-yī-líng nián Bā yuè jiǔ hào
  August 9, 1910
- 2001 年 7 月 20 日
  èr-líng-líng-yī nián Qī yuè èrshí rì
  July 20th, 2001
- 1 月 1 日 是新年。
  Yī yuè yī rì shì Xīnnián.
  January 1st is New Year's Day.

- 12 月 24 日 是平安夜。
  Shí-èr yuè èrshí-sì rì shì Píng'ān Yè.
  December 24th is Christmas Eve.
- 10 月 1 号 我们去上海。
  Shí yuè yī hào wǒmen qù Shànghǎi.
  We will go to Shanghai on October 1st.
- 我 1990 年 7 月 出生。
  Wǒ Yī-jiǔ-jiǔ-líng nián Qī yuè chūshēng.
  I was born in July 1990.
- 你的生日是 11 月 11 号 吗?
  Nǐ de shēngrì shì Shíyī yuè shíyī hào ma?
  Is your birthday November 11th?
- 我 2006 年 4 月 17 号 认识了他。
  Wǒ èr-líng-líng-liù nián Sì yuè shíqī hào rènshi le tā.
  I met him on April 17, 2006.
- 1980 年 9 月 4 号 我们结婚了。
  Yī-jiǔ-bā-líng nián Jiǔ yuè sì hào wǒmen jiéhūn le.
  We got married on September 4th, 1980.

Similar to

- Structure of days of the week (A1), page 33
- Structure of numbers (A1), page 36
- Structure of times (basic) (A1), page 42
- Structure of times (advanced) (A2), page 218

Structure of days of the week (A1)

星期 (xīngqī) means "week" in Chinese. This is also used to indicate which weekday you are talking about.

Structure

Days of the week in Chinese are formed by the word "week" followed by a number:

English	Chinese
Monday	星期一 Xīngqīyī
Tuesday	星期二 Xīngqī'èr
Wednesday	星期三 Xīngqīsān
Thursday	星期四 Xīngqīsì
Friday	星期五 Xīngqīwǔ
Saturday	星期六 Xīngqīliù
Sunday	星期天 Xīngqītiān

Notice that Sunday is the only exception. Rather than a number, 天 (tiān) is used. More formally, Sunday is also referred to as 星期日 (Xīngqīrì).

One other implication of this system that you may not have noticed: "day one" is Monday. In Chinese culture, the first day of the week is Monday, and *not* Sunday.

Examples

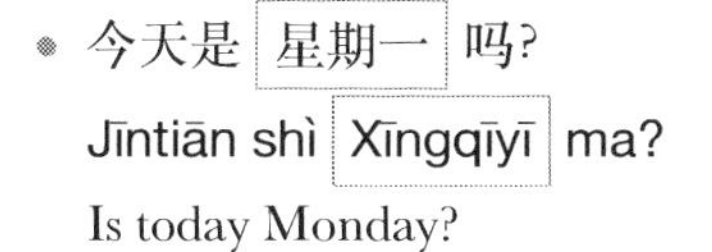

- 今天是 星期一 吗?
  Jīntiān shì Xīngqīyī ma?
  Is today Monday?

是 is optional

- 明天 星期五 ，太高兴了。
  Míngtiān Xīngqīwǔ, tài gāoxìng le.
  Tomorrow is Friday. I'm so happy.

  Optional 是 omitted

- 星期三 我不在上海。
  Xīngqīsān wǒ bù zài Shànghǎi.
  I'm not here in Shanghai on Wednesday.

- 星期二 早上我很忙。
  Xīngqī'èr zǎoshang wǒ hěn máng.
  I am busy on Tuesday morning.

- 你 星期天 要做什么?
  Nǐ Xīngqītiān yào zuò shénme?
  What are you doing on Sunday?

- 上个 星期五 我跟他见面了。
  Shàng gè Xīngqīwǔ wǒ gēn tā jiànmiàn le.
  I met him last Friday.

- 这个 星期三 晚上你有空吗?
  Zhège Xīngqīsān wǎnshang nǐ yǒu kòng ma?
  Are you free this Wednesday evening?

- 下个 星期四 是我的生日。
  Xià gè Xīngqīsì shì wǒ de shēngrì.
  My birthday is on next Thursday.

- 这个 星期五 晚上我们要去酒吧。
  Zhège Xīngqīwǔ wǎnshang wǒmen yào qù jiǔbā.
  We're going to a bar this Friday night.

- 星期六 和 星期天 我们不上班。
  Xīngqīliù hé Xīngqītiān wǒmen bù shàngbān.
  Saturday and Sunday we don't work.

Other Words for "Week"

Hopefully this doesn't freak you out, but there are actually two other ways to say "week" in Chinese. You should still learn 星期 (xīngqī) first, and that's really all you need as a beginner.

The other words for "week" are 礼拜 (lǐbài) and 周 (zhōu). Skip them for now unless you really need them.

Similar to

- Structure of dates (A1), page 31
- Structure of numbers (A1), page 36
- Structure of times (basic) (A1), page 42
- Structure of times (advanced) (A2), page 218

Structure of numbers (A1)

Chinese handles numbers in a very consistent and logical way. Once you've mastered just a few tricky parts, you will know how to read out any number in Chinese.

One to One Hundred

Structure for the First Ten

You just have to memorize these ten; nothing tricky there.

Numeral	Character	Pinyin
1	一	yī
2	二	èr
3	三	sān
4	四	sì
5	五	wǔ
6	六	liù
7	七	qī
8	八	bā
9	九	jiǔ
10	十	shí

Phone Numbers

Like in American English, Chinese phone numbers are given as a string of individual numbers, using the digits 0-9. The only trick is that the number 1 is often pronounced "yāo" instead of "yī" to avoid confusion with number 7, which is pronounced "qī."

- 110 *Number for the police in the PRC*

  yāo yāo líng

- 120 *Number for an ambulance in the PRC*

  yāo èr líng

- 119 *Number to report a fire in the PRC*

  yāo yāo jiǔ

- 13501200120 *Cell phone numbers are 11 digits in the PRC*

  yāo sān wǔ, líng yāo èr líng, líng yāo èr líng

Structure for Teens

Eleven, twelve and the teens are handled very logically. They're formed with 十 (shí) followed by a digit 一 (yī) to 九 (jiǔ). So eleven is 十一 (shíyī), twelve is 十二 (shí'èr), thirteen is 十三 (shísān), and so on up to nineteen, which is 十九 (shíjiǔ).

Numeral	Character	Pinyin
11	十一	shíyī
12	十二	shí'èr
13	十三	shísān
14	十四	shísì
15	十五	shíwǔ
16	十六	shíliù
17	十七	shíqī
18	十八	shíbā
19	十九	shíjiǔ

Structure for Tens

All the tens are also formed very logically. Twenty is 二十 (èrshí), thirty is 三十 (sānshí), and so on. Units in the tens are simply added on the end. So twenty one is 二十一 (èrshí-yī), thirty four is 三十四 (sānshí-sì), and ninety-nine is 九十九 (jiǔshí-jiǔ). All very logical and consistent.

Examples

Numeral	Character	Pinyin
20	二十	èrshí
23	二十三	èrshí-sān
30	三十	sānshí
39	三十九	sānshí-jiǔ
40	四十	sìshí
44	四十四	sìshí-sì
50	五十	wǔshí
73	七十三	qīshí-sān
82	八十二	bāshí-èr
97	九十七	jiǔshí-qī

And one hundred is simply 一百 (yībǎi), as in English. So you now know how to count to one hundred in Chinese.

After One Hundred

Dealing with Zeroes

Note: when there's a "0" in the middle of a number, you read it as 零 (líng), and don't put a unit (like "ten" or "hundred") after it. In the following examples, we'll show what happens when the "tens" place is a zero in a three-digit number.

Structure

x + 百 + 零 + y

Examples

Numeral	Character	Pinyin
101	一百零一	yībǎi líng yī
202	二百零二	èrbǎi líng èr
206	二百零六	èrbǎi líng liù
305	三百零五	sānbǎi líng wǔ
407	四百零七	sìbǎi líng qī
504	五百零四	wǔbǎi líng sì
602	六百零二	liùbǎi líng èr
701	七百零一	qībǎi líng yī
803	八百零三	bābǎi líng sān
909	九百零九	jiǔbǎi líng jiǔ

For Numbers 110 and Greater

For numbers greater than 100, if the number ends in zero (110, 230, 370, 450, etc.), a number like 150 can be read as 一百五十 (yībǎi wǔshí), but is often read as 一百五 (yībǎi wǔ). In fact, reading it as 一百五 (yībǎi wǔ) *always* means 150, never 105. As described above, 105 would be read as 一百零五 (yībǎi líng wǔ).

For numbers greater than 100 that end in a number in the teens, it's normal to pronounce the ten as "yīshí" rather than just "shí" (see the examples below).

Also, sometimes the number "200" is read as 二百 (èrbǎi), but often it is read as 两百 (liǎngbǎi). Both are OK. (This is an 二 (èr) vs. 两 (liǎng) issue[1] which you may or may not have encountered before.)

Structure

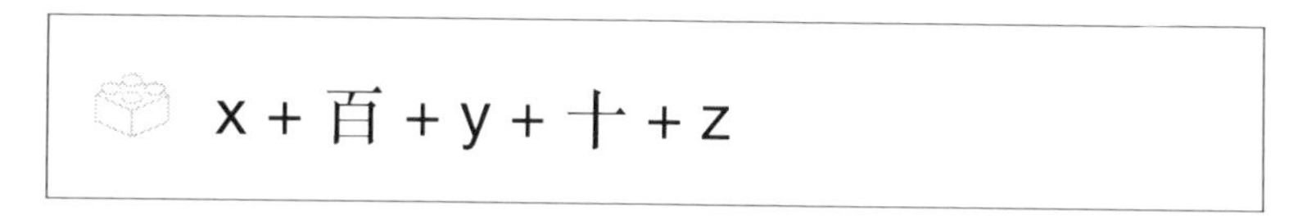

1. Comparing "er" and "liang" (A1), page 124

Examples

Numeral	Character	Pinyin
110	一百一十	yībǎi yīshí
111	一百一十一	yībǎi yīshí-yī
210	二百一十	èrbǎi yīshí
350	三百五十	sānbǎi wǔshí
480	四百八十	sìbǎi bāshí
550	五百五十	wǔbǎi wǔshí
635	六百三十五	liùbǎi sānshí-wǔ
777	七百七十七	qībǎi qīshí-qī
832	八百三十二	bābǎi sānshí-èr
999	九百九十九	jiǔbǎi jiǔshí-jiǔ

After One Thousand

千 (qiān) means "thousand" in Chinese. Its rules of usage are similar to the rules for "hundred." Just note that no matter how many zeroes are in the middle of the number, you just say 零 (líng) once.

Examples

Numeral	Character	Pinyin
1001	一千零一	yīqiān líng yī
1010	一千零一十	yīqiān líng yīshí
1019	一千零一十九	yīqiān líng yīshí-jiǔ
1020	一千零二十	yīqiān líng èrshí
1100	一千一百	yīqiān yībǎi
1101	一千一百零一	yīqiān yībǎi líng yī
1234	一千二百三十四	yīqiān èrbǎi sānshí-sì
2345	两千三百四十五	liǎngqiān sānbǎi sìshí-wǔ

8765	八千七百六十五	bāqiān qībǎi liùshí-wǔ
9999	九千九百九十九	jiǔqiān jiǔbǎi jiǔshí-jiǔ

10,000 and beyond

Things get a little trickier once you get to 10,000. If you're ready for it, you can move on to big numbers[1].

Similar to

- Comparing "er" and "liang" (A1), page 124
- Structure of dates (A1), page 31
- Structure of days of the week (A1), page 33
- Structure of times (basic) (A1), page 42
- Approximating with sequential numbers (A2), page 213
- Structure of times (advanced) (A2), page 218

1. Big numbers in Chinese (A2), page 215

Structure of times (basic) (A1)

Time in Chinese, just like in English, is expressed by stating the hour first, and then the minute (big to small).

On the Hour

The time of day in Chinese is formed with a number[1] 1 to 12 (一 (yī) to 十二 (shí'èr)) followed by 点 (diǎn). This 点 (diǎn) is equivalent to *o'clock* in English. In China, people generally use a twelve-hour clock, preceded by 上午 (shàngwǔ) for "a.m." or 下午 (xiàwǔ) for "p.m." when necessary.

Structure

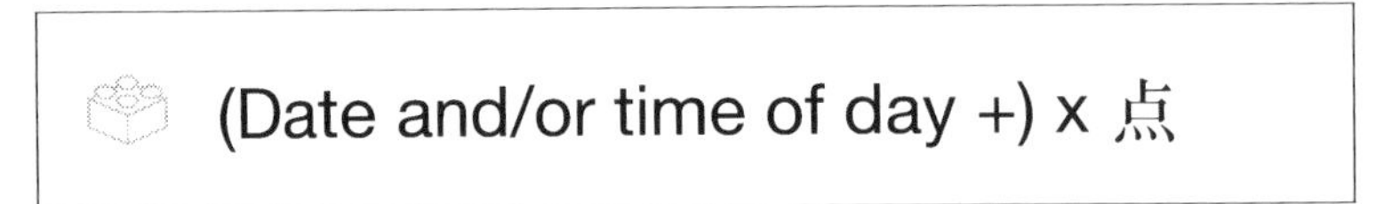

Sometimes people use the longer 点钟 (diǎnzhōng) instead of just 点 (diǎn), but you're fine using the short form.

Examples

If you want to include more specific information, start with the day or date, followed by the general time of day, with the exact clock time last. (This is the big-to-small pattern.) This is how Chinese gets around the need for "a.m." or "p.m.": use 上午 (shàngwǔ) for times in the morning, and 下午 (xiàwǔ) for times in the afternoon.

- 九点
  jiǔ diǎn
  9 o'clock
- 上午七点
  shàngwǔ qī diǎn
  7 o'clock a.m.
- 下午四点
  xiàwǔ sì diǎn
  4 o'clock p.m.
- 中午十二点
  zhōngwǔ shí'èr diǎn
  12 o'clock noon

1. Structure of numbers (A1), page 36

- 明天晚上七 点
  míngtiān wǎnshang qī diǎn
  7 o'clock p.m. tomorrow evening
- 9 月 9 号早上六 点
  jiǔ yuè jiǔ hào zǎoshang liù diǎn
  September 9th, 6 o'clock a.m.
- 星期三上午九 点
  Xīngqīsān shàngwǔ jiǔ diǎn
  Wednesday at 9 o'clock a.m.

Note that **two o'clock is 两点** (liǎng diǎn), not 二点 (èr diǎn). (For more information on when to use 两 (liǎng) vs. 二 (èr), see our article on comparing "er" and "liang"[1]).

"*Twelve* o'clock," however, is still 十二点 (shí'èr diǎn).

Half Hours

Half hours are added after 点 (diǎn) and are indicated with 半 (bàn).

Structure

X 点 + 半

Examples

- 五 点半
  wǔ diǎn bàn
  5:30
- 下午两 点半
  xiàwǔ liǎng diǎn bàn
  2:30 p.m.
- 星期天上午十 点半
  Xīngqītiān shàngwǔ shí diǎn bàn
  Sunday at 10:30 a.m.

---

1. Comparing "er" and "liang" (A1), page 124

- 昨天晚上七 点半
  zuótiān wǎnshang qī diǎn bàn
  7:30 yesterday evening
- 今天下午四 点半
  jīntiān xiàwǔ sì diǎn bàn
  4:30 p.m. this afternoon.

As a beginner, that should be all you need. If you've mastered all of these structures and want to get a little more advanced, see structure of times (advanced)[1].

Similar to

- Structure of dates (A1), page 31
- Structure of numbers (A1), page 36
- Before a specific time with "yiqian" (A2), page 201
- Structure of times (advanced) (A2), page 218

1. Structure of times (advanced) (A2), page 218

Expressing close possession without "de" (A1)

Expressing possession[1] in Chinese is accomplished with the particle 的 (de). But sometimes when certain (especially close) relationships are involved, it's more natural to drop the 的 (de).

Structure

Normally possession[1] is expressed using the particle 的 (de). However, you can omit 的 (de) in these cases:

- A close personal relationship is involved (family, close friends, boyfriends or girlfriends)
- An institutional or organizational relationship is involved (school, work)

In these cases 的 (de) **should be** omitted. It doesn't sound as natural if you leave it in.

Examples

- 我家 很大。
  Wǒ jiā hěn dà.
  My house is very big.
- 你哥哥 很高。
  Nǐ gēge hěn gāo.
  Your big brother is very tall.
- 这是 我女朋友 。
  Zhè shì wǒ nǚpéngyou .
  This is my girlfriend.
- 她妈妈 很漂亮。
  Tā māma hěn piàoliang.
  Her mom is very pretty.

---

1. Expressing possession with "de" (A1), page 47

- 我们学校 很大。
  Wǒmen xuéxiào hěn dà.
  Our school is big.
- 他们公司 在北京。
  Tāmen gōngsī zài Běijīng.
  Their company is in Bejing.
- 你男朋友 很帅。
  Nǐ nánpéngyou hěn shuài.
  Your boyfriend is very handsome.
- 他儿子 很有名。
  Tā érzi hěn yǒumíng.
  His son is really famous.
- 我女儿 会说英语。
  Wǒ nǚ'ér huì shuō Yīngyǔ.
  My daughter can speak English.
- 他爸爸 是 我们公司 的老板。
  Tā bàba shì wǒmen gōngsī de lǎobǎn.
  His dad is the boss of our company.

If 的 (de) was used in the above examples, it would create an unnatural sense of distance between the two.

Similar to

- Expressing possession with "de" (A1), page 47
- Expressing possession with "you" (A1), page 58

Expressing possession with "de" (A1)

In Chinese, possession is marked with the particle 的 (de), placed after the "owner" noun or noun phrase. This particle works in a similar way to apostrophe-"s" in English, but is used much more broadly in Chinese. This article highlights one of its simplest and most common usages.

Structure

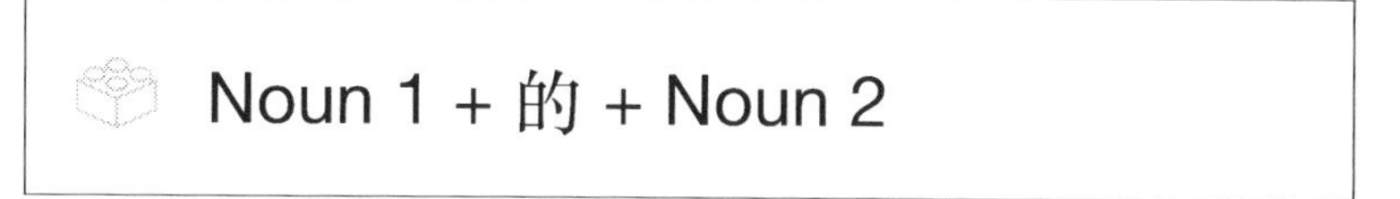

This means "**Noun 1's Noun 2**" (where Noun 2 belongs to Noun 1).

The structure is super simple. It will take a bit of time before you realize how truly universal this pattern is. It doesn't matter whether the "Noun 1" is a person, place, or thing, or even if it's a pronoun (like "he," "she," or "it"). The structure stays consistent.

Examples

- 我 的 老师
  wǒ de lǎoshī
  my teacher
- 你 的 手机
  nǐ de shǒujī
  your cell phone
- 我们 的 钱
  wǒmen de qián
  our money
- 他们 的 东西
  tāmen de dōngxi
  their stuff
- 爸爸 的 车
  bàba de chē
  dad's car

- 你们 的 菜
  nǐmen de cài
  your food
- 北京 的 空气
  Běijīng de kōngqì
  Beijing's air
- 公司 的 老板
  gōngsī de lǎobǎn
  the company's boss
- 上海 的 天气
  Shànghǎi de tiānqì
  Shanghai's weather
- 老师 的 朋友
  lǎoshī de péngyou
  teacher's friend

Similar to

- Expressing close possession without “de” (A1), page 45
- Expressing possession with “you” (A1), page 58

Questions with "ne" (A1)

The particle 呢 (ne) can be used to ask reciprocal questions, also known as "bounce back" questions. 呢 (ne) can also be used to form simple questions asking "what about...?" or "how about...?"

General Questions with 呢 (ne)

Structure

And it's as simple as that. Say what you want to ask about, then stick 呢 (ne) on the end. A very common way to use this is to return a question after being asked it. The classic example is this exchange:

A: 你好吗?

Nǐ hǎo ma?

B: 我很好。你 呢 ?

Wǒ hěn hǎo. Nǐ ne ?

A: 我也很好。

Wǒ yě hěn hǎo.

Examples

More 呢 (ne) examples (each of these can be translated as a "what about" question):

- 这个很好，那个 呢 ?

  Zhège hěn hǎo, nàge ne ?

  This one is good. What about that one?

- 这个用中文怎么说? 那个 呢 ?

  Zhège yòng Zhōngwén zěnme shuō? Nàge ne ?

  How do I say this in Chinese? And that?

- 我在家，你 呢 ?

  Wǒ zài jiā. Nǐ ne ?

  I'm at home. What about you?

- 你爸爸是上海人，你妈妈 呢 ？
  Nǐ bàba shì Shànghǎi rén, nǐ māma ne ?
  Your father is Shanghainese. And your mom?
- 你哥哥有工作，弟弟 呢 ？
  Nǐ gēge yǒu gōngzuò. Dìdi ne ?
  Your big brother has a job. What about your little brother?
- 北京下雨了。上海 呢 ？
  Běijīng xiàyǔ le. Shànghǎi ne ?
  It's raining in Beijing. How about in Shanghai?
- 我现在要出去。你 呢 ？
  Wǒ xiànzài yào chūqù. Nǐ ne ?
  I'm going to go out now. How about you?
- 我知道你会说中文。你老公 呢 ？
  Wǒ zhīdào nǐ huì shuō Zhōngwén. Nǐ lǎogōng ne ?
  I know you can speak Chinese. What about your husband?
- 这个周末我想去酒吧。你们 呢 ？
  Zhège zhōumò wǒ xiǎng qù jiǔbā. Nǐmen ne ?
  I want to go to a bar this weekend. What about you all?
- 今天晚上没空？明天晚上 呢 ？
  Jīntiān wǎnshang méi kòng? Míngtiān wǎnshang ne ?
  You don't have time tonight? What about tomorrow evening?

Asking "Where" with 呢 (ne)

You'll occasionally hear someone seemingly using 呢 (ne) out of the blue. When this happens, they're usually asking *where* someone or something is, and they expect that you know what they're talking about and know where that person or thing is.

Structure

[Missing Person / Thing] + 呢？

Examples

This one is simple, so just a few examples are needed:

- 钱 呢 ?
  Qián ne ?
  Where's the money?
- 你妈妈 呢 ?
  Nǐ māma ne ?
  Where's your mom?
- 我的手机 呢 ?
  Wǒ de shǒujī ne ?
  Where's my cell phone?

Similar to

- Tag questions with "ma" (A1), page 118
- Yes-no questions with "ma" (A1), page 120
- Sentence-final interjection "a" (A2), page 241
- Advanced yes-no questions with "ma"
- Softening the tone of questions with "ne"

Suggestions with “ba” (A1)

The particle 吧 (ba) has a number of different uses. Here we'll talk about the simplest way to use 吧 (ba): making suggestions.

Structure

Note that in Chinese, whenever you have a command with the subject “we,” you're basically just saying, “**let's** (do something).” 吧 (ba) just makes the suggestion sound more tentative and more polite.

Examples

- 我们走 吧 。
  Wǒmen zǒu ba.
  Let's go.
  This is a suggestion.
- 你说 吧 。
  Nǐ shuō ba.
  You say it.
  This is a suggestion.
- 快点吃 吧 。
  Kuài diǎn chī ba.
  Hurry up and eat.
  This is a suggestion.
- 给我两个 吧 。
  Gěi wǒ liǎng gè ba.
  Give me two.
  This is a suggestion.
- 喝水 吧 。
  Hē shuǐ ba.
  Have some water.
  This is a suggestion.
- 我们去香港 吧 。
  Wǒmen qù Xiānggǎng ba.
  Let's go to Hong Kong.
  This is a great suggestion!

- 我们六点去 吧 ？
  Wǒmen liù diǎn qù ba ?
  We're going at 6 o'clock (right)?
  This is more of a confirmation than a suggestion.
- 休息一下 吧 。
  Xiūxi yīxià ba .
  Take a break.
  This is a suggestion.
- 我们结婚 吧 。
  Wǒmen jiéhūn ba .
  Let's get married.
  This is a also suggestion, believe it or not!
- 老板，便宜一点 吧 。
  Lǎobǎn, piányi yīdiǎn ba .
  Boss, can you make it cheaper?
  This is more of a request, made to a shopkeeper.

Similar to

- Conceding with “ba” (A2), page 228
- Sentence-final interjection “a” (A2), page 241
- Softening speech with “ba” (A2), page 243
- Expressing “otherwise” with “yaobu”
- Reviewing options with “ba”

Expressing existence in a place with "zai" (A1)

The verb 在 (zài) expresses existence in a location, similar to how we say in English, "to be at" or "to be in."

Structure

The verb 在 (zài) is used to express existence in a place. English does not have a verb exclusively for this purpose, and instead uses "to be" with a preposition. In Chinese, 在 (zài) can cover both of these roles.

Subj. + 在 + Place

Remember that you don't need another verb in this construction. It can be tempting to try use 是 (shì), as English uses "to be," but this is not correct. 在 (zài) is the only verb needed.

Examples

- 我 在 上海。
  Wǒ zài Shànghǎi.
  I'm in Shanghai.
- 他们 在 英国。
  Tāmen zài Yīngguó.
  They're in England.
- 老板 在 外面。
  Lǎobǎn zài wàimiàn.
  The boss is outside.
- 他不 在 学校。
  Tā bù zài xuéxiào.
  He's not at school.
- 她现在 在 家吗?
  Tā xiànzài zài jiā ma?
  Is she at home now?
- 你 在 公司吗?
  Nǐ zài gōngsī ma?
  Are you at the office?

Literally, "Are you at the company?"

- 老师不 在 办公室吗?
  Lǎoshī bù zài bàngōngshì ma?
  Is the teacher not in the office?
- 谁 在 楼上?
  Shéi zài lóushàng?
  Who is upstairs?
- 我和朋友 在 酒吧。
  Wǒ hé péngyou zài jiǔbā.
  I'm with a friend at a bar.
- 你们明天 在 北京吗?
  Nǐ míngtiān zài Běijīng ma?
  Are you in Beijing tomorrow?

Similar to

- Expressing location with “zai… shang / xia / li” (A2), page 355
- Indicating location with “zai” before verbs (A2), page 288
- Special cases of “zai” following verbs (A2), page 293

- Idiomatic phrases with “zai”

Expressing existence with "you" (A1)

The verb 有 (yǒu), which means "to have," can also be used to express existence. This is similar to saying "there is" or "there are" in English.

Structure

Literally, this structure expresses that a place "has" a thing, which is to say, that thing is in the place.

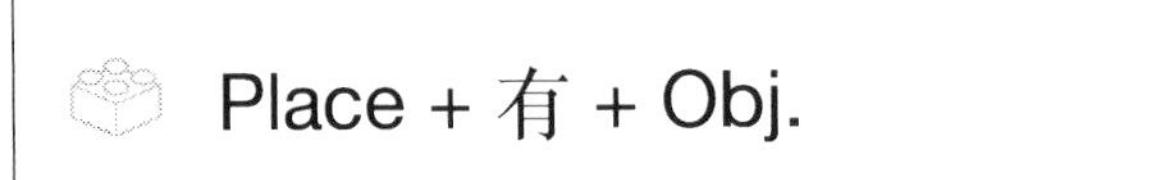

Examples

- 我家 有 很多小狗。
  Wǒ jiā yǒu hěn duō xiǎo gǒu.
  There are a lot of puppies in my home.
- 我们学校 有 很多帅哥。
  Wǒmen xuéxiào yǒu hěn duō shuàigē.
  There are a lot of cute guys in our school.
- 日本 有 很多中国人。
  Rìběn yǒu hěn duō Zhōngguó rén.
  There are many Chinese people in Japan.
- 这个酒吧 有 很多美女。
  Zhège jiǔbā yǒu hěn duō měinǚ.
  There are a lot of pretty girls in this bar.
- 你家 有 牛奶吗?
  Nǐ jiā yǒu niúnǎi ma?
  Is there milk in your house?
- 这里 有 一个问题。
  Zhèlǐ yǒu yī gè wèntí.
  There is a problem here.

- 房间里 有 人吗?
  Fángjiān lǐ yǒu rén ma?
  Is there anyone in the room?
- 杯子里 有 水吗?
  Bēizi lǐ yǒu shuǐ ma?
  Is there any water in the cup?
- 我的手机里 有 你的号码。
  Wǒ de shǒujī lǐ yǒu nǐ de hàomǎ.
  Your number is in my cell phone.
- 现在办公室里 有 人吗?
  Xiànzài bàngōngshì lǐ yǒu rén ma?
  Is there anyone in the office now?

Similar to

- Expressing possession with "you" (A1), page 58
- Negation of "you" with "mei" (A1), page 12

Expressing possession with "you" (A1)

有 (yǒu) can be used in various ways, but the most basic meaning of this verb you need to know is "to have."

Structure

Subj. + 有 + Obj.

Examples

- 我 有 钱。
  Wǒ yǒu qián.
  I have money.
- 你 有 房子吗?
  Nǐ yǒu fángzi ma?
  Do you have a house?
- 她没 有 车。
  Tā méi yǒu chē.
  She doesn't have a car.
- 他 有 女朋友吗?
  Tā yǒu nǚpéngyou ma?
  Does he have a girlfriend?
- 我们 有 三个女儿。
  Wǒmen yǒu sān gè nǚ'ér.
  We have three daughters.
- 我们家 有 两个公司。
  Wǒmen jiā yǒu liǎng gè gōngsī.
  Our family has two companies.
- 你 有 一百块钱吗?
  Nǐ yǒu yī bǎi kuài qián ma?
  Do you have 100 kuài RMB?

- 你的老师 有 iPad 吗?
  Nǐ de lǎoshī yǒu iPad ma?
  Does your teacher have an iPad?
- 我爸爸没 有 工作。
  Wǒ bàba méi yǒu gōngzuò.
  My dad doesn't have a job.
- 今天你 有 课吗?
  Jīntiān nǐ yǒu kè ma?
  Do you have classes today?

Negating 有 (yǒu)

The verb 有 (yǒu) is negated in a special way. Unlike most verbs, it is negated with 没 (méi) instead of 不 (bù). The negative form of 有 (yǒu) then, is 没有 (méiyǒu). For more on that topic, see our article on negation of "you" with "mei."[1]

Similar to

- Expressing existence with "you" (A1), page 56

1. Negation of "you" with "mei" (A1), page 12

Using the verb "jiao" (A1)

The verb 叫 (jiào) is used to indicate what someone or something is called, or what someone or something's name is. Its usage can seem a little weird to beginners, so it gets its own grammar point.

Structure

The verb 叫 (jiào) means both "to call" and "to be called." It's an easy way to give names, using the following structure:

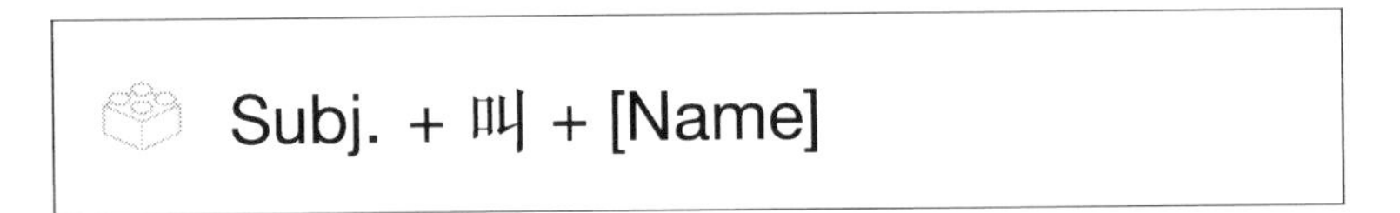

This can be used to give your full name or just your first name.

Examples

- 我 叫 Tom。
  Wǒ jiào Tom.
  My name is Tom.
  Note: it even works if you don't have a Chinese name!
- 他 叫 李小龙。
  Tā jiào Lǐ Xiǎolóng.
  His name is Li Xiaolong.
  Note: this is the real name of Bruce Lee
- 我哥哥 叫 老马。
  Wǒ gēge jiào Lǎo Mǎ.
  My brother is called Lao Ma.
  Note: this is probably not his real name
- 那个 叫 什么?
  Nàge jiào shénme?
  What is that called?
- 这个美女 叫 Alana。
  Zhège měinǚ jiào Alana.
  This pretty girl is named Alana.
- 我们的老板 叫 John。
  Wǒmen de lǎobǎn jiào John.
  Our boss is named John.

- 我的狗 叫 Max。
  Wǒ de gǒu jiào Max.
  My dog is called Max.
- 这种手机 叫 iPhone。
  Zhè zhǒng shǒujī jiào iPhone.
  This kind of cell phone is called an iPhone.
- 你爸爸 叫 什么?
  Nǐ bàba jiào 什么?
  What is your dad's name?
- 这个地方 叫 外滩。
  Zhège dìfang jiào Wàitān.
  This place is called the Bund.

You can also ask people their names using 叫 (jiào):

- 你 叫 什么名字?
  Nǐ jiào shénme míngzi?
  What's your name?

Similar to

- Using the verb "xing" (A1), page 65
- Causative verbs

Using the verb “qu” (A1)

You can use 去 (qù) whenever you have somewhere to go. It’s pretty easy to get a handle on this verb; the only trick is getting used to not needing a word for “to” before the destination.

去 (qù) with Just a Place

The verb 去 (qù) means “to go,” and is an easy way to talk about going to places.

Structure

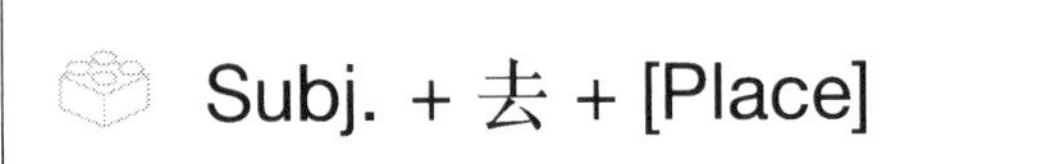

Subj. + 去 + [Place]

Notice that you don’t need a word to express “to.”

Examples

公司 literally means “company” but is often used to mean “office.”

- 我 去 公司。
  Wǒ qù gōngsī.
  I'm going to the office.
- 你 去 洗手间吗?
  Nǐ qù xǐshǒujiān ma?
  Are you going to the restroom?
- 下午我会 去 超市。
  Xiàwǔ wǒ huì qù chāoshì.
  In the afternoon, I'll go to the supermarket.
- 我们现在 去 公园。
  Wǒmen xiànzài qù gōngyuán.
  We're going to the park now.
- 晚上我们 去 酒吧。你去吗?
  Wǎnshang wǒmen qù jiǔbā. Nǐ qù ma?
  Tonight we're going to the bar. Are you going?

You can also use 去 (qù) for asking questions. (Note the use of question words and question particles.)

A: 你 去 哪儿 ?

Nǐ qù nǎr ?

Where are you going?

B: 我 去 学校 。

Wǒ qù xuéxiào .

I am going to school.

B: 你 去 我家 吗 ?

Nǐ qù wǒ jiā ma ?

Are you going to my place?

A: 我 去 。

Wǒ qù.

Yes.

literally, "I'm going."

When answering a yes-no question that uses 去 (qù) you don't need anything following it. However, it's important to note that you cannot just use 去 (qù) when there is no context.

去 (qù) with a Verb

Instead of a place, 去 (qù) can also be followed by some sort of action. The structure then means "go to do (something)," and "go and do (something)."

Structure

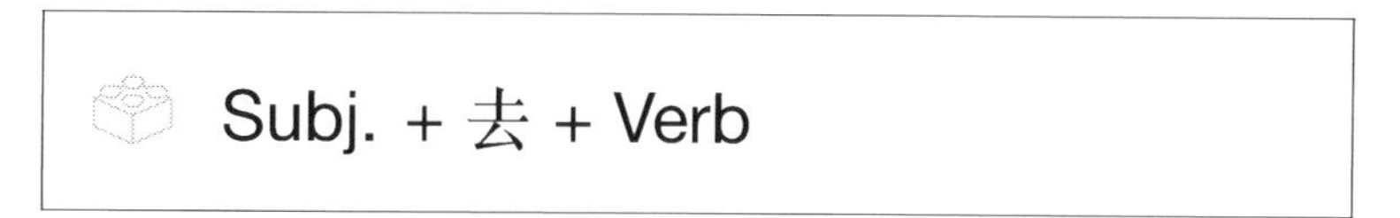

Examples

- 我 去 工作。

  Wǒ qù gōngzuò.

  I'm going to work.

- 他 去 上课。

  Tā qù shàngkè.

  He's going to class.

- 你想 去 旅行吗?

  Nǐ xiǎng qù lǚxíng ma?

  Would you like to go travel?

- 我们 去 吃饭吧。

  Wǒmen qù chīfàn ba.

  Let's go cat.

- 九点我们 去 买。

  Jiǔ diǎn wǒmen qù mǎi.

  At 9 o'clock, we'll go buy it.

Similar to

- Using “dao” to mean “to go to” (A2), page 298

Using the verb “xing” (A1)

The verb 姓 (xìng) literally means “to be surnamed” or “to have the surname.” It may seem awkward at first that there’s a verb just for this, but you’ll find that it’s used quite often in Chinese.

Giving One’s Surname

姓 (xìng) is used most often to tell someone your own surname (“family name” or “last name”), or to ask the surname of someone else.

Structure

Subj. + 姓 + [Surname]

Examples

- 我 姓 王。
  Wǒ xìng Wáng.
  My family name is Wang.
- 你老板 姓 李吗?
  Nǐ lǎobǎn xìng Lǐ ma?
  Is your boss's last name Li?
- 那个帅哥 姓 张。
  Nàge shuàigē xìng Zhāng.
  That handsome guy's last name is Zhang.
- 我爸爸 姓 周，我妈妈 姓 林。
  Wǒ bàba xìng Zhōu, wǒ māma xìng Lín.
  My father's family name is Zhou. My mother's family name is Lin.
- 他女朋友 姓 钱。
  Tā nǚpéngyou xìng Qián.
  His girlfriend's last name is Qian.
- 你好，我 姓 毛。
  Nǐ hǎo, wǒ xìng Máo.
  Hello. My last name is Mao.

- 我 姓 赵，我太太也 姓 赵。

  Wǒ xìng Zhào, wǒ tàitai yě xìng Zhào.

  My last name is Zhao. My wife's last name is also Zhao.

- 我的中文老师 姓 陈。

  Wǒ de Zhōngwén lǎoshī xìng Chén.

  My Chinese teacher's surname is Chen.

- 你奶奶也 姓 陈吗？

  Nǐ nǎinai yě xìng Chén ma?

  Is your grandma's family name also Chen?

- 他们都 姓 李。

  Tāmen dōu xìng Lǐ.

  All of their surnames are Li.

Asking Someone's Surname

You can also use 姓 (xìng) to ask people their surnames. You could do this quite directly by saying:

- 你姓什么？

  Nǐ xìng shénme?

  What is your last name?

However, the formal way to ask has a set form:

- 您贵姓？

  Nín guì xìng?

  What is your honorable surname?

Literally this means "What is your honorable surname?" Use this form to be polite when asking people their surnames.

Similar to

- Using the verb "jiao" (A1), page 60

Expressing "be going to" with "yao" (A1)

The auxiliary verb 要 (yào) has several different meanings[1], and here we'll tackle the "be going to" meaning. You'll use this when you are discussing your plans with someone.

Structure

The idea behind this usage of 要 (yào) is that someone is "planning to" or "going to" or "preparing to" do something. It's not that they just *want to*, or *have to*, it's that they fully expect to do it. It's in their plan.

This usage of 要 (yào) typically includes a time word of some sort, which may be placed before or after the subject. This is fairly logical; if you're discussing plans for the future, you're quite likely to say when you plan to do things.

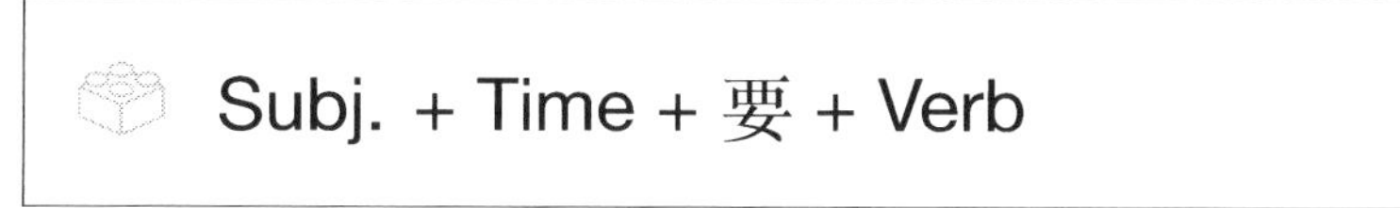

Time + Subj. + 要 + Verb

Note that the time word is not strictly required, and when it's missing, you may at first find yourself wondering which usage of 要 (yào)[1] you're dealing with. This is normal; it just takes some getting used to.

Examples

- 我 明天 要 买一个 iPhone。
  Wǒ míngtiān yào mǎi yī gè iPhone.
  I am going to buy an iPhone tomorrow.
- 你们 现在 要 出去吗?
  Nǐmen xiànzài yào chūqù ma?
  Are you all going out now?
- 我们 今年 要 去美国。
  Wǒmen jīnnián yào qù Měiguó.
  We are planning to go to the U.S. this year.

1. Auxiliary verb "yao" and its multiple meanings (A2), page 262

- 他 下个月 要 来中国工作。
  Tā xià gè yuè yào lái Zhōngguó gōngzuò.
  He is coming to China to work next month.
- 你 下个星期 要 去她家吃晚饭吗?
  Nǐ xià gè xīngqī yào qù tā jiā chī wǎnfàn ma?
  Are you going to her place for dinner next week?
- 这个 星期天 你 要 做什么?
  Zhège Xīngqītiān nǐ yào zuò shénme?
  What are you doing this Sunday?
- 我 晚上 要 给妈妈打电话。
  Wǒ wǎnshang yào gěi māma dǎ diànhuà.
  I am going to call my mom this evening.
- 下午 老师 要 来我家。
  Xiàwǔ lǎoshī yào lái wǒ jiā.
  The teacher is coming to my place this afternoon.
- 老板 明天 要 见他们吗?
  Lǎobǎn míngtiān yào jiàn tāmen ma?
  Is the boss going to meet them tomorrow?
- 下班以后 你 要 回家吗?
  Xiàbān yǐhòu nǐ yào huíjiā ma?
  Are you planning to go home after getting off work?

Similar to

- Expressing "about to happen" with "le" (A2), page 347
- Expressing "would like to" with "xiang" (A2), page 270
- Expressing "about to" with "jiuyao"

Expressing a learned skill with "hui" (A1)

The word 会 (huì) can be used to express an ability that has been learned (a skill). In this case 会 (huì) is an auxiliary verb.

Basic Usage

Structure

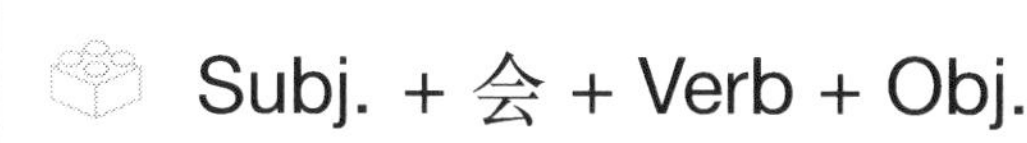

This structure is the easiest way to express all kinds of skills, from languages, to sports, to skills in daily life such as cooking, and driving.

Examples

- 他 会 说中文。
  Tā huì shuō Zhōngwén.
  He can speak Chinese.
- 我 会 写汉字。
  Wǒ huì xiě Hànzì.
  I can write Chinese characters.
- 你 会 做饭吗?
  Nǐ huì zuòfàn ma?
  Can you cook food?
- 狗 会 唱歌吗?
  Gǒu huì chànggē ma?
  Can dogs sing?
- 爸爸 会 开车。
  Bàba huì kāichē.
  Dad can drive.

Negating 会 (huì) Sentences

Structure

会 (huì) sentences are negated with 不 (bù)[1], which is inserted in front of 会 (huì):

> Subj. + 不 + 会 + Verb + Obj.

Again, this is the simplest way to express the lack of a learned ability. So while "can't" is a natural translation for "不会" (bù huì) in English, "don't know how to" is equally correct (and perhaps more helpful).

Also, due to a tone change rule for "不" (bù), the phrase "不会" (bù huì) is actually pronounced "bú huì."

Examples

- 我 不会 说英文。
  Wǒ bù huì shuō Yīngwén.
  I can't speak English.
- 妈妈 不会 做中国菜。
  Māma bù huì zuò Zhōngguó cài.
  Mom can't cook Chinese food.
- 你 不会 游泳吗?
  Nǐ bù huì yóuyǒng ma?
  You can't swim?
- 我奶奶 不会 用电脑。
  Wǒ nǎinai bù huì yòng diànnǎo.
  My grandmother can't use a computer.
- 你 不会 开车吗?
  Nǐ bù huì kāichē ma?
  You can't drive a car?

Note that if we say 我不能说中文 (wǒ bù néng shuō Zhōngwén), the speaker is saying that he can't speak Chinese for some reason other than his own ability[2], perhaps because speaking Chinese in English class is forbidden.

---

1. Standard negation with "bu" (A1), page 85
2. Expressing ability or possibility with "neng" (A1), page 72

Similar to

- Expressing ability or possibility with “neng” (A1), page 72
- Expressing permission with “keyi” (A1), page 75
- Expressing “will” with “hui” (A2), page 268

Expressing ability or possibility with "neng" (A1)

能 (néng) is one of several Chinese words that is normally translated as "can" in English. However, 能 (néng) is used to emphasize one's ability or the possibility of something happening.

Expressing Ability

能 (néng) indicates ability when used with activities that are not consciously learned or studied.

Structure

The structure to use 能 (néng) to express "ability" is:

Examples

- 我 能 吃四十个饺子。
  Wǒ néng chī sìshí gè jiǎozi.
  I can eat 40 dumplings.
- 他 能 工作 24 个小时。
  Tā néng gōngzuò èrshí-sì gè xiǎoshí.
  He can work 24 hours.
- 你 能 帮我找到他吗?
  Nǐ néng bāng wǒ zhǎodào tā ma?
  Can you help me find him?
- 你的手机 能 上网吗?
  Nǐ de shǒujī néng shàngwǎng ma?
  Can your cell phone go on the internet?
- 一岁的宝宝 能 说话吗?
  Yī suì de bǎobao néng shuōhuà ma?
  Can a one year old baby talk?

Expressing Possibility

When used with activities that are consciously learned or studied, 能 (néng) generally means that circumstances do not allow execution of the action. In other words, it's *not possible.*

Structure

The structure to use 能 (néng) to express possibility is exactly the same:

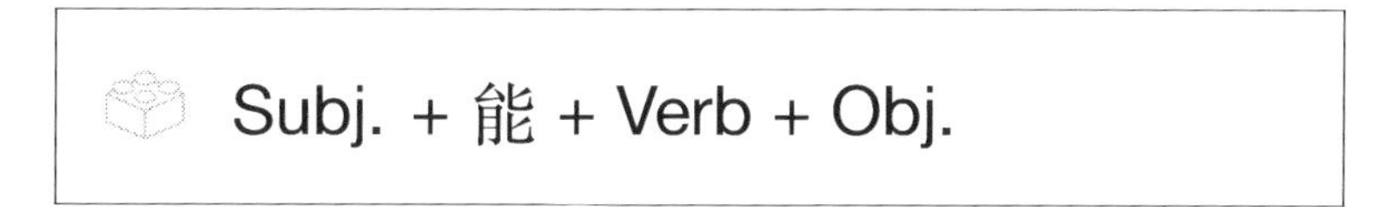

Examples

- 开车一个小时能到家吗?
  Kāichē yī gè xiǎoshí néng dào jiā ma?
  Is it possible to drive home in one hour?
- 他们明天能早点来吗?
  Tāmen míngtiān néng zǎo diǎn lái ma?
  Would it be possible for them to come a little earlier tomorrow?
- 你们能小声一点吗?
  Nǐmen néng xiǎo shēng yīdiǎn ma?
  Could you all lower your voices a bit?
- 你能告诉我她的手机号码吗?
  Nǐ néng gàosu wǒ tā de shǒujī hàomǎ ma?
  Could you tell me her cell phone number?
- 一千块能买一个手机吗?
  Yīqiān kuài néng mǎi yī gè shǒujī ma?
  Is it possible to buy a cell phone with one thousand RMB?

Other Usages

From these examples we can see such circumstances might be pertaining to getting someone's consent or reliant on the speaker's health. If the speaker wishes to express that they are able to execute an action requiring a consciously studied skill, 会 (huì) can be used instead.

Because 能 (néng) can express possibility, it is often used to form polite questions, something like "would it be possible" in English:

Examples

- 我 能 问你一个问题吗?
  Wǒ néng wèn nǐ yī gè wèntí ma?
  Could I ask you a question?
- 我 能 坐在这里吗?
  Wǒ néng zuò zài zhèlǐ ma?
  Could I sit here?
- 这里不 能 游泳。
  Zhèlǐ bù néng yóuyǒng.
  You can't swim here.
- 上课的时候不 能 说英文。
  Shàngkè de shíhou bù néng shuō Yīngwén.
  In class, you can't speak English.
- 工作的时候不 能 玩手机。
  Gōngzuò de shíhou bù néng wán shǒujī.
  When working, you can't play with your cell phone.

Similar to

- Expressing a learned skill with “hui” (A1), page 69
- Expressing permission with “keyi” (A1), page 75

Expressing permission with "keyi" (A1)

可以 (kěyǐ) is an auxiliary verb primarily used for expressing permission. It's often translated as "can," but in order to not get it confused with other words, it's best to think of it as "may" to emphasize the *permission* aspect.

Basic Usage

Just put 可以 (kěyǐ) in directly before a verb to create a meaning of "may" (plus the verb). It's the same structure whether it's a statement or a question.

Structure

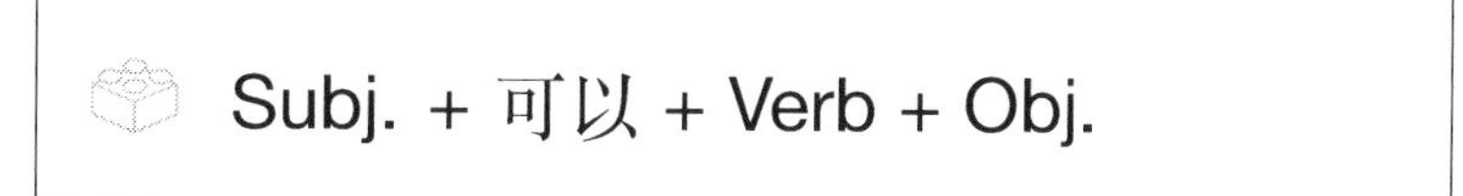

Use this structure to express permission to do things.

Examples

- 我 可以 进来吗?
  Wǒ kěyǐ jìnlái ma?
  May I come in?
- 二十一岁以后 可以 喝酒。
  Èrshí-yī suì yǐhòu kěyǐ hējiǔ.
  After you are 21 years old, you may drink alcohol.
- 妈妈，我 可以 出去玩吗?
  Māma, wǒ kěyǐ chūqù wán ma?
  Mom, may I go out and play?
- 我们 可以 在办公室吃饭吗?
  Wǒmen kěyǐ zài bàngōngshì chīfàn ma?
  Can we eat in the office?
- 我 可以 在这里停车吗?
  Wǒ kěyǐ zài zhèlǐ tíngchē ma?
  Can I park here?

Negating 可以 (kěyǐ) Sentences

可以 (kěyǐ) sentences are negated with 不 (bù)[1], which is inserted before 可以 (kěyǐ).

Structure

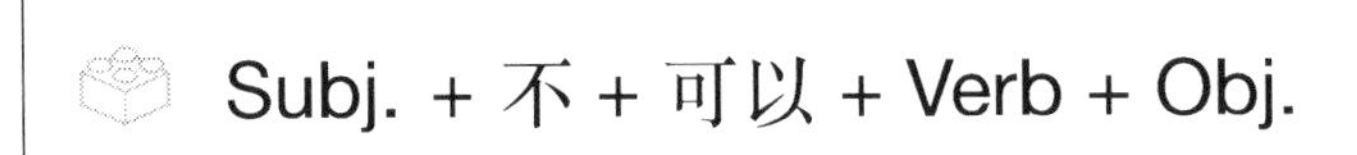

Examples

- 孩子 不可以 看这个。
  Háizi bù kěyǐ kàn zhège.
  Children can't watch this.
- 你现在 不可以 进去。
  Nǐ xiànzài bù kěyǐ jìnqù.
  You can't go in right now.
- 这里 不可以 抽烟。
  Zhèlǐ bù kěyǐ chōuyān.
  You can't smoke here.
- 我们都 不可以 去。
  Wǒmen dōu bù kěyǐ qù.
  None of us may go.
- 你 不可以 说脏话。
  Nǐ bù kěyǐ shuō zānghuà.
  You can't say swear words.

Similar to

- Expressing ability or possibility with "neng" (A1), page 72

1. Standard negation with "bu" (A1), page 85

Wanting to do something with “yao” (A1)

The auxiliary verb 要 (yào) has several different meanings[1], and here we'll tackle the “want to” meaning. To express “wanting to do” something, use 要 (yào) before the verb.

Structure

The verb 要 (yào) can be used as an auxiliary verb to indicate *wanting to do* something.

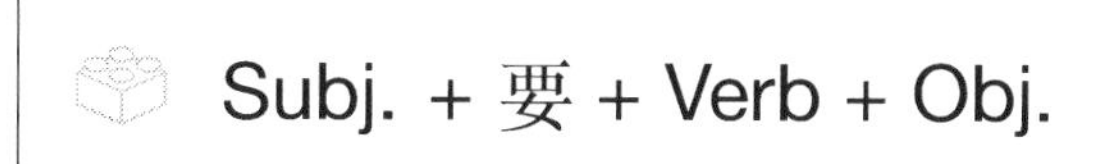

Subj. + 要 + Verb + Obj.

Examples

- 他 要 学中文。
  Tā yào xué Zhōngwén.
  He wants to study Chinese.
- 宝宝 要 睡觉。
  Bǎobao yào shuìjiào.
  The baby wants to sleep.
- 早饭我 要 吃肉。
  Zǎofàn wǒ yào chī ròu.
  For breakfast I want to eat meat.
- 今天很累，我 要 休息。
  Jīntiān hěn lèi, wǒ yào xiūxi.
  Today I'm very tired. I want to rest.
- 这个周末你们 要 做什么？
  Zhège zhōumò nǐmen yào zuò shénme?
  This weekend what do you want to do?

要 (yào) and 想 (xiǎng)

Instead of using 要 (yào), it is also possible to use the word 想 (xiǎng). These two words are largely interchangeable, and both can mean “to want.” The

1. Auxiliary verb “yao” and its multiple meanings (A2), page 262

small difference is that 要 (yào) is often used for something you want to or *need* to do, and *plan to take action on*. It can sound a bit more demanding (and less polite). 想 (xiǎng) on the other hand, often conveys an idea on one's mind, that one *may or may not take action on*. You can think of it as meaning "would like to."

Examples

- 我 要 喝咖啡。
  Wǒ yào hē kāfēi.
  I want to drink coffee.
  I am going to get my hands on some coffee

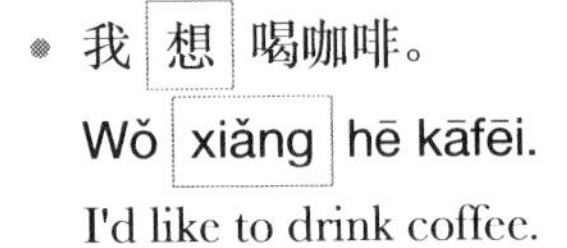

- 我 想 喝咖啡。
  Wǒ xiǎng hē kāfēi.
  I'd like to drink coffee.
  I want to drink a cup of coffee, but may or may not act on that
- 你 要 吃什么？
  Nǐ yào chī shénme?
  What do you want to eat?
- 你 想 吃什么？
  Nǐ xiǎng chī shénme?
  What would you like to eat?

Similar to

- Expressing "should" with "yinggai" (A2), page 266
- Expressing "must" with "dei"

How to do something with "zenme" (A1)

怎么 (zěnme) means "how" in Chinese, and it's not hard to use at all: just put it before a verb.

The Basic "How to Verb" Usage

Structure

The question word 怎么 (zěnme) is used to ask *how* in Chinese. It is inserted in front of the verb that's being asked about:

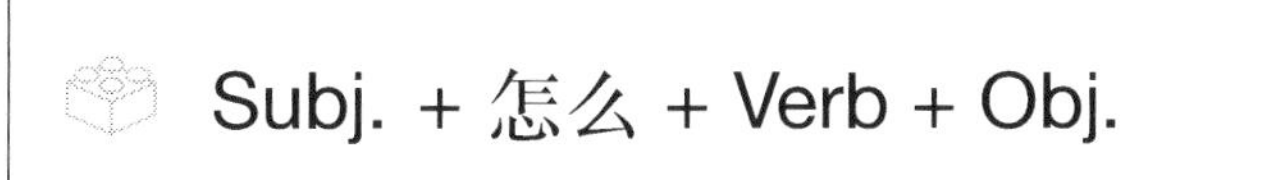

Note that the subject can often be omitted from general "how to" questions, and there doesn't always have to be an object.

Examples

- 你们 怎么 学中文?
  Nǐmen zěnme xué Zhōngwén?
  How do you study Chinese?
- 你 怎么 上班? 坐地铁吗?
  Nǐ zěnme shàngbān? Zuò dìtiě ma?
  How do you get to work? By metro?
- 你知道 怎么 去外滩吗?
  Nǐ zhīdào zěnme qù Wàitān ma?
  Do you know how to get to the Bund?
- 你 怎么 知道我喜欢旅行?
  Nǐ zěnme zhīdào wǒ xǐhuan lǚxíng?
  How did you know I like to travel?
- 我不知道 怎么 跟女孩子说话。
  Wǒ bù zhīdào zěnme gēn nǚháizi shuōhuà.
  I don't know how to talk to girls.

Topic First

Starting a "how to" question with the topic at the beginning of the question is very common. That is, the thing being asked about is introduced first, then a question is asked about how to do something involving it.

Structure

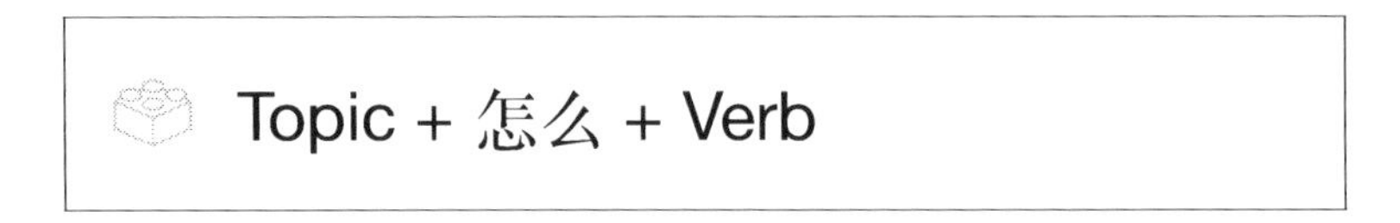

The object doesn't have to come after the verb. Sometimes it moves to the front of the question, establishing what the question is going to be about, before getting specific with the "how" question.

Examples

- 芒果 怎么 吃?
  Mángguǒ zěnme chī?
  How do you eat mangos?
- iPad 怎么 用?
  iPad zěnme yòng?
  How do you use an iPad?
- 语法 怎么 学?
  Yǔfǎ zěnme xué?
  How do you study grammar?
- 中国菜 怎么 做?
  Zhōngguó cài zěnme zuò?
  How do you cook Chinese food?
- "Apple" 怎么 说?
  "Apple" zěnme shuō?
  How do you say apple?

the "in Chinese" is implied

Similar to

- Placement of question words (A1), page 105
- Asking why with "zenme" (A2), page 339
- Expressing "not often" with "bu zenme"
- Expressing "not very" with "bu zenme"

Negation of past actions with “meiyou” (A1)

Use 没有 (méiyǒu) to negate past actions (to say that someone *didn’t do* something, or something *didn’t happen*).

Structure

Usually verbs can be negated with 不 (bù)[1], but that construction is used for habitual or present actions. If the verb is about an action **in the past**, though, 没有 (méiyǒu) should be used:

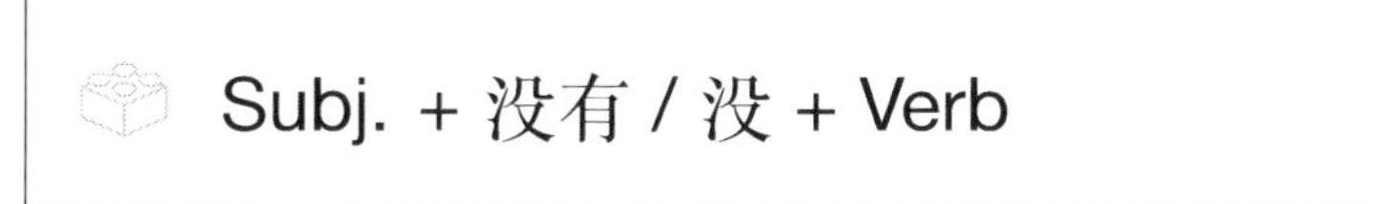

Note that you can shorten 没有 (méiyǒu) to just 没 (méi).

Examples

- 我 没有 去上班。
  Wǒ méiyǒu qù shàngbān.
  I didn't go to work.
- 他们 没有 说话。
  Tāmen méiyǒu shuōhuà.
  They didn't speak.
- 我 没有 喝你的啤酒。
  Wǒ méiyǒu hē nǐ de píjiǔ.
  I didn't drink your beer.
- 她 没有 看到你。
  Tā méiyǒu kàndào nǐ.
  She didn't see you.
- 我 没有 吃早饭。
  Wǒ méiyǒu chī zǎofàn.
  I didn't eat breakfast.

1. Standard negation with “bu” (A1), page 85

- 宝宝 没 哭。
  Bǎobao méi kū.
  The baby didn't cry.

有 has been omitted here.

- 你昨天 没 回家吗?
  Nǐ zuótiān méi huíjiā ma?
  You didn't go back home yesterday?
- 老板今天 没 来吗?
  Lǎobǎn jīntiān méi lái ma?
  The boss didn't come today?
- 老师今天 没 生气。
  Lǎoshī jīntiān méi shēngqì.
  The teacher didn't get angry today.
- 妈妈晚上 没 做饭。
  Māma wǎnshang méi zuòfàn.
  Mom didn't cook food this evening.

Go Easy on the 了 (le)

One thing you need to remember when using 没有 (méiyǒu) is that **了 (le) is not normally used with 没有 (méiyǒu)**. 了 (le) marks completed actions, while 没有 (méiyǒu) is used for actions that *didn't happen* (so of course they're not completed). These two don't work together. This is a very common mistake for beginner learners of Chinese.

✗ 我 没有 做 了 。
Wǒ méiyǒu zuò le .

✓ 我 没有 做。
Wǒ méiyǒu zuò.
I didn't do it.

Similar to

- Negation of "you" with "mei" (A1), page 12
- Standard negation with "bu" (A1), page 85
- Comparing "bu" and "mei" (A2), page 358

Negative commands with “buyao” (A1)

You can use 不要 (bùyào) to command someone: “don’t” (do something). This is similar to the other negative command “别 (bié)[1].”

Note: The pinyin for 不要 is written “bùyào” but pronounced “búyào” due to a tone change rule.

Structure

Negative commands in Chinese (“do not” or “don’t”) are formed with 不要. Usually the subject is omitted, as in English.

Examples

- 不要走。
  Bùyào zǒu.
  Don't leave.
- 不要打我！
  Bùyào dǎ wǒ!
  Don't hit me!
- 不要生气，好吗?
  Bùyào shēngqì, hǎo ma?
  Don't get angry, OK?
- 不要哭！
  Bùyào kū!
  Don't cry!
- 不要吃很多肉。
  Bùyào chī hěn duō ròu.
  Don't eat a lot of meat.

---

1. Negative commands with “bie” (A2), page 156

- 你们 不要 喝酒。
  Nǐmen bùyào hējiǔ.
  You guys, don't drink alcohol.
- 不要 说英文。
  Bùyào shuō Yīngwén.
  Don't speak English.
- 晚上 不要 喝咖啡。
  Wǎnshang bùyào hē kāfēi.
  Don't drink coffee at night.
- 上课的时候 不要 玩手机！
  Shàngkè de shíhou bùyào wán shǒujī!
  In class don't play with your phone!
- 不要 很晚睡觉！
  Bùyào hěn wǎn shuìjiào.
  Don't go to bed too late.

Similar to

- Negative commands with “bie” (A2), page 156
- Alternative existential sentences
- Expressing “don’t need to” with “buyong”

Standard negation with “bu” (A1)

不 (bù) is generally used to negate a verb in the present or future, or to talk about what you do not do, as a habit. So expressing things like “I don’t want to go” or “I’m not going” or “I don’t eat meat” would be typical uses of 不 (bù).

Negating Verbs

Structure

The standard way to negate verbs in Chinese is with 不 (bù). To negate a verb, simply place 不 (bù) before it:

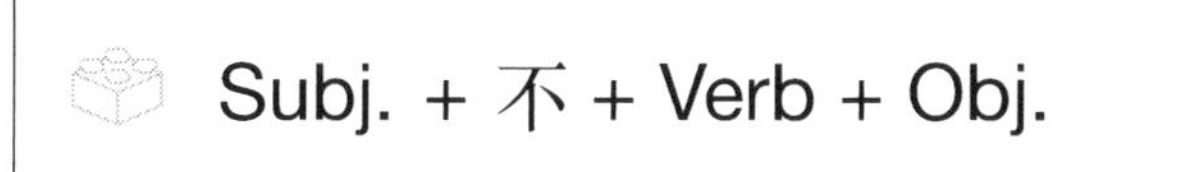

Subj. + 不 + Verb + Obj.

Examples

- 他们 不 是 坏孩子。
  Tāmen bù shì huài háizi.
  They are not bad kids.
- 我们 不 喝 酒。
  Wǒmen bù hē jiǔ.
  We don't drink alcohol.
- 我今天 不 想工作 。
  Wǒ jīntiān bù xiǎng gōngzuò .
  I don't want to work today.
- 你 不 喜欢 我吗?
  Nǐ bù xǐhuan wǒ ma?
  Do you not like me?
- 为什么你 不 喜欢喝 咖啡?
  Wèishénme nǐ bù xǐhuan hē kāfēi?
  Why don't you like to drink coffee?

Almost all verbs can be negated with 不 (bù) (unless you're talking about the past[1]). The only verb that can never be negated with 不 (bù) is 有 (yǒu)[2].

- ✗ 我不有时间。
  Wǒ bù yǒu shíjiān.
- ✓ 我没有时间。
  Wǒ méi yǒu shíjiān.
  I don't have time.

Negating Adjectives

As it turns out, the structure with an adjective is basically the same as the one with a verb.

Structure

Subj. + 不 + Adj.

Examples

- 我不饿。
  Wǒ bù è.
  I'm not hungry.
- 这个不贵。
  Zhège bù guì.
  This is not expensive.
- 公司不大。
  Gōngsī bù dà.
  The company is not big.
- 老板今天很不高兴。
  Lǎobǎn jīntiān hěn bù gāoxìng.
  The boss is very unhappy today.

1. Negation of past actions with "meiyou" (A1), page 81
2. Negation of "you" with "mei" (A1), page 12

- 我哥哥 不 高 ，但是很帅。
  Wǒ gēge bù gāo, dànshì hěn shuài.
  My older brother is not tall, but he is very handsome.

Similar to

- Connecting nouns with "shi" (A1), page 91
- Negation of "you" with "mei" (A1), page 12
- Negation of past actions with "meiyou" (A1), page 81
- Comparing "bu" and "mei" (A2), page 358

Basic sentence order (A1)

In its most basic form, Chinese word order is very similar to English word order. These similarities definitely have their limits, though; don't expect the two languages' word orders to stay consistent much beyond the very basic sentence orders outlined below.

Subject-Predicate

A simple predicate can be just a verb. The most basic word order in Chinese is:

Structure

You can form very simple sentences with just two words.

Examples

Subject	Verb	Translation
你们 Nǐmen	吃。 chī.	You eat.
他 Tā	笑。 xiào.	He laughs.
我 Wǒ	读。 dú.	I read.
你 Nǐ	去。 qù.	You go.
你们 Nǐmen	看。 kàn.	You look.
你 Nǐ	来。 lái.	You come here!
我 Wǒ	说。 shuō.	I speak.
孩子 Háizi	哭。 kū.	Children cry.

谁 Shéi	要学? yào xué?	Who wants to study?
谁 Shéi	想玩? xiǎng wán?	Who wants to play?

Subject-Verb-Object

A slightly longer predicate might be a verb with an object. A sentence with both a verb and an object is formed with this structure:

Structure

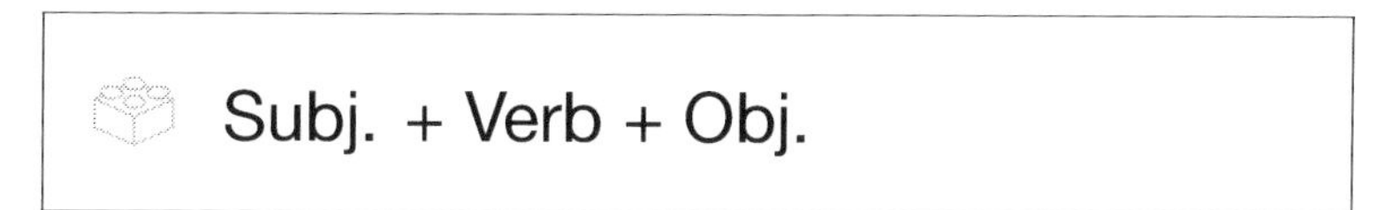

This is the same as in English, and is commonly referred to as SVO word order. You can express a huge variety of things with this simple structure.

Examples

Subject	Verb	Object	Translation
他们 Tāmen	吃 chī	肉。 ròu.	They eat meat.
你 Nǐ	喝 hē	茶吗? chá ma?	Do you drink tea?
我 Wǒ	去 qù	学校。 xuéxiào.	I go to school.
他 Tā	说 shuō	中文。 Zhōngwén.	He speaks Chinese.
你 Nǐ	喜欢 xǐhuan	孩子吗? háizi ma?	Do you like kids?
我们 Wǒmen	要买 yào mǎi	电脑。 diànnǎo.	We want to buy a computer.
你们 Nǐmen	想吃 xiǎng chī	中国菜吗? Zhōngguó cài ma?	Do you want to eat Chinese food?

我 Wǒ	爱 ài	你和爸爸。 nǐ hé bàba.	I love you and dad.
他们 Tāmen	要做 yào zuò	什么? shénme?	What do they want to do?
你 Nǐ	想去 xiǎng qù	什么地方? shénme dìfang?	What place do you want to go to?

When Things Get Tricky

Despite the convenient word order similarities highlighted above, things start to break down as soon as you start adding in such simple sentence elements as the "also" adverb 也 (yě)[1], a time word[2], or a location where something happened[3].

Don't worry; the more complicated Chinese structures aren't hard, they're just different! (If Chinese word order were really the same as English word order, that would be just a little too convenient, wouldn't it?)

Similar to

- Connecting nouns with "shi" (A1), page 91
- Placement of question words (A1), page 105
- Simple "noun + adjective" sentences (A1), page 96
- Standard negation with "bu" (A1), page 85
- Wanting to do something with "yao" (A1), page 77
- Actions in a row (A2), page 272
- Indicating location with "zai" before verbs (A2), page 288

1. The "also" adverb "ye" (A1), page 17
2. Time words and word order (A2), page 211
3. Indicating location with "zai" before verbs (A2), page 288

Connecting nouns with "shi" (A1)

The verb *to be* is not used in Chinese the same way as it is in English. In Chinese, 是 (shì) is for connecting nouns, and is generally not used with adjectives.

Basic Usage

Structure

The structure for connecting nouns with 是 (shì) is:

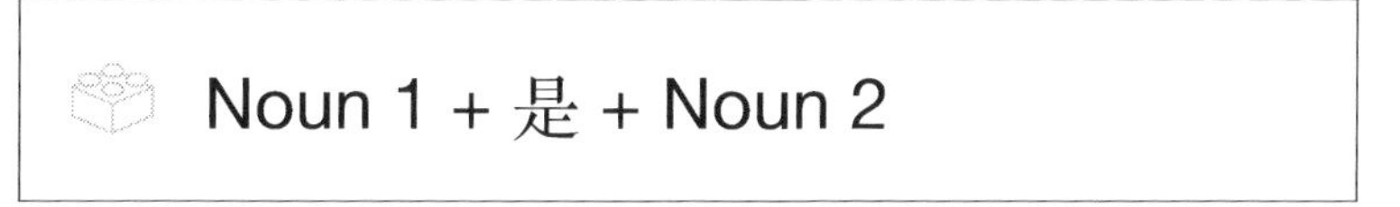

This is equivalent to "Noun 1 **is** Noun 2" in English.

Chinese does not conjugate verbs. That is, the form of the verb is the same no matter who is doing it. In this case, it is always 是 (shì) and never changes. As you can see, it's easy to form simple sentences expressing *to be* in Chinese. The only tricky thing about 是 (shì) in Chinese is that it's used to link *two nouns*, so you can't rely too much on translating directly from English when it comes to expressing the English verb "to be" in Chinese.

Examples

- 我 是 学生。
  Wǒ shì xuésheng.
  I am a student.
- 你 是 John 吗?
  Nǐ shì John ma?
  Are you John?
- 他们 是 有钱人。
  Tāmen shì yǒuqián rén.
  They are rich people.
- 你 是 老板吗?
  Nǐ shì lǎobǎn ma?
  Are you the boss?

- 这 是 我男朋友。
  Zhè shì wǒ nánpéngyou.
  This is my boyfriend.
- 那 是 你们公司吗?
  Nà shì nǐmen gōngsī ma?
  Is that your company?
- 你妈妈 是 老师吗?
  Nǐ māma shì lǎoshī ma?
  Is your mother a teacher?
- 这都 是 你的钱。
  Zhè dōu shì nǐ de qián.
  This is all your money.
- 那 是 什么菜?
  Nà shì shénme cài?
  What food is that?
- 我也 是 他的朋友。
  Wǒ yě shì tā de péngyou.
  I am also his friend.

Other Uses of 是 (shì)

Be careful and take note. As you can see above, 是 (shì) is only used to link two nouns. It cannot be used to link a noun and an adjective. This is a very common mistake for people just beginning to learn Chinese. For that kind of sentence, you'll want to use a different structure with the linking word 很 (hěn)[1].

In Chinese it is also possible to use the phrase "是不是 (shì bu shì)?" It can be used at the beginning or end of a sentence. It's meaning is quite similar to the English expressions "right" and "aren't you?" This is very useful if you want to express concern for a person, or if you want to mix up your sentence structure a bit and make it more interesting. The 是不是 (shì bu shì) pattern is also part of affirmative-negative questions[2].

Another way to use 是 (shì) is to use it as a tag question[3]. You can add "是吗?" (shì ma?) to the end of a question to mean the English equivalent of "is

1. Simple "noun + adjective" sentences (A1), page 96
2. Affirmative-negative question (A1), page 99
3. Tag questions with "ma" (A1), page 118

it" or "yeah?". Using this in a question usually allows the speaker to get a confirmation answer.

Examples

- 他没听到，是不是？
  Tā méi tīngdào, shì bu shì?
  He didn't hear you, right?
- 你是不是还没吃饭？
  Nǐ shì bu shì hái méi chīfàn?
  Haven't you eaten yet?
- 你们是不是中国人？
  Nǐmen shì bu shì Zhōngguó rén?
  Are you Chinese?
- 你到了，是吗？
  Nǐ dào le, shì ma?
  You have arrived, yeah?
- 你有两个孩子，是吗？
  Nǐ yǒu liǎng gè háizi, shì ma?
  You have two kids, yeah?

Similar to

- Simple "noun + adjective" sentences (A1), page 96
- Standard negation with "bu" (A1), page 85

Expressing "excessively" with "tai" (A1)

In Chinese, the simplest structure for expressing "too" in the sense of "excessively" is by using the word 太 (tài). Don't forget to also add 了 (le) after the adjective to keep your Chinese sounding natural.

Structure

太 + Adj. + 了

As in English, this can express that something really is excessive (often as a complaint), or can also colloquially express the meaning of "so" or "very."

Examples

The following examples sound a little bit like a complaint, or a reason for not doing something. They're similar to how we would use "too" in English, and the translations are straightforward.

- 米饭太多了。
  Mǐfàn tài duō le.
  There is too much rice.
- 现在太晚了。
  Xiànzài tài wǎn le.
  Now it's too late.
- 老板太忙了。
  Lǎobǎn tài máng le.
  The boss is too busy.
- 老师太累了。
  Lǎoshī tài lèi le.
  The teacher is too tired.
- 这个厕所太脏了。
  Zhège cèsuǒ tài zāng le.
  This restroom is too dirty.

In the following examples, the same exact pattern is used to exclaim how *good* something is, so these uses are totally *not* complaints. The English translations have to get a little more creative to express the same feeling in English.

- 你 太 好 了 。
  Nǐ tài hǎo le.
  You are so great.
- 他 太 帅 了 。
  Tā tài shuài le.
  He is very handsome.
- 这个女孩 太 漂亮 了 。
  Zhège nǚhái tài piàoliang le.
  This girl is so pretty.
- 小猫 太 可爱 了 ！
  Xiǎomāo tài kě'ài le!
  The kitten is so cute!
- 你的孩子 太 聪明 了 。
  Nǐ de háizi tài cōngming le.
  Your kids are wicked smart.

Note for the more advanced learner: This pattern can be used with modal verbs (e.g. 会 (huì), 能 (néng)) as well as psychological verbs (e.g. 喜欢 (xǐhuan), 想 (xiǎng), 爱 (ài)) to intensify the degree.

Similar to

- Expressing "a little too" with "you dian" (A2), page 165
- Expressing "not very" with "bu tai" (A2), page 169
- Expressing "really" with "zhen" (A2), page 171
- Special verbs with "hen" (A2), page 296
- Superlative "zui" (A2), page 185
- Positive adjectives with "-ji le"
- Expressing "a bit too"

Simple "noun + adjective" sentences (A1)

In English, nouns can be "linked" to adjectives and other nouns with the verb "to be." In Chinese, nouns are linked to other nouns in one way, but linked to adjectives in a completely different way. Nouns are linked to other nouns with 是 (shì)[1]. Nouns are linked to adjectives with 很 (hěn).

Structure

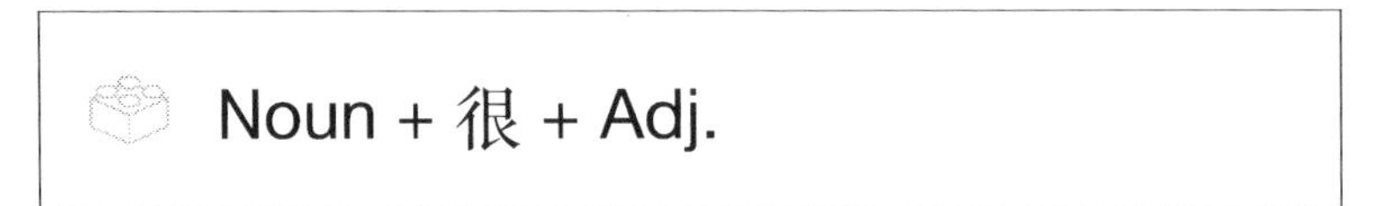

The noun in this structure is the subject of the sentence. Sometimes the 很 (hěn) in this structure is translated as "very," but often it is just a way to link a noun to an adjective.

Examples

In the following examples, 很 (hěn) is just a link (you could think of it as a substitute for the verb "to be"), and the sentences could be translated as "(Noun) is (adjective)."

- 我 很 好。
  Wǒ hěn hǎo.
  I'm good.
- 你 很 漂亮。
  Nǐ hěn piàoliang.
  You are pretty.
- 他 很 高兴。
  Tā hěn gāoxìng.
  He is happy.
- 中文 很 难。
  Zhōngwén hěn nán.
  Chinese is difficult.

1. Connecting nouns with "shi" (A1), page 91

- 老板很生气。
  Lǎobǎn hěn shēngqì.
  The boss is angry.
- 我们很累。
  Wǒmen hěn lèi.
  We're tired.
- 我哥哥也很高。
  Wǒ gēge yě hěn gāo.
  My older brother is also tall.
- 你家也很远吗?
  Nǐ jiā yě hěn yuǎn ma?
  Is your house also far away?
- 爸爸很忙，妈妈也很忙。
  Bàba hěn máng, māma yě hěn máng.
  Dad is busy, and mom is also busy.
- 他和他弟弟都很帅。
  Tā hé tā dìdi dōu hěn shuài.
  He and his younger brother are both handsome.

Remember that **是 (shì) is not used to link adjectives to nouns**. This is a classic mistake that almost everyone makes when learning Chinese. Make sure you use 很 (hěn) and not 是 (shì) to link adjectives to nouns, as shown below:

✘ 他是高。
Tā shì gāo.

✔ 他很高。
Tā hěn gāo.
He is tall.

What 很 (hěn) Really Means

If you're like most learners, when you first learn this pattern, you're thinking, *"How can 很 (hěn) mean "very" one minute, but then nothing but a "link" the next? How do I know if anything means anything in this language?"* That's a reasonable response. But in the case of these "Noun + Adj." sentences, you just have to think of this usage of 很 (hěn) as an exception. It's just part of the structure.

If you actually want to add the meaning of "very" into the sentence, you could use another adverb instead of 很 (hěn). One good choice is 非常 (fēicháng).

✔ 他 非常 高。
Tā fēicháng gāo.
He is very tall.

Similar to

- Age with "sui" (A1), page 26
- Connecting nouns with "shi" (A1), page 91
- The "also" adverb "ye" (A1), page 17
- Expressing "both A and B" with "you" (A2), page 167
- Special verbs with "hen" (A2), page 296
- Superlative "zui" (A2), page 185
- Adjectives with "name" and "zheme"
- Reduplication of adjectives

Affirmative-negative question (A1)

Also known as: 正反问句 (zhèng-fǎn wènjù) and alternative questions.

A common way to form questions in Chinese is to first use a verb in the positive, then repeat the same verb in its negative form, similar to how in English we can say, "Do you have money or not?" or "Have you or have you not been to the park?" This sentence pattern feels a lot more natural in Chinese than those admittedly awkward English equivalents, however.

Verb-Not-Verb

Structure

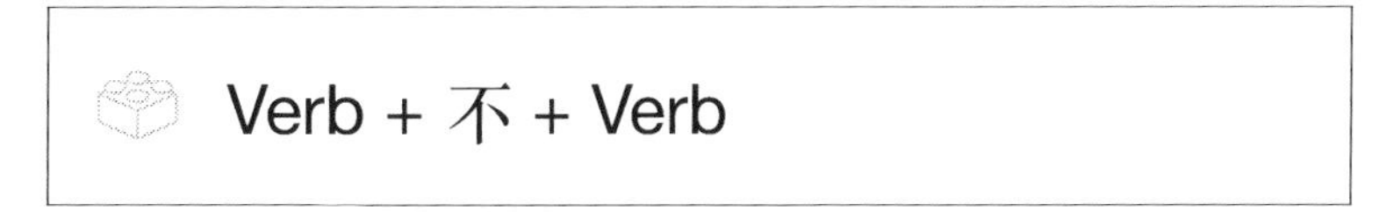

Examples

- 是不是？
  Shì bu shì?
  Is it (or not)?
- 他们来不来？
  Tāmen lái bu lái?
  Are they going to come or not?
- 你想不想我？
  Nǐ xiǎng bu xiǎng wǒ?
  Do you or do you not miss me?
- 我们要去酒吧，你去不去？
  Wǒmen yào qù jiǔbā, nǐ qù bu qù?
  We are going to the bar. Do you want to go?
- 我去买咖啡，你要不要？
  Wǒ qù mǎi kāfēi, yào bu yào?
  I'm going to buy coffee. Do you want some?

Note that the question provides the listener with both possible answers: it's either "Verb" or "不 (bù) Verb."

Verb-Not-Verb with an Object

Structure

If you want to add an object after the verb, the general sentence structure is:

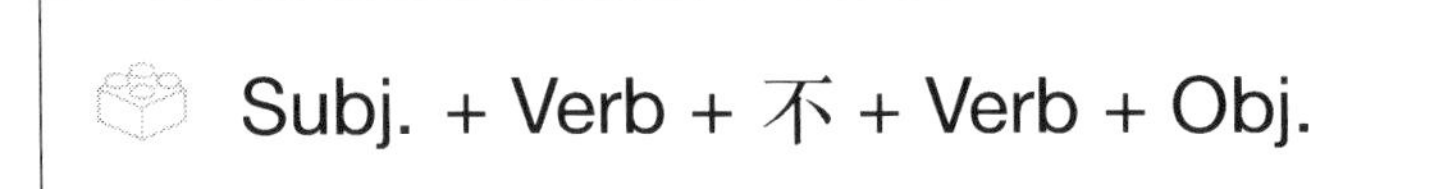

Examples

- 你 回不回 家？
  Nǐ huí bu huí jiā?
  Are you coming back home or not?
- 她 吃不吃 鱼？
  Tā chī bu chī yú?
  Does she eat fish?
- 你们 要不要 米饭？
  Nǐmen yào bu yào mǐfàn?
  Do you want rice?
- 你爸爸 喝不喝 酒？
  Nǐ bàba hē bu hē jiǔ?
  Does your dad drink alcohol or not?
- 今天老板 来不来 办公室？
  Jīntiān lǎobǎn lái bu lái bàngōngshì?
  Is the boss coming to the office today?

Adjective-Not-Adjective

Structure

It can also be done with adjectives (adjectives often behave like verbs in Chinese):

Examples

- 好不好？
  Hǎo bu hǎo?
  Is it good?
- 热不热？
  Rè bu rè?
  Is it hot?
- 他帅不帅？
  Tā shuài bu shuài?
  Is he handsome?
- 这里的咖啡贵不贵？
  Zhèlǐ de kāfēi guì bu guì?
  Is the coffee expensive here?
- 中国菜辣不辣？
  Zhōngguó cài là bu là?
  Is Chinese food spicy?

Literally, "good or not good?"

Again, the question provides the listener with both possible answers: it's either "Adjective" or "不 (bù) Adjective."

These are something like adding tag questions in English, in this case "Are you an adult or not?" If you wanted to translate it very literally, it would be, "Are you or are you not an adult?" In any case, the structure is a very common way to ask questions in Chinese.

Two-Character Verbs and Adjectives

All of the verbs used so far have been single-character verbs. Using two-characters verbs in affirmative-negative questions is slightly trickier. You usually put 不 (bù) after just the first character, then put the entire verb. For example 喜不喜欢 (xǐ bu xǐhuan) is the usual question form of 喜欢 (xǐhuan). You can repeat the whole two-character verb twice, but it's more common (and more elegant) to insert 不 (bù) after the first character (and the same is generally true of two-character adjectives).

Structure

It can be done with verbs:

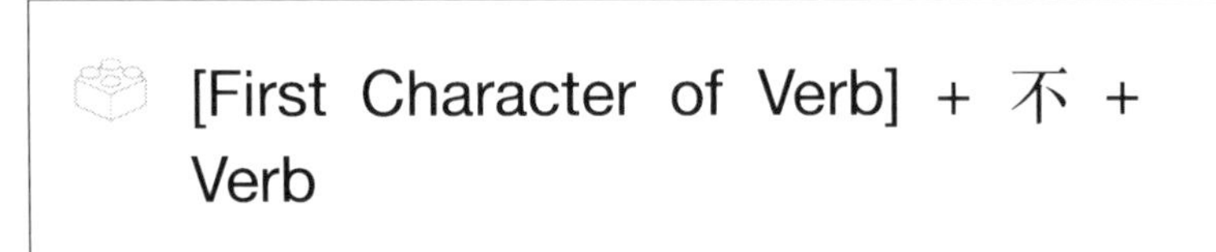

It can also be done with adjectives:

Examples

- 喜欢不喜欢 ? *whole word repeated*
  Xǐhuan bu xǐhuan ?
  Do you like it?
- 喜不喜欢 ? *only the first character repeated*
  Xǐ bu xǐhuan ?
  Do you like it?
- 高兴不高兴 ? *whole word repeated*
  Gāoxìng bu gāoxìng ?
  Are you happy?
- 高不高兴 ? *only the first character repeated*
  Gāo bu gāoxìng ?
  Are you happy?
- 他女朋友 漂亮不漂亮 ? *whole word repeated*
  Tā nǚpéngyou piàoliang bu piàoliang ?
  Is his girlfriend pretty?
- 他女朋友 漂不漂亮 ? *only the first character repeated*
  Tā nǚpéngyou piào bu piàoliang ?
  Is his girlfriend pretty?

- 中国菜 好吃不好吃 ? *whole word repeated*
  Zhōngguó cài hǎochī bu hǎochī ?
  Is Chinese food good?
- 中国菜 好不好吃 ? *only the first character repeated*
  Zhōngguó cài hǎo bu hǎochī ?
  Is Chinese food good?
- 那个地方 好玩不好玩 ? *whole word repeated*
  Nàge dìfang hǎowán bu hǎowán ?
  Is that place fun?
- 那个地方 好不好玩 ? *only the first character repeated*
  Nàge dìfang hǎo bu hǎowán ?
  Is that place fun?

有 (yǒu) is a Special Case

Structure

Because the verb 有 (yǒu) is negated with 没 (méi)[1] and not 不 (bù), the structure for affirmative-negative questions with 有 (yǒu) is:

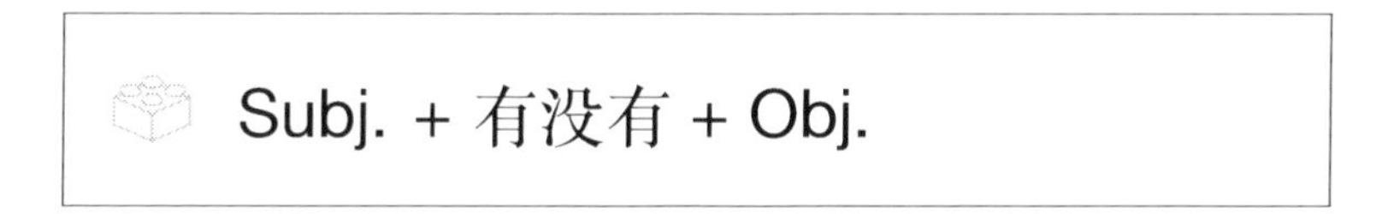

The possible answers are: "有 (yǒu)" or "没有 (méiyǒu)."

The questions could be be asking about current possession ("Do you have it or not?"), or to ask about verbs in the past[2] ("Did you do it or not?").

Examples

- 你哥哥 有没有 女朋友?
  Nǐ gēge yǒu méiyǒu nǚpéngyou?
  Does your older brother have a girlfriend?
- 你们 有没有 孩子?
  Nǐmen yǒu méiyǒu háizi?
  Do you have children?

1. Negation of "you" with "mei" (A1), page 12
2. Negation of past actions with "meiyou" (A1), page 81

- 奶奶 有没有 坐过飞机?
  Nǎinai yǒu méiyǒu zuò guo fēijī?
  Has grandma been on a plane?
- 他 有没有 上过大学?
  Tā yǒu méiyǒu shàng guo dàxué?
  Has he been to college?

Similar to

- Placement of question words (A1), page 105
- Comparing "bu" and "mei" (A2), page 358

Placement of question words (A1)

Who, what, when, where, why, and how. These question words are also to forming questions in Chinese. The important thing to remember is that word order is the same in Chinese for questions and statements.

Overview

Common Question Words List

In English, question words are also known as *wh-words*, as the majority of them begin with *wh*:

- 什么

  shénme

  what

- 哪里、哪儿

  nǎlǐ, nǎr

  where

- 哪个

  nǎge

  which

- 谁

  shéi

  who

  In spoken Chinese, people normally say "shéi," not "shuí"

- 什么时候

  shénme shíhou

  when

- 为什么

  wèishénme

  why

- 怎么

  zěnme

  how

- 多少

  duōshao

  how many / how much

Rules

In English, question words have to be placed at the beginning of the sentence. This involves changing the word order to allow this rearrangement. In Chinese, using question words is a lot simpler. You simply place a question word in the place of the thing you want to ask about. *Nothing needs to be rearranged.*

So if the statement is

- 我是 小李 。
  Wǒ shì Xiǎo Lǐ.
  I am Xiao Li.

the question form - "who are you?" - has the same word order:

- 你是 谁 ?
  Nǐ shì shéi ?
  Who are you? (you are who?)

This works for whatever it is you want to ask about. The question form has the same word order as the statement form.

Expressing "What" with 什么 (shénme)

Structure

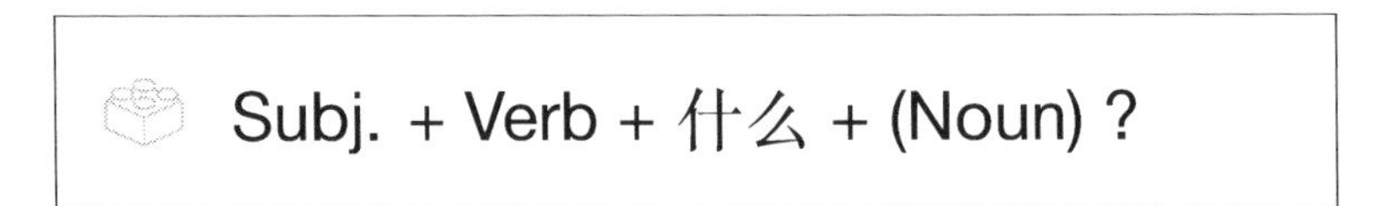

Examples

A: 这是 什么 ?
Zhè shì shénme ?
What is this?

B: 这是 我的 iPad 。
Zhè shì wǒ de iPad .
This is my iPad.

A: 你喜欢吃 什么 菜?
Nǐ xǐhuan chī shénme cài?
What kind of food do you like?

B: 我喜欢吃 中国菜 。

Wǒ xǐhuan chī Zhōngguó cài.

I like Chinese food.

A: 你用 什么 手机?

Nǐ yòng shénme shǒujī?

What kind of cell phone do you use?

B: 我用 iPhone 。

Wǒ yòng iPhone.

I use an iPhone.

A: 你在看 什么 书?

Nǐ zài kàn shénme shū?

What kind of book are you reading?

B: 我在看 小说 。

Wǒ zài kàn xiǎoshuō.

I am reading a novel.

A: 他开 什么 车?

Tā kāi shénme chē?

What kind of car does he drive?

B: 他开 宝马 。

Tā kāi Bǎomǎ.

He drives a BMW.

Expressing "Where" with 哪里 (nǎlǐ) / 哪儿 (nǎr)

The words 哪里 (nǎlǐ) and 哪儿 (nǎr) mean the same thing. The difference is simply regional preference: 哪里 (nǎlǐ) is preferred in the south (Shanghai, Taiwan), whereas 哪儿 (nǎr) is preferred in the north (Beijing, Xi'an).

Structure

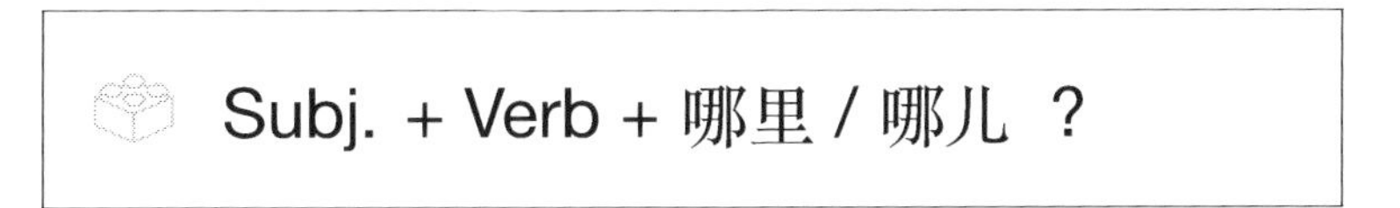

Examples

A: 你在 哪里 ?
Nǐ zài nǎlǐ ?
Where are you?

B: 我在 家 。
Wǒ zài jiā .
I'm at home.

A: 你要去 哪儿 ?
Nǐ yào qù nǎr ?
Where are you going now?

B: 我要去 洗手间 。
Wǒ yào qù xǐshǒujiān .
I'm going to the bathroom.

A: 我们在 哪儿 ?
Wǒmen zài nǎr ?
Where are we?

B: 我们在 南京西路 。
Wǒmen zài Nánjīng Xī Lù .
We are at West Nanjing road.

A: 这个周末你想去 哪儿 ?
Zhège zhōumò nǐ xiǎng qù nǎr ?
Where do you want to go this weekend?

B: 我想去 公园 。
Wǒ xiǎng qù gōngyuán .
I want to go to the park.

A: 你好，你要去 哪儿 ?
Nǐhǎo, nǐ yào qù nǎr ?
Hello, where do you want to go?

B: 我要去 外滩 。
Wǒ yào qù Wàitān .
I want to go to the Bund.

Expressing "Which" with 哪个 (nǎge)

Structure

Subj. + Verb + 哪个 (+ Noun) ?

Examples

A: 你要 哪个 ？

Nǐ yào nǎge ?

Which one do you want?

B: 我要 这个 。

Wǒ yào zhège .

I want this one.

A: 你喜欢 哪个菜 ？

Nǐ xǐhuan nǎge cài ?

Which dish do you like?

B: 我喜欢 这个菜 。

Wǒ xǐhuan zhège cài .

I like this dish.

A: 我们去 哪个饭店 ？

Wǒmen qù nǎge fàndiàn ?

Which restaurant are we going to?

B: 我们去 你妈妈的饭店 。

Wǒmen qù nǐ māma de fàndiàn .

We are going to your mom's restaurant.

A: 你在 哪个房间 ？

Nǐ zài nǎge fángjiān ?

Which room are you in?

B: 我在 你的房间 。

Wǒ zài nǐ de fángjiān .

I'm in your room.

A: 你住在 哪个区 ?

Nǐ zhù zài nǎge qū?

Which district do you live in?

B: 我住在 静安区 。

Wǒ zhù zài Jìng'ān Qū.

I live in Jing'an District.

Expressing "Who" with 谁 (shéi)

Structure

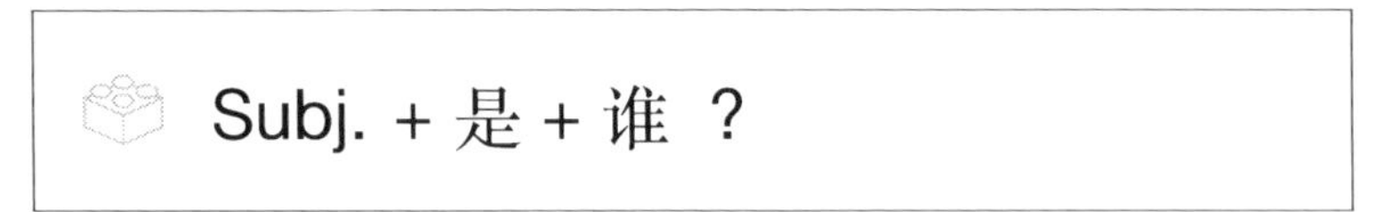

Examples

A: 你是 谁 ?

Nǐ shì shéi?

Who are you?

B: 我是 他女朋友 。

Wǒ shì tā nǚpéngyou.

I'm his girlfriend.

A: 她是 谁 ?

Tā shì shéi?

Who is she?

B: 她是 我的老师 。

Tā shì wǒ de lǎoshī.

She's my teacher.

A: 你不喜欢 谁 ?

Nǐ bù xǐhuan shéi?

Who do you not like?

B: 我不喜欢 我的老板 。
Wǒ bù xǐhuan wǒ de lǎobǎn.
I don't like my boss.

A: 谁 想去？
Shéi xiǎng qù?
Who wants to go?

B: 我 想去。
Wǒ xiǎng qù.
I want to go.

A: 谁 想喝咖啡？
Shéi xiǎng hē kāfēi?
Who wants to drink coffee?

B: 我 想喝咖啡。
Wǒ xiǎng hē kāfēi.
I want to drink coffee.

Expressing "When" with 什么时候 (shénme shíhou)

Structure

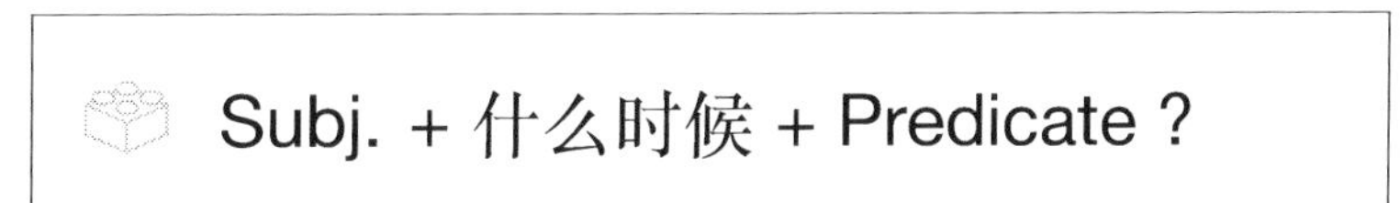

Examples for asking and telling *when* (to keep things simple, we'll just include questions about the future; asking questions about the past can be slightly more complicated and may involve the "shi… de" construction).

Examples

A: 你 什么时候 来？
Nǐ shénme shíhou lái?
When are you coming?

B: 我 明天 来。
Wǒ míngtiān lái.
I'm coming tomorrow.

A: 你们 什么时候 走？
Nǐmen shénme shíhou zǒu?
When are you guys leaving?

B: 我们 下个月 走。
Wǒmen xià gè yuè zǒu.
We're leaving next month.

A: 我们 什么时候 吃饭？
Wǒmen shénme shíhou chīfàn?
When are we eating?

B: 我们 6 点 吃饭。
Wǒmen liù diǎn chīfàn.
We're eating at 6:00.

A: 爸爸 什么时候 回来？
Bàba shénme shíhou huílái?
When is dad coming back?

B: 爸爸 周末 回来。
Bàba zhōumò huílái.
Dad is coming back this weekend.

A: 你的飞机 什么时候 到上海？
Nǐ de fēijī shénme shíhou dào Shànghǎi?
When is your airplane arriving in Shanghai?

B: 晚上八点 。
Wǎnshang bā diǎn.
Eight o'clock this evening.

Expressing "Why" with 为什么 (wèishénme)

Structure

Subj. + 为什么 + Predicate ?

Examples

A: 你 为什么 学中文？
Nǐ wèishénme xué Zhōngwén?
Why do you study Chinese?

B: 因为 我在中国工作。
Yīnwèi wǒ zài Zhōngguó gōngzuò.
Because I'm working in China.

A: 他们 为什么 不喝咖啡?
Nǐ wèishénme bù hē kāfēi?
Why don't you drink coffee?

B: 因为 咖啡很苦。
Yīnwèi kāfēi hěn kǔ.
Because coffee is bitter.

A: 他 为什么 不来?
Tā wèishénme bù lái?
Why isn't he coming?

B: 因为 他很忙。
Yīnwèi tā hěn máng.
Because he is busy.

A: 你早上 为什么 不在?
Nǐ zǎoshang wèishénme bù zài?
Why were you not here this morning?

B: 因为 我出去见朋友了。
Yīnwèi wǒ chūqù jiàn péngyou le.
Because I went out to meet some friends.

A: 这些外国人 为什么 不喜欢中国?
Zhèxiē wàiguó rén wèishénme bù xǐhuan Zhōngguó?
Why do these foreigners not like China?

B: 因为 中国人太多。
Yīnwèi Zhōngguó rén tài duō.
Because China has a lot of people.

Expressing "How" with 怎么 (zěnme)

Structure

Subj. + 怎么 + Verb (+ Obj.) ?

Examples

A: 你 怎么 学习中文?
Nǐ zěnme xuéxí Zhōngwén?
How do you study Chinese?

B: 我 用 Grammar Wiki 学习中文。
Wǒ yòng Grammar Wiki xuéxí Zhōngwén.
I use the Grammar Wiki to study Chinese.

A: 你 怎么 上网?
Nǐ zěnme shàngwǎng?
How do you go online?

B: 我 用手机 上网。
Wǒ yòng shǒujī shàngwǎng.
I use my cell phone to go online.

A: 你 怎么 去北京?
Nǐ zěnme qù Běijīng?
How do you go to Beijing?

B: 我 坐火车 去。
Wǒ zuò huǒchē qù.
I take the train.

A: 你们 怎么 回家?
Nǐmen zěnme huíjiā?
How are you guys going to get home?

B: 我 开车 回家。
Wǒ kāichē huíjiā.
I'm driving home.

A: 你 怎么 买票?

Nǐ zěnme mǎi piào?

How do you buy tickets?

B: 我 上网 买票。

Wǒ shàngwǎng mǎi piào.

I go online to buy tickets.

Similar to

- Basic sentence order (A1), page 88
- How to do something with "zenme" (A1), page 79
- Asking why with "zenme" (A2), page 339

Tag questions with “bu” (A1)

In the same way you can tag questions with 吗 (ma)[1], tag questions can also be formed using 不 (bù). This is done by putting an affirmative-negative question[2] at the end of a sentence.

Structure

This can then be attached to the end of a sentence to form a tag question. Tag questions seek confirmation or acceptance of what has been said. In English, “right?” and “OK?” are often used as tag questions.

Examples

- 你会说中文，对不对？
  Nǐ huì shuō Zhōngwén, duì bu duì?
  You speak Chinese, right?
- 他是你的老板，对不对？
  Tā shì nǐ de lǎobǎn, duì bu duì?
  He's your boss, right?
- 我们是好朋友，对不对？
  Wǒmen shì hǎo péngyou, duì bu duì?
  We are good friends, right?
- 你昨天没回家，对不对？
  Nǐ zuótiān méi huíjiā, duì bu duì?
  You didn't come back home yesterday, right?
- 你有新女朋友了，是不是？
  Nǐ yǒu xīn nǚpéngyou le, shì bu shì?
  You have a new girlfriend, right?

---

1. Tag questions with “ma” (A1), page 118
2. Affirmative-negative question (A1), page 99

- 九点开会，是不是？
  Jiǔ diǎn kāihuì, shì bu shì?
  We are going to hold a meeting at 9, right?
- 你姓王，是不是？
  Nǐ xìng Wáng, shì bu shì?
  Your last name is Wang, is it not?
- 我们回家吧，好不好？
  Wǒmen huíjiā ba, hǎo bu hǎo?
  Let's go home, OK?
- 周末去看电影，好不好？
  Zhōumò qù kàn diànyǐng, hǎo bu hǎo?
  Let's go to a movie this weekend, OK?
- 你们明天来，好不好？
  Nǐmen míngtiān lái, hǎo bu hǎo?
  You come here tomorrow, OK?

Similar to

- Affirmative-negative question (A1), page 99
- Tag questions with "ma" (A1), page 118
- Comparing "bu" and "mei" (A2), page 358

Tag questions with "ma" (A1)

As well as yes/no questions[1], you can also form tag questions with 吗 (ma). Tag questions are quick questions that are tagged on the end of a sentence to ask for confirmation. In English, this is often done with "right?" or negatively with "isn't it?"

The easiest way to do this in Chinese is to add some kind of confirmation word and 吗 (ma) on the end of the sentence.

Structure

As you can see below, the pattern typically involves words like 好 (hǎo), 对 (duì), 是 (shì), or 可以 (kěyǐ), followed by 吗 (ma).

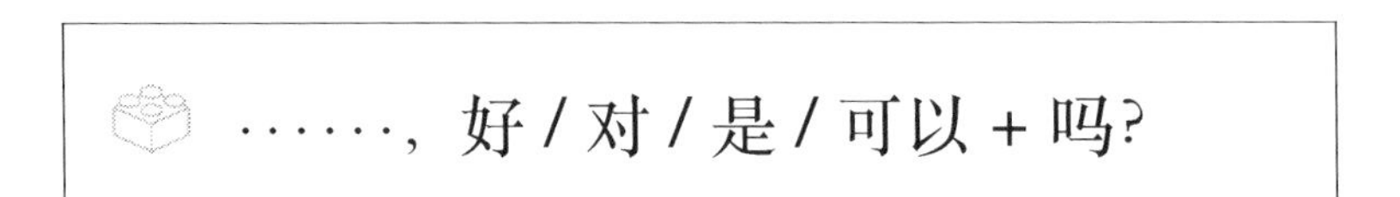

By placing these on the end of a sentence, you can soften a suggestion or request confirmation.

Examples

- 这样做，对吗？
  Zhèyàng zuò, duì ma?
  Do it like this, right?
- 你们见过，对吗？
  Nǐmen jiàn guo, duì ma?
  You've met, right?
- 他们昨天都没去，是吗？
  Tāmen zuótiān dōu méi qù, shì ma?
  They didn't go yesterday, right?
- 你没来过，是吗？
  Nǐ méi lái guo, shì ma?
  You haven't been here, right?

---

1. Yes-no questions with "ma" (A1), page 120

- 你喜欢我妹妹，是吗？
  Nǐ xǐhuan wǒ mèimei, shì ma?
  You like my younger sister, huh?
- 我们去你家，好吗？
  Wǒmen qù nǐ jiā, hǎo ma?
  Let's go to your place, OK?
- 不要告诉他，好吗？
  Bùyào gàosu tā, hǎo ma?
  Don't tell him, OK?
- 今天我们都不喝酒，好吗？
  Jīntiān wǒmen dōu bù hējiǔ, hǎo ma?
  Let's all not drink alcohol today, OK?
- 我现在想去洗手间，可以吗？
  Wǒ xiànzài xiǎng qù xǐshǒujiān, kěyǐ ma?
  I want to go to the bathroom now. Is that OK?
- 妈妈，我要吃巧克力，可以吗？
  Māma, wǒ yào chī qiǎokèlì, kěyǐ ma?
  Mom, I want to eat chocolate. May I?

Similar to

- Questions with “ne” (A1), page 49
- Tag questions with “bu” (A1), page 116
- Yes-no questions with “ma” (A1), page 120
- Advanced yes-no questions with “ma”

Yes-no questions with "ma" (A1)

The question particle 吗 (ma) is a simple way to form questions in Chinese. By placing 吗 (ma) on the end of a statement, you convert it into a *yes/no question* (questions that could be answered with "yes" or "no" in English).

Basic Usage

Structure

Any statement can be converted into a yes/no question with 吗 (ma). You could think of 吗 (ma) as being like a question mark you say out loud. So the basic structure is:

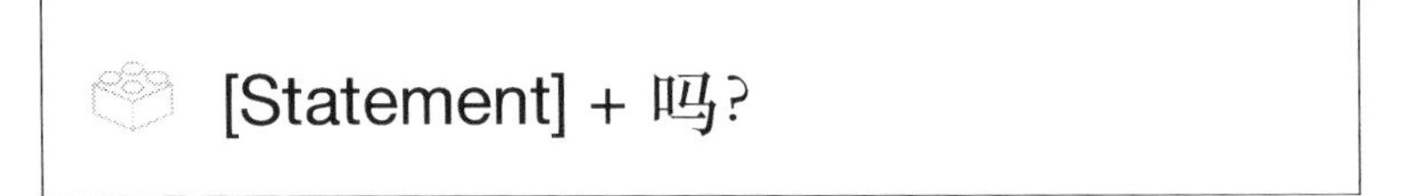

Examples

- 你喜欢咖啡。 *statement*

  Nǐ xǐhuan kāfēi.

  You like coffee.

The sentence "You like coffee" can easily be converted into the question "Do you like coffee?" by adding 吗 (ma):

- 你喜欢咖啡 吗 ? *question*

  Nǐ xǐhuan kāfēi ma ?

  Do you like coffee?

More examples of statements and their yes/no question forms:

- 你是大学生。 *statement*

  Nǐ shì dàxuéshēng.

  You are a college student.

- 你是大学生 吗 ? *question*

  Nǐ shì dàxuéshēng ma ?

  Are you a college student?

- 他是老板。 *statement*

  Tā shì lǎobǎn.

  He is the boss.

- 他是老板 吗 ? *question*
  Tā shì lǎobǎn ma ?
  Is he the boss?
- 你喜欢她。 *statement*
  Nǐ xǐhuan tā.
  You like her.
- 你喜欢她 吗 ? *question*
  Nǐ xǐhuan tā ma ?
  Do you like her?
- 你想家。 *statement*
  Nǐ xiǎng jiā.
  You miss home.
- 你想家 吗 ? *question*
  Nǐ xiǎng jiā ma ?
  Do you miss home?
- 爸爸喜欢喝茶。 *statement*
  Bàba xǐhuan hē chá.
  Dad likes drinking tea.
- 爸爸喜欢喝茶 吗 ? *question*
  Bàba xǐhuan hē chá ma ?
  Does dad like drinking tea?
- 你们也去。 *statement*
  Nǐmen yě qù.
  You also go.
- 你们也去 吗 ? *question*
  Nǐmen yě qù ma ?
  Are you also going?
- 他在你们学校学中文。 *statement*
  Tā zài nǐmen xuéxiào xué Zhōngwén.
  He studies Chinese in your school.

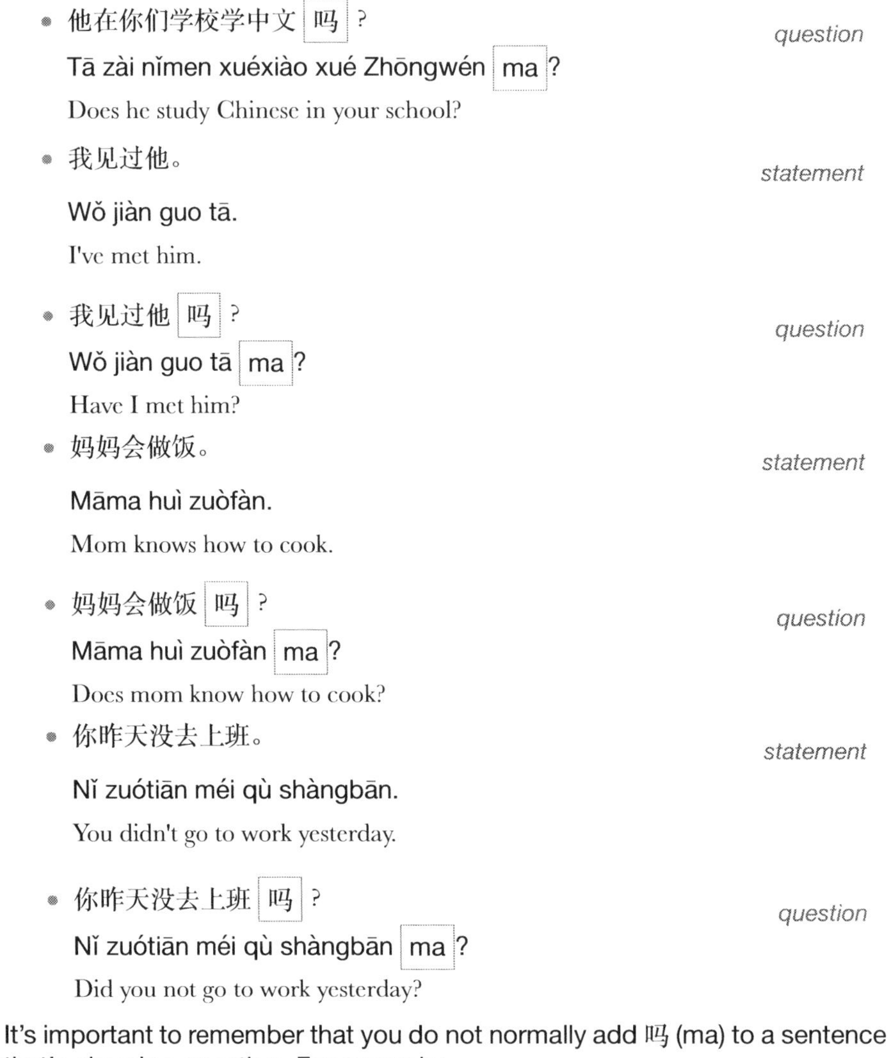

- 他在你们学校学中文 吗 ? *question*
  Tā zài nǐmen xuéxiào xué Zhōngwén ma ?
  Does he study Chinese in your school?
- 我见过他。 *statement*
  Wǒ jiàn guo tā.
  I've met him.
- 我见过他 吗 ? *question*
  Wǒ jiàn guo tā ma ?
  Have I met him?
- 妈妈会做饭。 *statement*
  Māma huì zuòfàn.
  Mom knows how to cook.
- 妈妈会做饭 吗 ? *question*
  Māma huì zuòfàn ma ?
  Does mom know how to cook?
- 你昨天没去上班。 *statement*
  Nǐ zuótiān méi qù shàngbān.
  You didn't go to work yesterday.
- 你昨天没去上班 吗 ? *question*
  Nǐ zuótiān méi qù shàngbān ma ?
  Did you not go to work yesterday?

It's important to remember that you do not normally add 吗 (ma) to a sentence that's *already a question*. For example:

✗ 你是谁 吗 ? *谁 is a question word*
Nǐ shì shéi ma ?

✗ 这是不是书 吗 ? *是不是 is a question pattern*
Zhè shì bu shì shū ma ?

These would be something like "Are you who are you?" and "Is this is a book?" in English, both obviously ungrammatical. Still, if you're not careful, you may find yourself throwing a 吗 (ma) onto the end of a question that doesn't need it. Many learners make this mistake, so don't worry if it happens every once in a while, just catch it and remember it the next time.

More Advanced Usage

However, this doesn't mean that a sentence *can't ever* have a question word and 吗 (ma). If a sentence contains verbs of understanding such as 知道 (zhīdào), 了解 (liǎojiě), 明白 (míngbai), 认识 (rènshi), etc., then 吗 (ma) can still be added at the end of the question. You will later learn more about these advanced yes-no questions with "ma".

Similar to

- Placement of question words (A1), page 105
- Expressing the self-evident with "ma"

Comparing “er” and “liang” (A1)

In Chinese, there are two words for “two.” They are 二 (èr) and 两 (liǎng), and each is used in different circumstances.

Uses of 二 (èr)

二 (èr) is for Numbers

The digit “2” is 二 (èr). This is used generally in numbers, when counting to ten, giving out a phone number, and so on.

Unlike 两 (liǎng), 二 (èr) is not used to say there are “two” of something, and does not generally occur with measure words by itself. Numbers like 十二 (12) (shí'èr) and 二十二 (22) (èrshí-èr) end with a “2” and can still be combined with measure words. In those cases, 两 (liǎng) is not needed.

Examples

Here are some common examples of 二 (èr) in action:

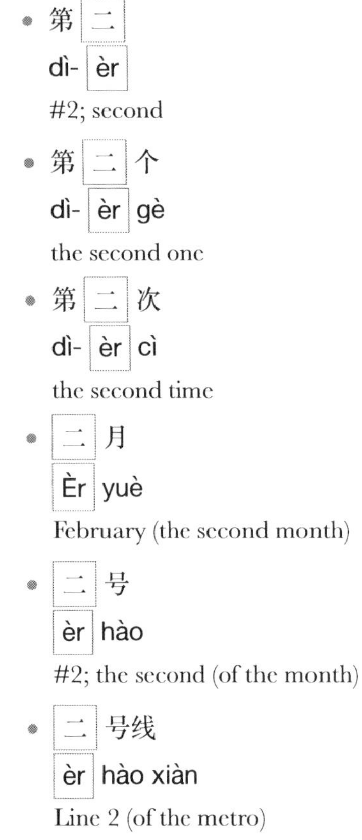

- 第二
  dì- èr
  #2; second
- 第二个
  dì- èr gè
  the second one
- 第二次
  dì- èr cì
  the second time
- 二月
  Èr yuè
  February (the second month)
- 二号
  èr hào
  #2; the second (of the month)
- 二号线
  èr hào xiàn
  Line 2 (of the metro)

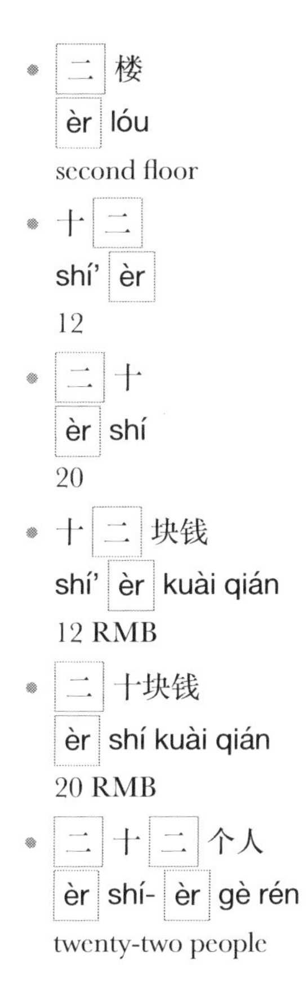

- 二楼
  èr lóu
  second floor
- 十二
  shí' èr
  12
- 二十
  èr shí
  20
- 十二块钱
  shí' èr kuài qián
  12 RMB
- 二十块钱
  èr shí kuài qián
  20 RMB
- 二十二个人
  èr shí- èr gè rén
  twenty-two people

Uses of 两 (liǎng)

两 (liǎng) is for Measure Words

When specifying quantities (and using measure words to do it), 两 (liǎng) is used. This is when you want to say "two of something" or "both."

Here are some common examples of 两 (liǎng) in action:

Examples

- 两个小时
  liǎng gè xiǎoshí
  two hours
- 两点
  liǎng diǎn
  2 o'clock
- 两天
  liǎng tiān
  two days

- 两 个星期
  liǎng gè xīngqī
  two weeks
- 两 个月
  liǎng gè yuè
  two months
- 两 年
  liǎng nián
  two years
- 两 次
  liǎng cì
  two times / twice
- 两 块钱
  liǎng kuài qián
  2 kuai / 2 RMB
- 两 百
  liǎng bǎi
  200

  note: 二百 (èrbǎi) is also acceptable.
- 两 千
  liǎng qiān
  2,000
- 我 两 个都要。
  Wǒ liǎng gè dōu yào.
  I want both of them.

Similar to

- Structure of numbers (A1), page 36

Negative adjectives with "-si le" (A2)

In English, you might use the expression "you scared me to death!" In Chinese, 死了 (sǐ le) is used similarly to intensify an adjective with an unpleasant connotation.

Structure

The "Subject" part below is actually optional, you can still make your over-the-top exclamations without it.

This structure is technically a kind of degree complement.

Examples

- 我饿死了。
  Wǒ è sǐ le!
  I'm starving!
  Literally, "hungry to death"
- 今天累死了。
  Jīntiān lèi sǐ le!
  Today was so exhausting!
  Literally, "tired to death"
- 热死了！
  Rè sǐ le!
  It's ridiculously hot!
  Literally, "hot to death"
- 这几天忙死了。
  Zhè jǐ tiān máng sǐ le!
  It's been so terribly busy these days!
  Literally, "busy to death"
- 这件衣服丑死了。
  Zhè jiàn yīfu chǒu sǐ le!
  This clothing is totally hideous!
  Literally, "ugly to death"
- 你的房间脏死了。
  Nǐ de fángjiān zāng sǐ le!
  Your room is absolutely filthy!
  Literally, "dirty to death"

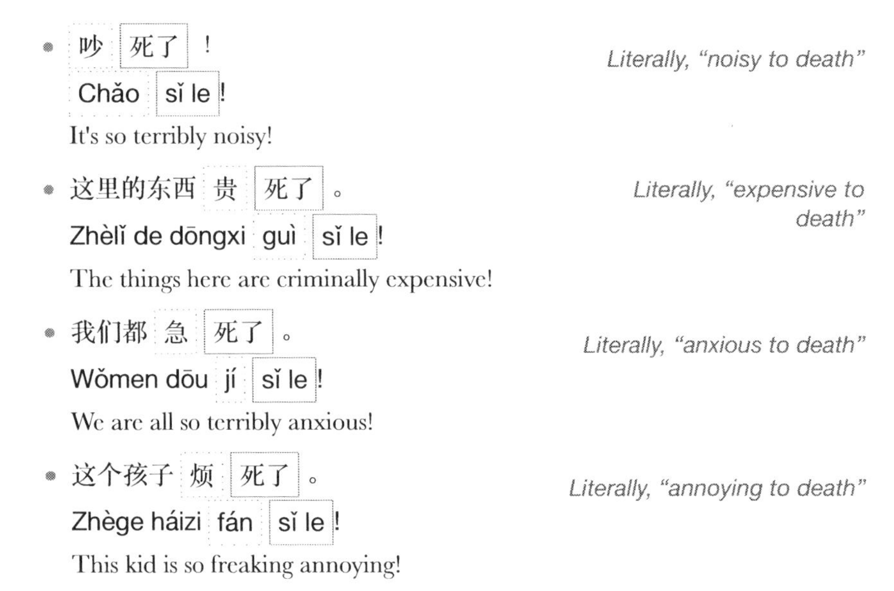

- 吵 死了 ！
  Chǎo sǐ le!
  It's so terribly noisy!
  Literally, "noisy to death"
- 这里的东西 贵 死了 。
  Zhèlǐ de dōngxi guì sǐ le!
  The things here are criminally expensive!
  Literally, "expensive to death"
- 我们都 急 死了 。
  Wǒmen dōu jí sǐ le!
  We are all so terribly anxious!
  Literally, "anxious to death"
- 这个孩子 烦 死了 。
  Zhège háizi fán sǐ le!
  This kid is so freaking annoying!
  Literally, "annoying to death"

None of these sentences actually refers to someone dying. Instead the word 死了 (sǐ le) and the structure is simply used to intensify an adjective. Notice how these are awkward to translate into English; the translations above took a number of different angles to create the same impact as -死了 (sǐ le) does in Chinese. You might say that -死了 (sǐ le) is much more versatile in Chinese than the English expression "to death."

For Positive Connotations

Traditionally, -死了 (sǐ le) is only for adjectives with negative connotations, while positive connotations use a similar degree complement, 极了 (jí le). In recent years, however, it's become quite popular to also use -死了 (sǐ le) with positive adjectives:

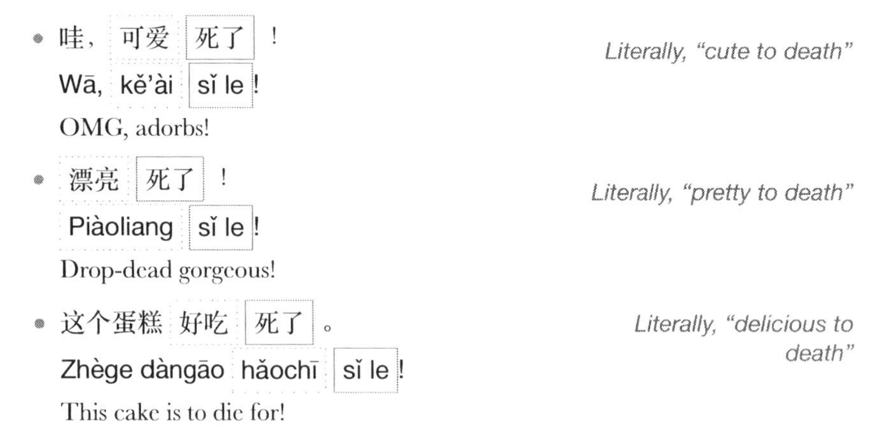

- 哇， 可爱 死了 ！
  Wā, kě'ài sǐ le!
  OMG, adorbs!
  Literally, "cute to death"
- 漂亮 死了 ！
  Piàoliang sǐ le!
  Drop-dead gorgeous!
  Literally, "pretty to death"
- 这个蛋糕 好吃 死了 。
  Zhège dàngāo hǎochī sǐ le!
  This cake is to die for!
  Literally, "delicious to death"

Approximations with “chabuduo” (A2)

差不多 (chàbuduō), translated literally, means “the difference is not much.” In practice it means something like “more or less,” and is useful for expressing rough approximations.

差不多 (chàbuduō) as a Predicate

As a predicate, 差不多 can be used pretty much all by itself to complete a sentence after you tell us what subject we’re talking about. When several things are 差不多 (chàbuduō), it means they are “more or less *the same*.” So actually 差不多 (chàbuduō) is often understood to mean 差不多一样 (chàbuduō yīyàng), but you don’t say the 一样 (yīyàng) part. You just say 差不多 (chàbuduō).

Simple Subject

Let’s first assume that the subject is an easily understood group of people or things.

Structure

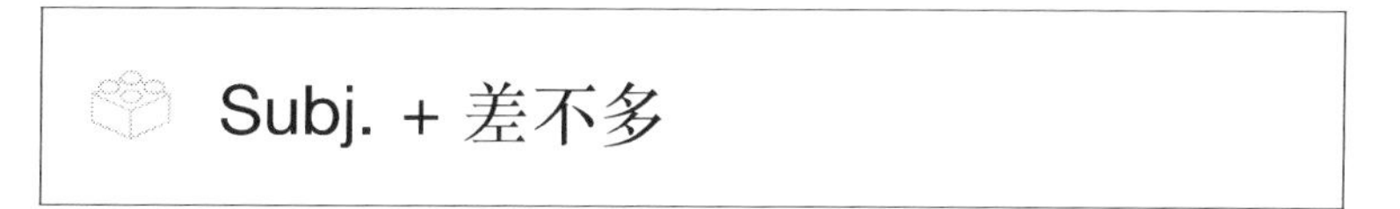

You might also add a 都 (dōu) in before 差不多 (chàbuduō) if there are more than two things being compared.

Examples

- 这几个地方都 差不多 。
  Zhè jǐ gè dìfang dōu chàbuduō .
  These places are all pretty much the same.
- 这两个词的意思 差不多 。
  Zhè liǎng gè cí de yìsi chàbuduō .
  The meanings of these two words are pretty much the same.
- 我们的想法 差不多 。
  Wǒmen de xiǎngfǎ chàbuduō .
  Our ways of thinking are pretty much the same.
- 那两家餐厅的菜 差不多 。
  Nà liǎng jiā cāntīng de cài chàbuduō .
  Those two restaurants' dishes are almost the same.

- 你们的中文水平 差不多 。
  Nǐmen de Zhōngwén shuǐpíng chàbuduō.
  Your Chinese levels are almost the same.

Several Subjects

Let's add in a few different subjects now, using the Chinese word for "and."

Structure

Another often used structure is:

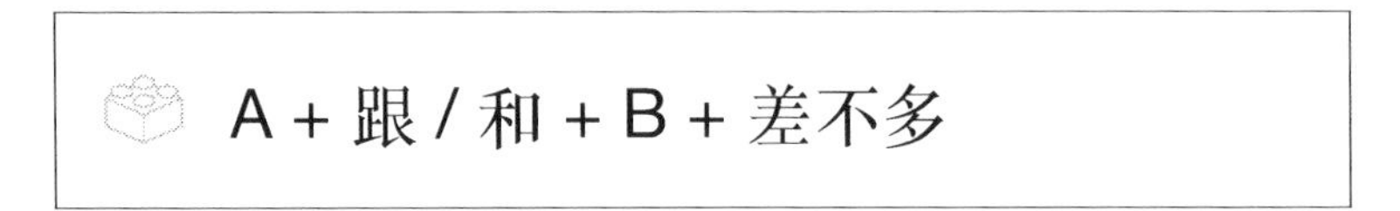

Examples

- 上海 和 纽约 差不多 。
  Shànghǎi hé Niǔyuē chàbuduō.
  Shanghai and New York are basically the same.
- Starbucks 和 Costa 差不多 。
  Starbucks hé Costa chàbuduō.
  Starbucks and Costa are almost the same.
- 这里的天气 跟 台湾的天气 差不多 。
  Zhèlǐ de tiānqì gēn Táiwān de tiānqì chàbuduō.
  The weather here is pretty much like Taiwan's.
- 你的工作 跟 我的工作 差不多 。
  Nǐ de gōngzuò gēn wǒ de gōngzuò chàbuduō.
  Your job and my job are almost the same.
- 你的新手机 跟 我的旧手机 差不多 。
  Nǐ de xīn shǒujī gēn wǒ de jiù shǒujī chàbuduō.
  Your new cell phone is pretty much like my old cell phone.

差不多 (chàbuduō) as an Adverb

When using 差不多 (chàbuduō) as an adverb, place it before the adjective or verb.

Structure

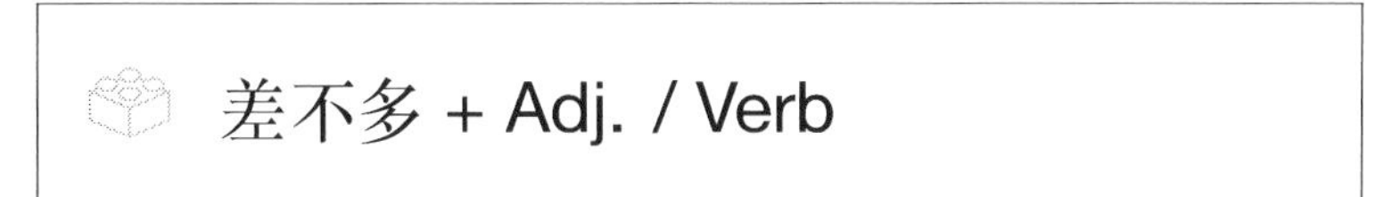

Examples

- 这两个孩子差不多大。
  Zhè liǎng gè háizi chàbuduō dà.
  These two children are more or less the same age.
- 我跟我哥哥差不多高。
  Wǒ gēn wǒ gēge chàbuduō gāo.
  My older brother and I are more or less the same height.
- 我差不多到公园门口了。
  Wǒ chàbuduō dào gōngyuán ménkǒu le.
  I'm almost at the entrance of the park.
- 电影差不多要开始了。
  Diànyǐng chàbuduō yào kāishǐ le.
  The movie is almost about to start.
- 今天的工作差不多做完了。
  Jīntiān de gōngzuò chàbuduō zuò wán le.
  Today's work is almost done.

差不多 (chàbuduō) with a Quantity or Time Phrase

After 差不多 (chàbuduō) you can also add a phrase that expresses quantity or time. This makes it clear that you're giving a rough estimate.

Structure

Examples

- 你儿子 差不多 五岁了吧?
  Nǐ érzi chàbuduō wǔ suì le ba?
  Your son should be about 5 years old, right?
- 他住在上海 差不多 三个月了。
  Tā zhù zài Shànghǎi chàbuduō sān gè yuè le.
  He has lived in Shanghai for about three months.
- 我在这家公司工作了 差不多 十年了。
  Wǒ zài zhè jiā gōngsī gōngzuò le chàbuduō shí nián le.
  I've worked for this company for almost ten years.
- 我父母结婚 差不多 二十年了。
  Wǒ fùmǔ jiéhūn chàbuduō èrshí nián le.
  My parents have been married for about twenty years.
- 差不多 两个星期以前，我在北京见过他。
  Chàbuduō liǎng gè xīngqí yǐqián, wǒ zài Běijīng jiàn guo tā.
  About two weeks ago I met with him in Beijing.

Similar to

- Expressing “nearly” with “jihu”

Emphasizing quantity with "dou" (A2)

都 (dōu) is one of those words that on the surface may seem simple, but actually has many different subtle uses. In this article, we will look at using 都 (dōu) to emphasize quantity.

Structure

You can use 都 (dōu) to emphasize the large quantity of something. The subject should be some sort of large group (like a majority of people or things), e.g. 很多人 (hěn duō rén) or 大家 (dàjiā).

Examples with 很多 (hěn duō)

First let's look at some typical examples using 很多 (hěn duō) to emphasize that it's "a lot." Note that in English, it would be totally redundant and unnecessary to add "all" into these sentences, but in Chinese it's *totally natural* (and kind of weird not to). If you remember to follow the rule and keep using the 都 (dōu), eventually it will become more natural for you too.

- 很多地方都有 wifi。
  Hěn duō dìfang dōu yǒu wifi.
  A lot of places have wifi.
- 我的很多朋友都有车。
  Wǒ de hěn duō péngyou dōu yǒu chē.
  A lot of my friends have cars.
- 很多美国人都喜欢喝咖啡。
  Hěn duō Měiguó rén dōu xǐhuan hē kāfēi.
  A lot of Americans like drinking coffee.
- 很多孩子都不喜欢上学。
  Hěn duō háizi dōu bù xǐhuan shàngxué.
  A lot of kids don't like to go to school.
- 很多年轻人都想在大城市工作。
  Hěn duō niánqīng rén dōu xiǎng zài dà chéngshì gōngzuò.
  A lot of young people want to go to work in big cities.

Examples with 大家 (dàjiā)

Now let's look at some examples using 大家 (dàjiā) or "everyone." Again, in English, it would be totally redundant and unnecessary to add "all" into these sentences, but in Chinese it's *totally natural* (and kind of weird not to). You just have to get used to it.

- 大家 都 来了吗?
  Dàjiā dōu lái le ma?
  Is everyone here?
- 大家 都 应该知道。
  Dàjiā dōu yīnggāi zhīdào.
  Everyone should know.
- 大家 都 说你很聪明。
  Dàjiā dōu shuō nǐ hěn cōngming.
  Everyone says you're smart.
- 大家 都 忘了他的名字。
  Dàjiā dōu wàng le tā de míngzi.
  Everyone forgot his name.
- 大家 都 喜欢吃辣吗?
  Dàjiā dōu xǐhuan chī là ma?
  Does everyone like eating spicy food?

Examples with 每天 (měi tiān)

One other common way to use 都 (dōu) is when you're talking about something that happens really often, such as "every day": 每天 (měi tiān). Use 都 (dōu) here in Chinese, even if it feels unnatural. (Fake it 'til you make it!)

- 我 每天 都 要上班。
  Wǒ měi tiān dōu yào shàngbān.
  I have to go to work every day.
- 老师 每天 都 迟到。
  Lǎoshī měi tiān dōu chídào.
  The teacher comes late every day.
- 她 每天 都 不吃早饭。
  Tā měi tiān dōu bù chī zǎofàn.
  Every day, she does not eat breakfast.

- 我女朋友 每天 都 上淘宝。

  Wǒ nǚpéngyou měi tiān dōu shàng Táobǎo.

  My girlfriend goes on *Taobao* every day.

- 妈妈 每天 都 给我们做晚饭。

  Māma měi tiān dōu gěi wǒmen zuò wǎnfàn.

  Mom cooks dinner for us every day.

For more uses with 每 (měi), see also: Expressing "every" with "mei"[1].

Other Examples

Here are some other examples that don't use 很多 (hěn duō) or 大家 (dàjiā) or 每天 (měi tiān), but are still quite typical:

- 美国人 都 说英文。

  Měiguó rén dōu shuō Yīngwén.

  Americans all speak English.

- 我们五个人 都 去。

  Wǒmen wǔ gè rén dōu qù.

  All five of us are going.

- 四川人 都 喜欢吃辣。

  Sìchuān rén dōu xǐhuan chī là.

  Sichuanese people all like eating spicy food.

- 我的家人 都 没去过中国。

  Wǒ de jiārén dōu méi qù guo Zhōngguó.

  None of my family members has been to China.

- 我的学生 都 喜欢问问题。

  Wǒ de xuéshēng dōu xǐhuan wèn wèntí.

  My students all like to ask questions.

Similar to

- The "all" adverb "dou" (A1), page 15
- Expressing "every time" with "mei" and "dou"
- Referring to "all" using "suoyou"

1. Expressing "every" with "mei" (A2), page 322

Expressing "all along" with "yizhi" (A2)

一直 (yīzhí) literally means "straight." Used as an adverb, 一直 (yīzhí) can also be used to express that you have been doing something all along, have been continuously doing something since a certain time, or that something will continuously happen in the future.

Structure

This structure expresses the continuous nature of an action or a circumstance.

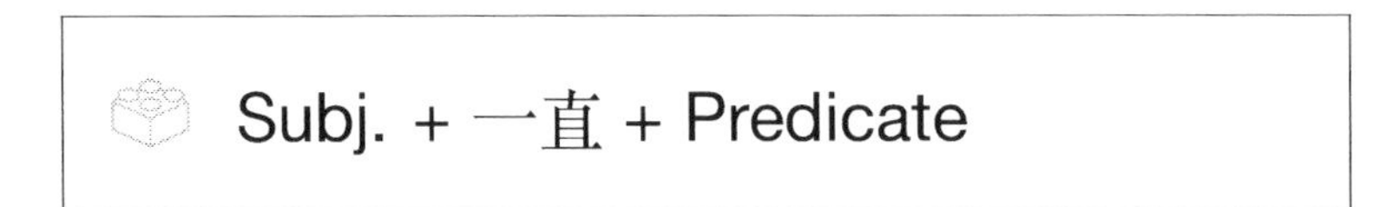

Also note that although 一直 (yīzhí) means "continuously," it is frequently more natural to use the word "always" in the English translation.

Examples

- 我 一直 在学习中文。
  Wǒ yīzhí zài xuéxí Zhōngwén.
  I've been studying Chinese all along.
- 昨天晚上我 一直 在做作业。
  Zuótiān wǎnshang wǒ yīzhí zài zuò zuòyè.
  Yesterday evening I was continuously doing homework.
- 老板 一直 很忙。
  Lǎobǎn yīzhí hěn máng.
  The boss is always very busy.

"Always" is more natural than "continuously."

- 我 一直 很喜欢你。
  Wǒ yīzhí hěn xǐhuan nǐ.
  I've always liked you a lot.
- 爸爸 一直 都不抽烟。
  Bàba yīzhí dōu bù chōuyān.
  Dad has never smoked cigarettes.
- 我男朋友 一直 在中国教英文。
  Wǒ nánpéngyou yīzhí zài Zhōngguó jiāo Yīngwén.
  My boyfriend has always been teaching English in China.

- 18 岁以后，他 一直 一个人住。
  Shíbā suì yǐhòu, tā yīzhí yīgèrén zhù.
  Since he was 18, he has always lived alone.
- 你 一直 在这家公司工作吗?
  Nǐ yīzhí zài zhè jiā gōngsī gōngzuò ma?
  Have you always worked in this company?
- 你们 一直 住在一起吗?
  Nǐmen yīzhí zhù zài yīqǐ ma?
  Have you always been living together?
- 北京的空气 一直 很不好。
  Běijīng de kōngqì yīzhí hěn bù hǎo.
  The air in Beijing has been bad for a while.

Similar to

- Expressing “always” with “zongshi” (A2), page 142
- Comparing “buduan” and “buting”
- Comparing “yizhi” and “yixiang”
- Expressing “since the beginning” with “yixiang”

Expressing "already" with "yijing" (A2)

已经…… 了 (yǐjīng... le) is the basic pattern used to express "already" in Chinese. It's easy to forget the 了 (le) on the end, but using it will make your Chinese more natural.

Basic Usages

已经 (yǐjīng) with Verb Phrases

Structure

The most common structure is to use 已经…… 了 (yǐjīng... le) with a verb phrase.

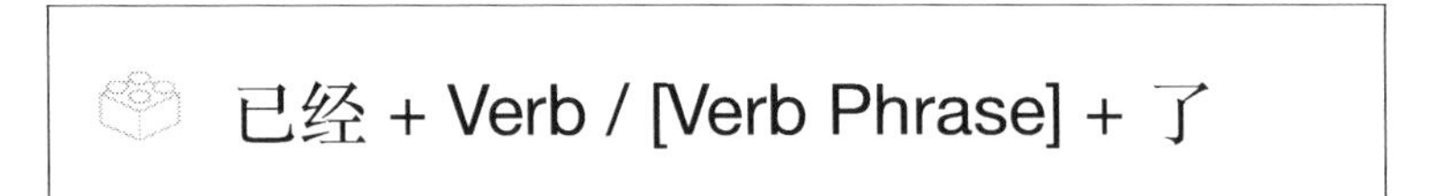

Examples

- 他们 已经 走 了 。 *with just a verb*
  Tāmen yǐjīng zǒu le.
  They've already left.
- 我 已经 有男朋友 了 。 *with a verb phrase*
  Wǒ yǐjīng yǒu nánpéngyou le.
  I already have a boyfriend.
- 宝宝 已经 会说话 了 。 *with a verb phrase*
  Bǎobao yǐjīng huì shuōhuà le.
  The baby can already speak.
- 妈妈 已经 回来 了 。 *with just a verb*
  Māma yǐjīng huílái le.
  Mom has already come back.
- 他 已经 上飞机 了 。 *with a verb phrase*
  Tā yǐjīng shàng fēijī le.
  He's already gotten on the plane.

已经 (yǐjīng) with Adjectives

Structure

Sometimes an adjective or a time noun is used instead of a typical verb phrase:

> 已经 + (很 +) Adj. + 了

Examples

- 爸爸妈妈已经老了。
  Bàba māma yǐjīng lǎo le.
  Mom and dad are already old.
- 已经很便宜了。
  Yǐjīng hěn piányi le.
  It is already very cheap.
- 你女朋友已经很漂亮了！
  Nǐ nǚpéngyou yǐjīng hěn piàoliang le!
  Your girlfriend is already very beautiful!
- 你的感冒已经好了吗?
  Nǐ de gǎnmào yǐjīng hǎo le ma?
  Is your cold already better?
- 已经很晚了，我们走吧。
  Yǐjīng hěn wǎn le, wǒmen zǒu ba.
  It's already really late. Let's go.

已经 (yǐjīng) with Time Nouns

A "time noun" simply refers to almost any word in Chinese indicating a time something happened.

Structure

Examples

- 已经 11 点 了 ，女儿还没回来。
  Yǐjīng shíyī diǎn le, nǚ'ér hái méi huílái.
  It is already 11 o'clock, and my daughter has not returned.
- 爷爷 已经 八十五岁 了 。
  Yéye yǐjīng bāshí-wǔ suì le.
  Grandpa is already eighty-five years old.
- 我学习中文 已经 一年 了 。
  Wǒ xuéxí Zhōngwén yǐjīng yī nián le.
  I have already been studying Chinese for a year.
- 他在洗手间里 已经 半个小时 了 。
  Tā zài xǐshǒujiān lǐ yǐjīng bàn gè xiǎoshí le.
  He has already been in the bathroom for half an hour.
- 爸爸去北京出差 已经 两天 了 。
  Bàba qù Běijīng chūchāi yǐjīng liǎng tiān le.
  It has already been two days since dad went to Beijing on business trip.

Negative Form

Structure

The negative structure simply adds a 不 (bù) after 已经 (yǐjīng), and before the verb (or possibly adjective).

> 已经 + 不 + [Verb Phrase] / Adj. + 了

Examples

Generally this negative 已经 (yǐjīng) structure is translated into English as "not… anymore" rather than using the word "already."

- 我 已经 不 喜欢你 了 。
  Wǒ yǐjīng bù xǐhuan nǐ le.
  I don't like you anymore.

- 他 已经 不 爱他的猫 了。
  Tā yǐjīng bù ài tā de māo le.
  He doesn't love his cat anymore.
- 他们 已经 不 住在中国 了。
  Tāmen yǐjīng bù zhù zài Zhōngguó le.
  They don't live in China anymore.
- 我 已经 不 需要父母的钱 了。
  Wǒ yǐjīng bù xūyào fùmǔ de qián le.
  I don't need my parents' money anymore.
- 你 已经 不 在 Google 工作 了 吗?
  Nǐ yǐjīng bù zài Google gōngzuò le ma?
  You don't work at Google anymore?

Similar to

- Expressing "already" with just "le" (A2), page 230
- Expressing "already" with "dou"

Expressing “always” with “zongshi” (A2)

If you are trying to describe a daily routine, a habit, or just something that consistently happens, you can use the word 总是 (zǒngshì). 总是 (zǒngshì) means “always,” and like other adverbs, comes before the verb in a sentence.

总是 (zǒngshì) with Verbs

总是 (zǒngshì) is an adverb that is often translated to English as “always.” It is placed before the verb that it modifies.

Structure

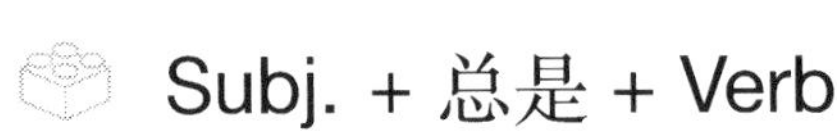

Examples

- 他 总是 迟到。

  Tā zǒngshì chídào.

  He is always late.

- 我 总是 忘记这个词。

  Wǒ zǒngshì wàngjì zhège cí.

  I always forget this word.

- 他 总是 一个人吃饭。

  Tā zǒngshì yīgèrén chīfàn.

  He always eats alone.

- 你男朋友 总是 说脏话。

  Nǐ nánpéngyou zǒngshì shuō zānghuà.

  Your boyfriend always uses foul language.

- 我的学生 总是 问我很多有意思的问题。

  Wǒ de xuéshēng zǒngshì wèn wǒ hěn duō yǒu yìsi de wèntí.

  My students always ask me lots of interesting questions.

总是 (zǒngshì) with Adjectives

Structure

When 总是 (zǒngshì) is used together with an adjective, you will need to add a modifier in the middle, such as 很 (hěn), 特别 (tèbié), 这么 (zhème), 那么 (nàme), etc.

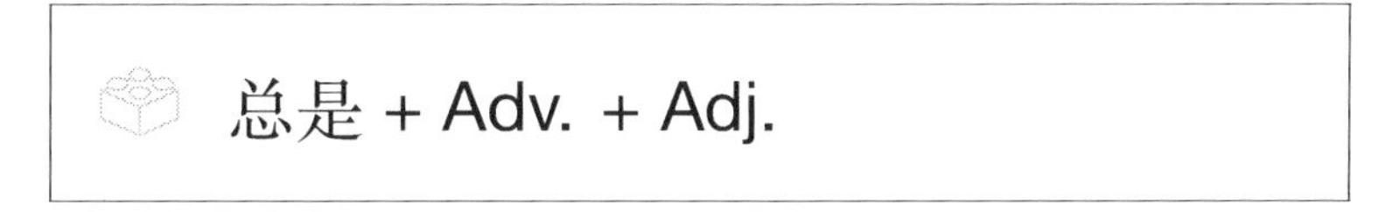

Examples

- 他 总是 很累。
  Tā zǒngshì hěn lèi.
  He is always tired.
- 你为什么 总是 很忙?
  Nǐ wèishénme zǒngshì hěn máng?
  Why are you always very busy?
- 你家 总是 很干净。
  Nǐ jiā zǒngshì hěn gānjìng.
  Your house is always very clean.
- 孩子们 总是 非常开心。
  Háizi men zǒngshì fēicháng kāixīn.
  The children are always very happy.
- 我的学生 总是 特别努力。
  Wǒ de xuéshēng zǒngshì tèbié nǔlì.
  My students are always very hard-working.

Similar to

- Expressing "all along" with "yizhi" (A2), page 136
- Expressing "always" with "conglai"
- Using "always" as a complaint with "laoshi"
- Comparing "yizhi" and "yixiang"

Expressing "and also" with "hai" (A2)

In English we use "and also" when we want to connect separate and different thoughts. We can do the same thing in Chinese by using 还 (hái).

Structure

The adverb 还 (hái) can be used to link two phrases together, in a similar way to "and also" in English. In this case, 还 (hái) begins a new phrase or clause.

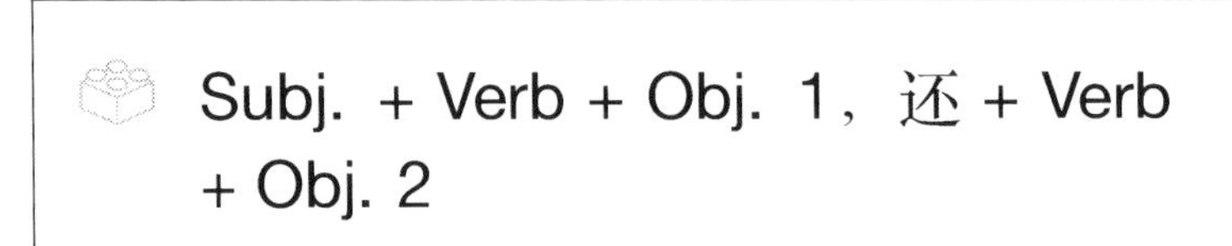

Examples

- 她有一个弟弟，还 有一个妹妹。
  Tā yǒu yī gè dìdi, hái yǒu yī gè mèimei.
  She has a younger brother and also has a younger sister.
- 我老板会说法语，还 会说日语。
  Wǒ lǎobǎn huì shuō Fǎyǔ, hái huì shuō Rìyǔ.
  My boss can speak French and can also speak Japanese.
- 你要一杯咖啡，还 要什么？
  Nǐ yào yī bēi kāfēi, hái yào shénme?
  You want a cup of coffee, and what else do you want?
- 我想吃冰淇淋，还 想吃汉堡。
  Wǒ xiǎng chī bīngqílín, hái xiǎng chī hànbǎo.
  I want to eat ice cream and I also want to eat a hamburger.
- 爸爸有一个小米手机，还 有一个 iPhone。
  Bàba yǒu yī gè Xiǎomǐ shǒujī, hái yǒu yī gè iPhone.
  Dad has a Xiaomi phone and also has an iPhone.
- 你晚上在家做了作业，还 做了什么？
  Nǐ wǎnshang zài jiā zuò le zuòyè, hái zuò le shénme?
  You did your homework at home tonight, and what else did you do?

- 他结婚的时候，请了同事，还请了谁？

  Tā jiéhūn de shíhou, qǐng le tóngshì, hái qǐng le shéi?

  When he got married, he invited his co-workers. Who else did he invite?

- 生日的时候，我们会吃蛋糕，还要送礼物。

  Shēngrì de shíhou, wǒmen huì chī dàngāo, hái yào sòng lǐwù.

  During a birthday, we eat cake and also give presents.

- 去美国要带钱、护照，还要带什么？

  Qù Měiguó yào dài qián, hùzhào, hái yào dài shénme?

  To go to the USA, you need to take money and a passport. What else do you need to take with you?

The Difference Between 还 (hái) and 也 (yě)

It should be noted that another common way to express "also" is with the word 也 (yě). What's the difference? With 还 (hái), ONE subject is doing TWO different things, whereas when 也 (yě)[1] is used, TWO subjects are doing ONE thing.

It's the difference between these two English sentences:

- He fixed dinner **and also** washed the dishes.
- She washed the dishes **too**.

If you translated these into Chinese, the first one (one subject, two actions) would use 还 (hái), and the second one (second subject, no new actions) would use 也 (yě). Let's do that!

- 他做了饭，还洗了碗。

  Tā zuò le fàn, hái xǐ le wǎn.

  He fixed dinner and also washed the dishes.

- 她也洗了碗。

  Tā yě xǐ le wǎn.

  She washed the dishes too.

How about a few more similar examples?

- 我洗了澡，还洗了衣服。

  Wǒ xǐ le zǎo, hái xǐ le yīfu.

  I took a shower and also did my laundry.

---

1. The "also" adverb "ye" (A1), page 17

- 她 也 洗了衣服。
  Tā yě xǐ le yīfu.
  She did her laundry too.
- 我们今天晚上出去吃饭了， 还 看了电影。
  Wǒmen jīntiān wǎnshang chūqù chīfàn le, hái kàn le diànyǐng.
  We went out for dinner tonight and also watched a movie.
- 他们今天晚上 也 看了电影。
  Tāmen jīntiān wǎnshang yě kàn le diànyǐng.
  They watched a movie tonight too.

Similar to

- The "also" adverb "ye" (A1), page 17
- Moderating positive adjectives with "hai" (A2), page 178
- Continuation with "hai"
- Expressing "in addition" with "haiyou"
- Expressing "not only… but also"
- Advanced usage of "hai"

Expressing "even more" with "geng" (A2)

To express "even more," (as in "even more expensive," "even more ridiculous," "even more badass"), you can use 更 (gèng). 更 (gèng) generally comes before adjectives.

Basic Usage

Structure

The pattern in Chinese is simple:

Note that this pattern is not simply a way of adding "-er" to an adjective or a substitute for 比 (bǐ) comparisons[1]. In each case, you're adding "even more" to an existing considerable amount, as in, "I'm already rich, but I want to be even richer."

Examples

- 这两个银行哪个 更 近？
  Zhè liǎng gè yínháng nǎge gèng jìn?
  Between these two banks, which one is closer?
- 我想找一个 更 帅的男朋友。
  Wǒ xiǎng zhǎo yī gè gèng shuài de nánpéngyou.
  I want to find a more handsome boyfriend.
- 我喜欢在网上买书，因为 更 便宜。
  Wǒ xǐhuan zài wǎngshàng mǎi shū, yīnwèi gèng piányi.
  I like buying books online because it's cheaper.
- 不要太高兴，我们还有 更 多的工作要做。
  Bùyào tài gāoxìng, wǒmen hái yǒu gèng duō de gōngzuò yào zuò.
  Don't get too excited. We still have more work to do.
- 结婚以后，她变得 更 漂亮了。
  Jiéhūn yǐhòu, tā biàn de gèng piàoliang le.
  She's become more beautiful after she got married.

1. Basic comparisons with "bi" (A2), page 253

Structure with 比 (bǐ)

While 更 (gèng) is not a substitute for 比 (bǐ) (the classic comparison word)[1], the two can be used together.

Structure

This expresses that “A is **even more** Adj. than B.”

Examples

- 北京的房子 比 上海 更 贵。
  Běijīng de fángzi bǐ Shànghǎi gèng guì.
  The houses in Beijing are even more expensive than those in Shanghai.
- 春节 比 中秋节 更 热闹。
  Chūnjié bǐ Zhōngqiūjié gèng rènao.
  Spring Festival is even more boisterous than Mid-autumn Festival.
- 汉字 比 声调 更 难。
  Hànzì bǐ shēngdiào gèng nán.
  Chinese characters are even more difficult than tones.
- 他现在的女朋友 比 以前的 更 漂亮。
  Tā xiànzài de nǚpéngyou bǐ yǐqián de gèng piàoliang.
  His current girlfriend is even more beautiful than his previous one.
- 中国的高铁 比 飞机 更 方便。
  Zhōngguó de gāotiě bǐ fēijī gèng fāngbiàn.
  China's high-speed trains are even more convenient than airplanes.

Similar to

- Basic comparisons with “bi” (A2), page 253
- Superlative “zui” (A2), page 185
- Expressing “more and more” with “yuelaiyue”

---

1. Basic comparisons with “bi” (A2), page 253

Expressing "just" with "gang" (A2)

For events that happened in the immediate past, in English we use the word "just." For example, if you pass a turn you were supposed to make, you might say, "I *just* passed it!" In Chinese, "just" can be expressed with 刚 (gāng) or 刚刚 (gānggāng).

Expressing "Just" Happened

Structure

刚 (gāng) expresses an action that happened not long ago. 刚刚 (gānggāng) is used the same way, with the same meaning.

Subj. + 刚 + Verb

or

Subj. + 刚刚 + Verb

Examples

- 我们 刚 知道。

  Wǒmen gāng zhīdào.

  We just found out.

- 她们 刚 走。

  Tāmen gāng zǒu.

  They just left.

- 老板 刚刚 到办公室。

  Lǎobǎn gānggāng dào bàngōngshì.

  The boss just arrived at the office.

- 我老婆 刚 生完孩子。

  Wǒ lǎopo gāng shēng wán háizi.

  My wife just finished giving birth to our baby.

- 你刚刚下班吗?
  Nǐ gānggāng xiàbān ma?
  Did you just get off work?

"Just" Within a Specific Time Period

This more complicated use of 刚 (gāng) is not nearly as essential as the one above, but you may find it useful to specify just *when* the event "just" occurred, specifically.

Structure

刚 (gāng) can also express "from the time an action happens until the present time."

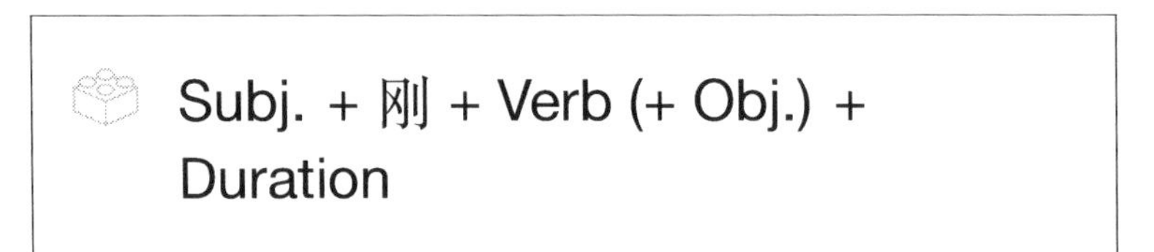

Note that although we need to say "ago" in English, in this pattern there's no need for a word that means "ago."

Examples

- 我刚认识她十天。
  Wǒ gāng rènshi tā shí tiān.
  I just met her ten days ago.
- 他刚来中国两个月。
  Tā gāng lái Zhōngguó liǎng gè yuè.
  He just got to China two months ago.
- 我弟弟刚工作半年。
  Wǒ dìdi gāng gōngzuò bàn nián.
  My younger brother just started working half a year ago.
- 她刚结婚三个月。
  Tā gāng jiéhūn sān gè yuè.
  She just got married three months ago.
- 我的车刚买两天，开的时候小心点。
  Wǒ de chē gāng mǎi liǎng tiān, kāi de shíhou xiǎoxīn diǎn.
  I just bought the car two days ago. Be careful when you drive.

Similar to

- Expressing "just now" with "gangcai" (A2), page 205
- Comparing "gang" and "gangcai"

Expressing "only" with "zhi" (A2)

There are a number of different ways to express "only" in Chinese, but 只 (zhǐ) is the most basic one you need to learn first. It's an adverb, so it normally comes before verbs.

Structure

The adverb 只 (zhǐ) can come directly before a verb, or before an auxiliary verb like 会 (huì) or 能 (néng).

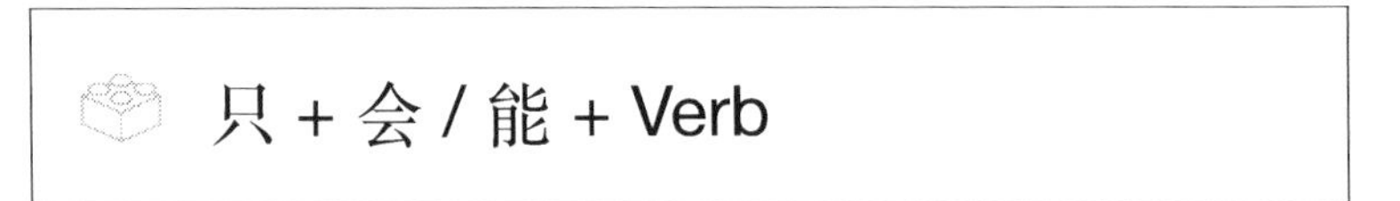

Examples

- 我 只 有一个哥哥。
  Wǒ zhǐ yǒu yī gè gēge.
  I only have one older brother.
- 我们 只 有十块钱。
  Wǒmen zhǐ yǒu shí kuài qián.
  We only have ten RMB.
- 我们公司 只 有两个员工。
  Wǒmen gōngsī zhǐ yǒu liǎng gè yuángōng.
  Our company only has two employees.
- 你 只 爱吃肉吗?
  Nǐ zhǐ ài chī ròu ma?
  Do you only like eating meat?
- 他们 只 会说英文。
  Tāmen zhǐ huì shuō Yīngwén.
  They can only speak English.

- 我 只 能说两句中文。
  Wǒ zhǐ néng shuō liǎng jù Zhōngwén.
  I can only say two sentences in Chinese.
- 你们 只 要咖啡吗?
  Nǐmen zhǐ yào kāfēi ma?
  Do you only want coffee?
- 我老婆 只 要一个孩子。
  Wǒ lǎopo zhǐ yào yī gè háizi.
  My wife only wants one child.
- 宝宝 只 会走，不会跑。
  Bǎobao zhǐ huì zǒu, bù huì pǎo.
  The baby can only walk. He can't run.
- 我 只 想跟你在一起。
  Wǒ zhǐ xiǎng gēn nǐ zài yīqǐ.
  I only want to be with you.

Similar to

- Expressing “just” with “jiu”

Expressing actions in progress with "zai" (A2)

在 (zài) and 正在 (zhèngzài) can be used as auxiliary verbs to express that an action is *ongoing* or *in progress*. This is often the equivalent of *present continuous* in English, which is how we express that an activity is happening *now*.

You can use 正在 (zhèngzài) instead of just 在 (zài) to put a little more emphasis on an action that is *in progress* ***right now***.

Structure

Subj. + 在 + Verb + Obj.

or

Subj. + 正在 + Verb + Obj.

Examples

- 她 在 看书。
  Tā zài kànshū.
  She is reading.
- 妈妈 在 打电话。
  Māma zài dǎ diànhuà.
  Mom is making a phone call.
- 谁 在 里面洗澡?
  Shéi zài lǐmiàn xǐzǎo?
  Who is taking a shower in there?
- 阿姨 正在 打扫我们的房间。
  Āyí zhèngzài dǎsǎo wǒmen de fángjiān.
  The cleaning lady is cleaning our room right now.

- 昨天晚上七点，我们 在 吃饭。
  Zuótiān wǎnshang qīdiǎn, wǒmen zài chīfàn.
  Yesterday at 7pm, we were eating dinner.
- 老板 在 开会，没有时间见你。
  Lǎobǎn zài kāihuì, méiyǒu shíjiān jiàn nǐ.
  The boss is currently in a meeting. He doesn't have time to see you.
- 我现在 在 上班，不方便离开。
  Wǒ xiànzài zài shàngbān, bù fāngbiàn líkāi.
  I am working now. It's not convenient for me to leave.
- 我们 正在 上课，请你等一会儿。
  Wǒmen zhèngzài shàngkè, qǐng nǐ děng yīhuìr.
  We are in class right now; please wait a moment.
- 你 正在 开车，不可以玩手机。
  Nǐ zhèngzài kāichē, bù kěyǐ wán shǒujī.
  You're driving right now; you can't play with your cell phone.
- 你给我打电话的时候，我 正在 跟朋友打游戏。
  Nǐ gěi wǒ dǎ diànhuà de shíhou, wǒ zhèngzài gēn péngyou dǎ yóuxì.
  When you called me, I was playing video games with friends.

There is no need to worry too much about when to use 在 (zài) or 正在 (zhèngzài), since they basically mean the same thing. 正在 (zhèngzài) usually shows that the action is in progress (*right now*). "在 (zài) + Verb" is more commonly used than "正在 (zhèngzài) + Verb," but both are fine to use.

Similar to

- Aspect particle "zhe"
- Expressing actions in progress (full form)

Negative commands with “bie” (A2)

Instead of saying “do not” with 不要 (bùyào)[1], we can say “don't” a little more quickly and forcefully by using 别 (bié).

Structure

As well as 不要 (bùyào)[1], negative commands can also be formed with 别 (bié). You could think of 别 (bié) as a contraction of 不要 (bùyào), as the structure is the same for both:

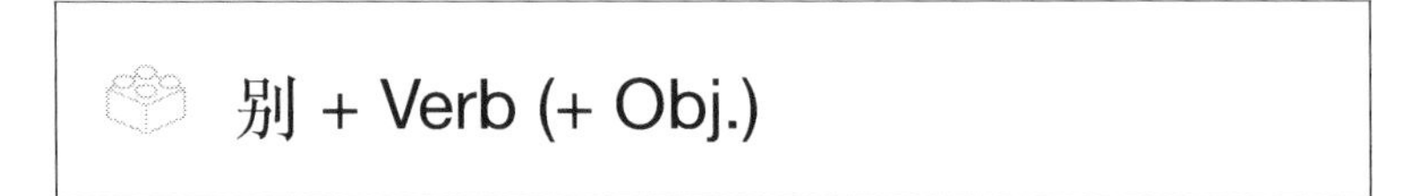

Examples

- 别走。
  Bié zǒu.
  Don't leave.
- 别说话！
  Bié shuōhuà!
  Don't speak!
- 别笑！
  Bié xiào!
  Don't laugh!
- 别动！
  Bié dòng!
  Don't move!
- 别过来！
  Bié guòlái!
  Don't come over here!
- 别打孩子！
  Bié dǎ háizi!
  Don't hit the child!

---

1. Negative commands with “buyao” (A1), page 83

- 别 喝太多。
  Bié hē tài duō.
  Don't drink too much.
- 喝酒以后 别 开车。
  Hējiǔ yǐhòu bié kāichē.
  After drinking alcohol, don't drive.
- 吃饭的时候 别 玩手机。
  Chīfàn de shíhou bié wán shǒujī.
  When eating, don't play with your cell phone.
- 上课的时候 别 说英文。
  Shàngkè de shíhou bié shuō Yīngwén.
  Don't speak English in class.

Similar to

- Negative commands with "buyao" (A1), page 83
- Expressing "stop doing" with "bie· · · le" (A2), page 353

- Alternative existential sentences
- Expressing "don't need to" with "buyong"

Simultaneous tasks with "yibian" (A2)

Multitasking is everywhere in the modern world (what else are you doing while you read this?), but you if can *focus* for just a minute, you can learn a way to express simultaneous tasks in Chinese! This can be done with 一边 (yībiān).

Structure

To express that one thing is done *while* doing something else, the word 一边 (yībiān) is used.

Subj. + 一边 + Verb （，） + 一边 + Verb

Note that you sometimes see 一边 (yībiān) shortened to 边 (biān) as well, which has a less formal feel.

Examples

- 不要 一边 吃东西， 一边 说话。
  Bùyào yībiān chī dōngxi, yībiān shuōhuà.
  Don't speak while eating.
- 我常常 一边 洗澡， 一边 唱歌。
  Wǒ chángcháng yībiān xǐzǎo, yībiān chànggē.
  I often sing songs while I take a shower.
- 孩子喜欢 一边 吃饭， 一边 玩。
  Háizi xǐhuan yībiān chīfàn, yībiān wán.
  Children like to play while eating.
- 你喜欢 一边 听音乐， 一边 做作业吗？
  Nǐ xǐhuan yībiān tīng yīnyuè, yībiān zuò zuòyè ma?
  Do you like to listen to music while doing homework?
- 我们 一边 走 一边 聊吧。
  Wǒmen yībiān zǒu yībiān liáo ba.
  Let's walk while we talk.

- 请你 一边 读 一边 写。
  Qǐng nǐ yībiān dú yībiān xiě.
  Please write as you read.
- 不要 一边 开车，一边 打电话。
  Bùyào yībiān kāichē, yībiān dǎ diànhuà.
  Don't talk on the phone while you drive.
- 老板喜欢 一边 抽烟，一边 工作。
  Lǎobǎn xǐhuan yībiān chōuyān, yībiān gōngzuò.
  The boss likes to smoke while working.
- 很多人都 一边 上班，一边 玩手机。
  Hěn duō rén dōu yībiān shàngbān, yībiān wán shǒujī.
  Many people play with their cell phones while working.
- 她常常 一边 做饭，一边 带孩子。
  Tā chángcháng yībiān zuòfàn, yībiān dài háizi.
  She often looks after the baby while cooking food.

You'll notice that the order of the two actions is sometimes different in the original Chinese and the English translations above. This is because the "main" action usually comes second in English (after the "while"), but first in Chinese. For example, "take a shower while singing" sounds strange in English, but "sing while taking a shower" doesn't.

Note that you must be actively doing both actions. That is, they have to be intentional. If you want to say something happened while another thing was happening, it would be better to use 的时候 (de shíhou)[1].

Similar to

- Expressing "both A and B" with "you" (A2), page 167
- Expressing "when" with "de shihou" (A2), page 207
- Expressing "when" with "shi"
- Expressing "along with···" with "suizhe"
- Expressing simultaneous actions with "yimian"

1. Expressing "when" with "de shihou" (A2), page 207

Asking about degree with "duo" (A2)

How big? How busy? How cold? Ask questions like these regarding the degree of an adjective with 多 (duō). This is just one of the many uses of this word.

Structure

多 (duō) is often used to ask about the degree or extent of something.

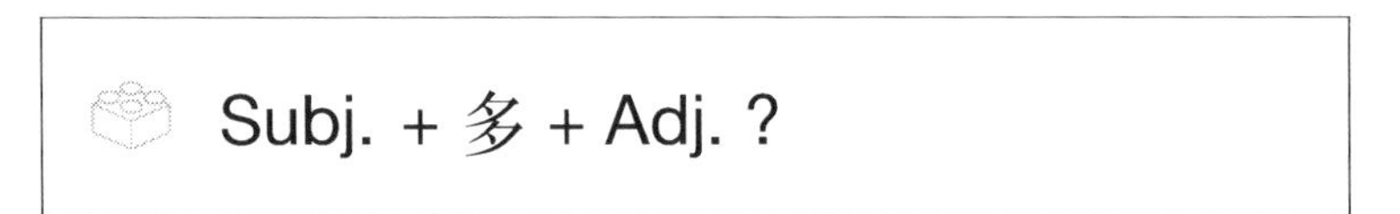

This is an easy way to ask "How [adjective] is [subject]?"

Examples

- 她 多 高?
  Tā duō gāo?
  How tall is she?
- 你家 多 大?
  Nǐ jiā duō dà?
  How large is your house?
- 你的孩子 多 大?
  Nǐ de háizi duō dà?
  How old is your child?
- 黄河 多 长?
  Huánghé duō cháng?
  How long is the Yellow River?
- 你家离这儿 多 远?
  Nǐ jiā lí zhèr duō yuǎn?
  How far is your house away from here?
- 你要在美国待 多 久?
  Nǐ yào zài Měiguó dāi duō jiǔ?
  How long are you going to stay in the USA?

- 这些东西 多 重？
  Zhèxiē dōngxi duō zhòng?
  How heavy are these things?
- 你知道我们现在 多 胖吗？
  Nǐ zhīdào wǒmen xiànzài duō pàng ma?
  Do you know how fat we are now?
- 你知道这里的冬天 多 冷吗？
  Nǐ zhīdào zhèlǐ de dōngtiān duō lěng ma?
  Do you know how cold it is here in winter?
- 你知道上海的房子 多 贵吗？
  Nǐ zhīdào Shànghǎi de fángzi duō guì ma?
  Do you know how expensive housing is in Shanghai?

大 (dà) and 小 (xiǎo) can also be used to describe ages. The question phrase 多大 (duō dà) is often used to ask "how old." However, it is an informal way to ask, usually reserved for peers, close friends, or children. The phrase 几岁 (jǐ suì) is most often used for children young enough to display their ages on one hand. Adults do not normally directly ask each other's ages in a formal setting.

Similar to

- Intensifying with "duo" (A2), page 176
- Doing something more with "duo"
- Indicating a number in excess

Basic comparisons with "yiyang" (A2)

Along with 比 (bǐ)[1] and 没有 (méiyǒu)[2], 一样 (yīyàng) is another way to make basic comparisons. However, 一样 (yīyàng) is used to express that two things are *the same* in some way.

Basic Usage

Structure

The simple structure is used for stating that two things are the same:

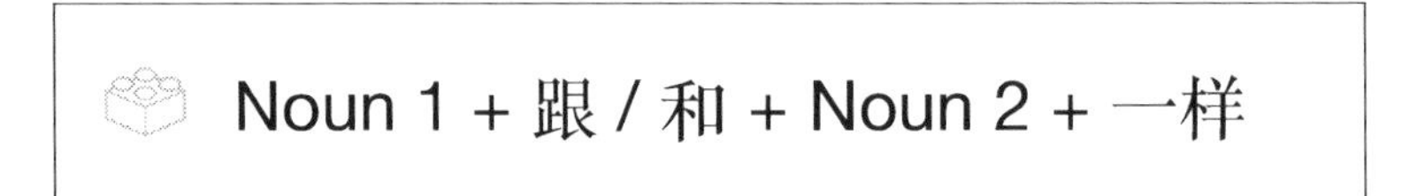

Examples

- 我 和 你 一样 。
  Wǒ hé nǐ yīyàng.
  I am the same as you.
- 他的性格 跟 他妈妈 一样 。
  Tā de xìnggé gēn tā māma yīyàng.
  He has the same personality as his mom.
- 北京的天气 和 上海不 一样 。
  Běijīng de tiānqì hé Shànghǎi bù yīyàng.
  The weather in Beijing and the weather in Shanghai are not alike.
- 这个词的意思 和 那个词 一样 吗?
  Zhège cí de yìsi hé nàge cí yīyàng ma?
  Are the meanings of this word and that word the same?
- 美国文化 跟 中国文化不 一样 。
  Měiguó wénhuà gēn Zhōngguó wénhuà bù yīyàng.
  American culture and Chinese culture are not the same.

---

1. Basic comparisons with "bi" (A2), page 253
2. Basic comparisons with "meiyou" (A2), page 258

- 啤酒 和 葡萄酒的味道 一样 吗?
  Píjiǔ hé pútaojiǔ de wèidào yīyàng ma?
  Do beer and red wine taste the same?

一样 (yīyàng) with Adjectives

Structure

To add an adjective into the mix, just place it after 一样 (yīyàng):

> Noun 1 + 跟 / 和 + Noun 2 + 一样 + Adj.

This describes Noun 1 as being as *adjective* as Noun 2.

Examples

- 你家 跟 我家 一样 大。
  Nǐ jiā gēn wǒ jiā yīyàng dà.
  Your house is just as big as mine.
- 她 和 她哥哥 一样 高。
  Tā hé tā gēge yīyàng gāo.
  She and her older brother are equally tall.
- 你的头发 和 我的头发 一样 长。
  Nǐ de tóufa hé wǒ de tóufa yīyàng cháng.
  You hair is as long as mine.
- 这里的天气 跟 我老家 一样 舒服。
  Zhèlǐ de tiānqì gēn wǒ lǎojiā yīyàng shūfu.
  The weather here is just as comfortable as my hometown's.
- 你 跟 老板 一样 忙吗?
  Nǐ gēn lǎobǎn yīyàng máng ma?
  Are you as busy as the boss is?

There is also a similar but more advanced usage of this pattern that uses 像 (xiàng).

Similar to

- Expressing "age difference" with "da and xiao"
- Expressing "compared with" with "gen"
- Comparing specifically with "xiang"

Expressing “a little too” with “you dian” (A2)

At times you may want to politely diss something using the phrase “a little too.” For example, if you are getting lunch with a friend who wants to be seated outside, you might say, “It is a little too hot” to suggest you sit inside. In a case like this, you can use 有一点 (yǒuyīdiǎn) or 有点 (yǒudiǎn). The two are interchangeable.

Structure

To say that something is “a little *too*...” or “a bit *too*...,” 有一点 (yǒuyīdiǎn) is often used. Its northern Chinese version is 有一点儿 (yǒuyīdiǎnr).

Subj. + 有一点 (儿) + Adj.

In spoken Chinese, the 一 (yī) in 有一点 (yǒuyīdiǎn) is often dropped, leaving 有点 (yǒudiǎn). In northern China, that’s usually pronounced 有点儿 (yǒudiǎnr).

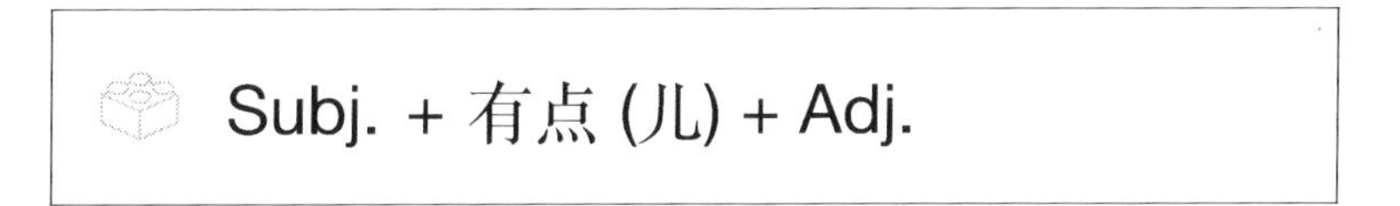

Examples

- 我 有一点 饿。
  Wǒ yǒuyīdiǎn è.
  I'm a little hungry.
- 这个菜 有一点 辣。
  Zhège cài yǒuyīdiǎn là.
  This dish is a little too spicy.
- 昨天 有一点 热。
  Zuótiān yǒuyīdiǎn rè.
  Yesterday it was a little too hot.
- 上海的冬天 有一点 冷。
  Shànghǎi de dōngtiān yǒuyīdiǎn lěng.
  Winter in Shanghai is a bit too cold.

- 我弟弟 有点 胖。
  Wǒ dìdi yǒudiǎn pàng.
  My younger brother is a bit fat.
- 今天 有点 累。
  Jīntiān yǒudiǎn lèi.
  Today I am a little bit tired.
- 这个月公司 有点 忙。
  Zhège yuè gōngsī yǒudiǎn máng.
  This month the company is a little bit busy.
- 这个地方 有点 吵，我们走吧。
  Zhège dìfang yǒudiǎn chǎo, wǒmen zǒu ba.
  This place is a little too noisy. Let's go.
- 爸爸回来 有点 晚，妈妈 有点 不高兴。
  Bàba huílái yǒudiǎn wǎn, māma yǒudiǎn bù gāoxìng.
  Dad came back home a bit too late, so mom was a little unhappy.
- 老师今天 有点 不舒服，所以没来上课。
  Lǎoshī jīntiān yǒudiǎn bù shūfu, suǒyǐ méi lái shàngkè.
  Today, the teacher felt a little unwell, so she didn't come to class.

Negative Connotation

Note that for the speaker, the adjective after 有点 (yǒudiǎn) expresses an unpleasant or undesirable meaning, so you won't hear things like 有点高兴 (yǒudiǎn gāoxìng), 有点舒服 (yǒudiǎn shūfu), 有点好玩儿 (yǒudiǎn hǎowánr), etc., because "happy," "comfortable," and "fun" are all adjectives with positive connotations.

Similar to

- Simple "noun + adjective" sentences (A1), page 96
- Expressing "some" with "yixie" (A2), page 315
- Using "youde" to mean "some" (A2), page 317
- Comparing "youdian" and "yidian"
- Expressing "rather" with "bijiao"

Expressing "both A and B" with "you" (A2)

When you're getting descriptive, you may find yourself wanting to use multiple adjectives at a time. The character 又 (yòu) can be used to give two qualities to something. Using the double 又 (yòu) structure is like saying that something is "both··· and···" in English.

Structure

The structure in Chinese is:

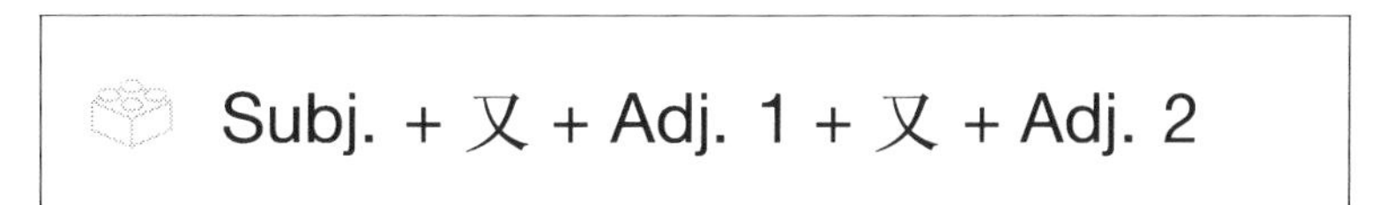

The two words shouldn't contrast in feeling. It is important to note they must both be bad or both be good.

Examples

- 她男朋友 又 高 又 帅。
  Tā nánpéngyou yòu gāo yòu shuài.
  Her boyfriend is both tall and handsome.
- 这个房子 又 大 又 亮。
  Zhège fángzi yòu dà yòu liàng.
  This house is both big and bright.
- 妈妈的头发 又 黑 又 亮。
  Māma de tóufa yòu hēi yòu liàng.
  Mom's hair is both black and shiny.
- 我姐姐 又 聪明 又 漂亮。
  Wǒ jiějie yòu cōngming yòu piàoliang.
  My older sister is both smart and beautiful.
- 中国菜 又 便宜 又 好吃。
  Zhōngguó cài yòu piányi yòu hǎochī.
  Chinese food is both cheap and good-tasting.
- 你们老板 又 年轻 又 有钱。
  Nǐmen lǎobǎn yòu niánqīng yòu yǒuqián.
  Your boss is both young and rich.

- 这里的咖啡 又 贵 又 难喝。
  Zhèlǐ de kāfēi yòu guì yòu nánhē.
  The coffee here is both expensive and bad-tasting.
- 我家小狗 又 可爱 又 听话。
  Wǒ jiā xiǎogǒu yòu kě'ài yòu tīnghuà.
  My family's dog is both cute and obedient.
- 上海的冬天 又 冷 又 湿。
  Shànghǎi de dōngtiān yòu lěng yòu shī.
  Winter here in Shanghai is both cold and humid.
- 她小时候 又 矮 又 瘦。
  Tā xiǎoshíhou yòu ǎi yòu shòu.
  She was both short and thin when she was young.

Similar to

- Simple "noun + adjective" sentences (A1), page 96
- Expressing "both... and..." with "ji...you"

Expressing "not very" with "bu tai" (A2)

You may be familiar with using 太 (tài) to express "too,"[1] such as when something is "too expensive" or "too hot." 不太 (bù tài) is a similar pattern for the negative, which just means "not very" or "not so" (literally "not too"). Note that this pattern does not normally use 了 (le).

不太 (bù tài) with Adjectives

Structure

Note: This pattern can also be used with non-adjectives. See below for more info.

Examples

- 我家 不太 大。
  Wǒ jiā bù tài dà.
  My house is not too big.
- 那个地方 不太 远。
  Nàge dìfang bù tài yuǎn.
  That place is not very far away.
- 老板今天 不太 高兴。
  Lǎobǎn jīntiān bù tài gāoxìng.
  The boss is not very happy today.
- 这个店的衣服 不太 贵。
  Zhège diàn de yīfu bù tài guì.
  The clothes in this shop are not too expensive.
- 我觉得他 不太 聪明。
  Wǒ juéde tā bù tài cōngming.
  I think he is not too smart.

1. Expressing "excessively" with "tai" (A1), page 94

不太 (bù tài) with Verbs

Structure

This pattern can be used with some psychological verbs (e.g. 喜欢 (xǐhuan), 想 (xiǎng), 明白 (míngbai)), as is the case with the next examples. These verbs are relatively limited.

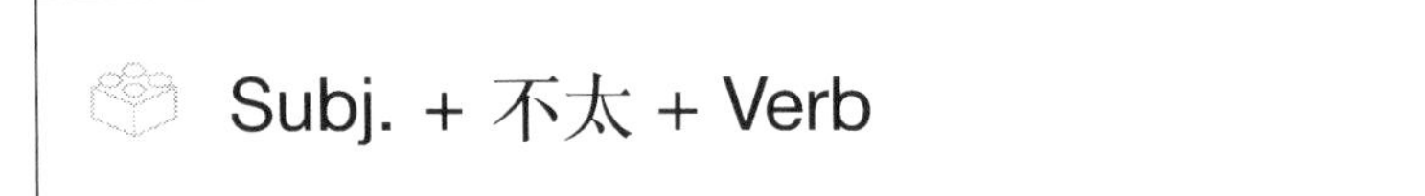

Examples

- 我 不太 懂。
  Wǒ bù tài dǒng.
  I don't really understand.
- 他们 不太 想去。
  Tāmen bù tài xiǎng qù.
  They don't really want to go.
- 我哥哥 不太 喜欢他的工作。
  Wǒ gēge bù tài xǐhuan tā de gōngzuò.
  My older brother doesn't really like his job.
- 他 不太 明白老板的意思。
  Tā bù tài míngbai lǎobǎn de yìsi.
  He didn't really understand what the boss meant.

Similar to

- Expressing "excessively" with "tai" (A1), page 94

Expressing "really" with "zhen" (A2)

As an adverb, the word 真 (zhēn) means "really" or "truly."

真 (zhēn) Before an Adjective

Structure

真 (zhēn) is used only in exclamatory sentences and comes before an adjective.

真 + Adj.

Example

- 你真好！
  Nǐ zhēn hǎo!
  You are so nice!
- 你女朋友真漂亮！
  Nǐ nǚpéngyou zhēn piàoliang!
  Your girlfriend is really pretty!
- 他家真有钱！
  Tā jiā zhēn yǒuqián!
  His family is really rich!
- 小狗真可爱！
  Xiǎogǒu zhēn kě'ài!
  This puppy is really cute!
- 今天真热！
  Jīntiān zhēn rè!
  It's truly hot today!

真 (zhēn) Before Certain Verbs or 能 (néng) / 会 (huì)

We don't want to get too technical on you, but there are certain other words that can be jazzed up with 真 (zhēn). One type of word is auxiliary verbs, like 能 (néng) and 会 (huì). The other type is psychological verbs like 喜欢 (xǐhuan).

Structure

真 + Verb

Example

- 你妈妈 真 爱你！
  Nǐ māma zhēn ài nǐ!
  Your mother really loves you!
- 我 真 喜欢住在中国！
  Wǒ zhēn xǐhuan zhù zài Zhōngguó!
  I really like living in China!
- 我 真 讨厌这种男人！
  Wǒ zhēn tǎoyàn zhè zhǒng nánrén!
  I really hate this kind of guy!
- 你 真 会说话！
  Nǐ zhēn huì shuōhuà!
  You are so good with words!
- 你 真 能吃！
  Nǐ zhēn néng chī!
  You ate so much!

Similar to

- Intensifying with “duo” (A2), page 176
- Superlative “zui” (A2), page 185

Expressing distance with "li" (A2)

Are we there yet? One of the ways to express distance is to use 离 (lí). The word order might seem a little tricky at first, but once you get it down, you'll be able to talk about distance with no problem.

Using 离 (lí) in a Statement

Structure

Unless you're talking about a very specific distance, you'll normally want to pair 离 (lí) with the adjective 近 (jìn) for "close," or 远 (yuǎn) for "far."

So this pattern is normally used to simply express that one place is (not) close or (not) far from another place. Easy, right? It's learning the sentence pattern that usually trips learners up, because it doesn't feel like natural word order to a speaker of English.

Examples

- 我家 离 公司很近。
  Wǒ jiā lí gōngsī hěn jìn.
  My house is close to my office.
- 美国 离 中国很远。
  Měiguó lí Zhōngguó hěn yuǎn.
  The USA is far from China.
- 这个酒店 离 火车站很近。
  Zhège jiǔdiàn lí huǒchēzhàn hěn jìn.
  This hotel is very close to the train station.
- 那个酒吧 离 这儿太远了，我不想去。
  Nàge jiǔbā lí zhèr tài yuǎn le, wǒ bù xiǎng qù.
  That bar is too far away from here. I don't want to go.
- 我不想去 离 家很远的地方工作。
  Wǒ bù xiǎng qù lí jiā hěn yuǎn de dìfang gōngzuò.
  I don't want to go work at a place very far away from home.

Using 离 (lí) in a Question

Structure

These two sentence patterns are extremely common in everyday conversations when discussing distances.

Place 1 + 离 + Place 2 (+ Adv.) + 近 / 远 + 吗?

Place 1 + 离 + Place 2 (+ 有) + 多远?

Note that in English, you can actually ask, "How close is it from here?" if the distance is obviously short. But in Chinese it's just, "How far is it from here?"

Examples

- 你家 离 超市远吗?
  Nǐ jiā lí chāoshì yuǎn ma?
  Is your house far away from the supermarket?
- 你的大学 离 你老家很远吗?
  Nǐ de dàxué lí nǐ lǎojiā hěn yuǎn ma?
  Is your college very far away from your hometown?
- 你们公司 离 地铁站近吗?
  Nǐmen gōngsī lí dìtiězhàn jìn ma?
  Is your company close to the metro station?
- 你家 离 学校多远?
  Nǐ jiā lí xuéxiào duō yuǎn?
  How far is it from your home to school?
- 这个酒店 离 机场有多远?
  Zhège jiǔdiàn lí jīchǎng yǒu duō yuǎn?
  How far is it from this hotel to the airport?

Expressing "Stay Away from Me" with 离 (lí)

One final example is a command, commonly heard in colloquial Chinese:

- 你 离 我远点儿！
  Nǐ lí wǒ yuǎn diǎnr!
  Stay away from me.

It's a somewhat atypical usage when compared with the others, because it uses two people rather than two places. The sentence literally means, "Distance yourself from me further." In other words, "Stay away from me," or "Don't come near me."

Intensifying with "duo" (A2)

One way to intensify a sentence is to make it an exclamation. To do this, you can use 多 (duō).

Structure

As well as asking about degree[1], you can also use 多 (duō) to intensify adjectives.

Examples

- 一个人 多 好！
  Yīgèrén duō hǎo!
  It's so nice being alone!
- 你女儿 多 聪明啊！
  Nǐ nǚér duō cōngming a!
  Your daughter is so smart!
- 今天天气 多 舒服！
  Jīntiān tiānqì duō shūfu!
  Today's weather is so nice!
- 你看这个地方， 多 美啊！
  Nǐ kàn zhège dìfang, duō měi a!
  Look at this place, it is so beautiful!
- 学中文 多 有意思啊！
  Xué Zhōngwén duō yǒu yìsi a!
  Studying Chinese is so interesting!
- 坐地铁 多 方便！
  Zuò dìtiě duō fāngbiàn!
  How convenient it is to take the metro!

---

1. Asking about degree with "duo" (A2), page 160

- 你看这个小狗，多 可爱！
  Nǐ kàn zhège xiǎogǒu, duō kě'ài!
  Look at this puppy! It is so cute!
- 这样做 多 麻烦！
  Zhèyàng zuò duō máfan!
  Doing it this way is so troublesome!
- 这些菜 多 好吃啊！
  Zhèxiē cài duō hǎochī a!
  These foods are so delicious!
- 你男朋友 多 帅啊！
  Nǐ nánpéngyou duō shuài a!
  Your boyfriend is so handsome!

多 (duō) can be compared to 很 (hěn) in this case. If you use 很 (hěn) instead of 多 (duō), the meaning is basically the same. However 很 (hěn) is also used to make simple "noun + adjective" sentences[1], which might not be exclamatory at all, whereas 多 (duō) is used only for excited exclamations.

Similar to

- Asking about degree with "duo" (A2), page 160
- Adjectives with "name" and "zheme"
- Doing something more with "duo"
- Indicating a number in excess

1. Simple "noun + adjective" sentences (A1), page 96

Moderating positive adjectives with "hai" (A2)

Whenever you want to imply that something is "good," but also kind of "meh," you can use 还 (hái) in front of the "good" adjective.

Commonly Used Expressions

Besides expressing continuation, 还 (hái) can also be used to weaken positive adjectives. Used with the adjective "good," this is similar to saying "fairly good" or "pretty good" in English. It's also sometimes used by a speaker to be more modest. Below are some of the most common adjectives that get "toned down" by 还 (hái) in this structure.

Structure

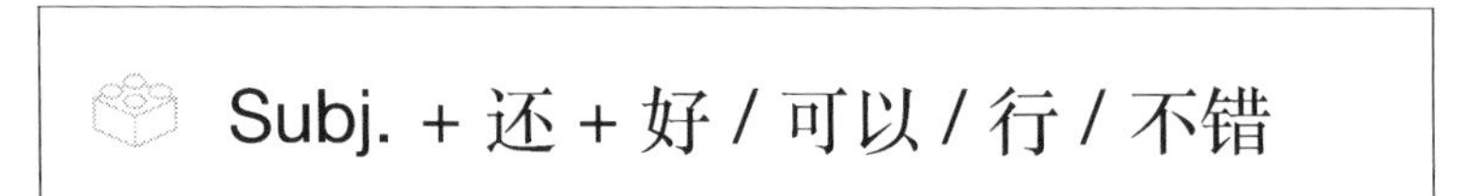

In this pattern, 好 (hǎo), 可以 (kěyǐ), 行 (xíng), and 不错 (bùcuò) combined with 还 ()hái can all be taken to mean "pretty good" or "all right" or "decent" (but also kind of *meh*... not *great*). As in English, intonation and facial expressions help convey the meaning. If expectations were already low to begin with, 还可以 (hái kěyǐ) can have the sense of "pretty darn good;" it all depends on context and tone of voice.

Examples

- 我 还好 。
  Wǒ hái hǎo.
  I'm OK.
- 爸爸做的菜 还可以 。
  Bàba zuò de cài hái kěyǐ.
  The food that dad cooks is OK.
- 我们老板 还不错 。
  Wǒmen lǎobǎn hái bùcuò.
  Our boss is not too bad.
- 这家店 还行 ，不太贵。
  Zhè jià diàn hái xíng, bù tài guì.
  This shop is OK. It's not too expensive.

- 我男朋友的工资 还可以 。
  Wǒ nánpéngyou de gōngzī hái kěyǐ.
  My boyfriend's salary is OK.
- 新的办公室 还不错 。
  Xīn de bàngōngshì hái bùcuò.
  The new office is OK.
- 我觉得这里的菜 还可以 ，没有那么难吃。
  Wǒ juéde zhèlǐ de cài hái kěyǐ, méiyǒu nàme nánchī.
  I think the food here is OK, it is not too bad-tasting.
- 这个牌子 还不错 ，很多年轻人喜欢。
  Zhège páizi hái bùcuò , hěn duō niánqīng rén xǐhuan.
  This brand is not too bad. Many young people like it.
- 房子 还可以 ，但是有点贵。
  Fángzi hái kěyǐ, dànshì yǒudiǎn guì.
  The apartment is not too bad, but it is a bit expensive.

Similar to

- Expressing “and also” with “hai” (A2), page 144
- Superlative “zui” (A2), page 185

- Continuation with “hai”
- Advanced usage of “hai”

Modifying nouns with adjective + “de” (A2)

One of the best ways to use the common character 的 (de) is to spice up your nouns with adjectives. By using 的 (de), we can connect sassy adjectives to otherwise boring nouns.

With a Noun

Structure

A very common way to modify nouns is to attach an adjective to them using 的 (de).

This structure comes up extremely frequently and is an easy way to attribute features to nouns. Occasionally you will see this 的 (de) omitted, but note that if the adjective has two characters (e.g. 漂亮 (piàoliang) or 高兴 (gāoxìng)), the 的 (de) is generally required.

Examples

- 漂亮的 女孩儿
  piàoliang de nǚháir
  beautiful girl
- 辣的 菜
  là de cài
  spicy food
- 可爱的 宝宝
  kě'ài de bǎobao
  a cute baby
- 我喜欢 新鲜的 果汁。
  Wǒ xǐhuan xīnxiān de guǒzhī.
  I like fresh fruit juice.
- 他常常买 便宜的 东西。
  Tā chángcháng mǎi piányi de dōngxi.
  He often buys cheap stuff.

Without a Noun

Structure

In some cases, it is possible to drop the noun from the pattern, and just use the adjective + 的 (de). This is kind of like saying "the big one" or "the red one" in English. In Chinese the 的 (de) serves the same purpose as the English word "one." By using this pattern, you can avoid repeating the same noun over and over again unnecessarily. Just be sure the other person is already clear which "one" you're referring to when using this pattern!

Examples

A: 孩子喜欢吃什么东西?

Háizi xǐhuan chī shénme dōngxi?

What food do children like to eat?
It is implied that a lot of work has already been done but there is still "even more" work left.

B: 甜的 。

Tián de.

Sweet food.

A: 你喜欢哪种女孩?

Nǐ xǐhuan nǎ zhǒng nǚhái?

What kind of girls do you like?

B: 漂亮的 。

Piàoliang de.

Pretty ones.

A: 你要喝冷水还是热水?

Nǐ xǐhuan hē lěng shuǐ háishì rè shuǐ ?

Do you want to drink cold or hot water?

B: 冷的 。

Lěng de.

Cold.

A: 你想找什么样的男朋友?

Nǐ xiǎng zhǎo shénmeyàng de nánpéngyou?

What kind of boyfriend do you want to find?

B: 有钱的 。

Yǒuqián de.

A rich one.

A: 你不喜欢吃什么菜?

Nǐ bù xǐhuan chī shénme cài?

Which foods do you not like to eat?

B: 辣的 。

Là de.

Spicy ones.

Similar to

- Expressing close possession without “de” (A1), page 45
- Expressing possession with “de” (A1), page 47
- Turning adjectives into adverbs

Modifying nouns with phrase + "de" (A2)

In addition to linking adjectives to nouns[1], 的 (de) can also be used to link a whole phrase to a noun, making the already useful 的 (de) even more useful.

Structure

As well as attaching adjectives to nouns[1], 的 (de) can be used to attach whole phrases to nouns. In English this is often achieved with "who" or "that." For example, "the man who went to Beijing" or "the book that I bought yesterday."

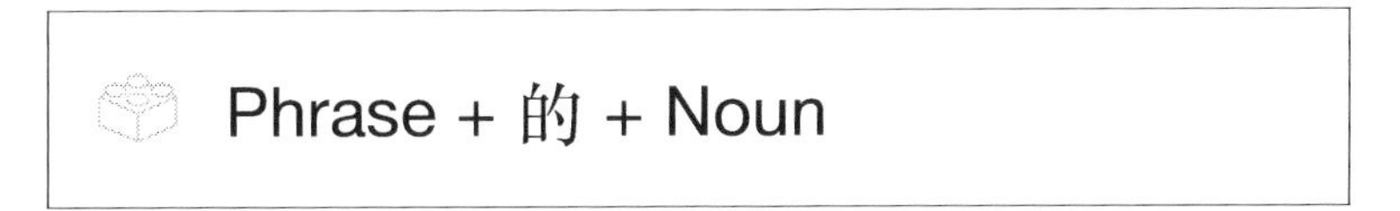

Here a phrase means *Verb + (Object)*.

Examples

- 妈妈做 的 菜
  māma zuò de cài
  the food that mom cooks
- 去北京 的 火车
  qù Běijīng de huǒchē
  the train that goes to Beijing
- 你教 的 学生
  nǐ jiāo de xuésheng
  the students that you teach
- 老板请 的 朋友
  lǎobǎn qǐng de péngyou
  the friends that the boss invited
- 我画 的 画
  wǒ huà de huà
  the pictures that I draw

---

1. Modifying nouns with adjective + "de" (A2), page 180

- 他写 的 书
  tā xiě de shū
  the books that he wrote
- 妈妈给我买 的 衣服
  māma gěi wǒ mǎi de yīfu
  the clothes that mom bought for me
- 客户问 的 问题
  kèhù wèn de wèntí
  the questions that the client asked
- 穿 Prada 的 女人
  chuān Prada de nǚrén
  women who wear Prada
- 不喜欢中国菜 的 老外
  bù xǐhuan Zhōngguó cài de lǎowài
  the foreigners that don't like Chinese food

Similar to

- Expressing close possession without "de" (A1), page 45
- Expressing possession with "de" (A1), page 47
- Modifying nouns with adjective + "de" (A2), page 180

Superlative "zui" (A2)

The most common way to form a superlative (best, worst, biggest, smallest, etc.) in Chinese is to use 最 (zuì) before an adjective (and a few select verbs).

最 (zuì) with Adjectives

Structure

The structure is:

And now you have the superlative form of the adjective. Unlike in English, this structure is consistent for all adjectives in Chinese. The inconsistencies in English sometimes confuse beginners, so note in the examples below how to say "best," "worst," "least," and "most" (meaning "greatest number").

Examples

- 哪个老师 最 好？
  Nǎge lǎoshī zuì hǎo?
  Which teacher is the best?
- 你们家谁 最 漂亮？
  Nǐmen jiā shéi zuì piàoliang?
  In your family who is the most beautiful?
- Zuckerberg 最 有钱。
  Zuckerberg zuì yǒuqián.
  Zuckerberg is the richest.
- 汉语 最 难。
  Hànyǔ zuì nán.
  The Chinese language is the most difficult.
- 这种事 最 麻烦。
  Zhè zhǒng shì zuì máfan.
  These kind of things are the most troublesome.

Optional 了 (le)

Occasionally you'll also see a 了 (le) added after the adjective. This simply adds emphasis to the "-est."

Structure

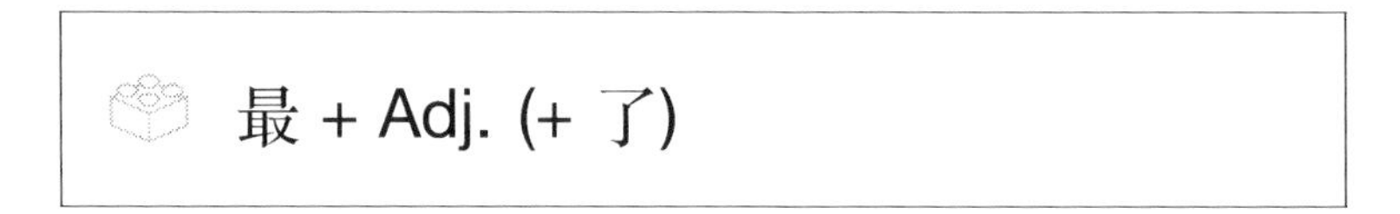

Examples

- 小狗 最 可爱 了 。 *This 了 is optional*
  Xiǎogǒu zuì kěài le .
  The puppy is the cutest.
- 四川菜 最 辣 了 。 *This 了 is optional*
  Sìchuān cài zuì là le .
  Sichuan food is the spiciest.
- 我的中国朋友 最 热情 了 。 *This 了 is optional*
  Wǒ de Zhōngguó péngyou zuì rèqíng le .
  My Chinese friend is the most enthusiastic.
- 他的学生 最 认真 了 。 *This 了 is optional*
  Tā de xuésheng zuì rènzhēn le .
  His student is the most serious.
- 黄山的风景 最 美 了 。 *This 了 is optional*
  Huángshān de fēngjǐng zuì měi le .
  Huang Mountain's landscape is the most beautiful.

最 (zuì) with Psychological Verbs

最 (zuì) can also come before psychological verbs, to express what one "most likes," "most hates," etc. It won't make sense if you try to use 最 (zuì) with non-psychological verbs, though.

Structure

The structure is:

Note the 了 (le) on the end there! It's not strictly required, but you'll hear it a lot in spoken Chinese.

Examples

- 老板 最 喜欢 你了！
  Lǎobǎn zuì xǐhuan nǐ le!
  The boss likes you the best!
- 你 最 怕 什么?
  Nǐ zuì pà shénme?
  What do you most fear?
- 我 最 爱 中国菜。
  Wǒ zuì ài Zhōngguó cài.
  I love Chinese food most.
- 谁 最 了解 你?
  Shéi zuì liǎojiě nǐ?
  Who knows you best?
- 她 最 讨厌 抽烟的男人了。
  Tā zuì tǎoyàn chōuyān de nánrén 了.
  She most hates men that smoke.

Although you could translate it as "like the best," pairing 最 (zuì) with the psychological verb 喜欢 (xǐhuan) is also a great way to talk about one's "favorite."

- 你 最 喜欢 什么颜色?
  Nǐ zuì xǐhuan shénme yánsè?
  What is your favorite color?

- 你 最 喜欢 什么动物?
  Nǐ zuì xǐhuan shénme dòngwù?
  What is your favorite animal?

Similar to

- Expressing “excessively” with “tai” (A1), page 94
- Simple “noun + adjective” sentences (A1), page 96
- Expressing “even more” with “geng” (A2), page 147
- Expressing “really” with “zhen” (A2), page 171
- Intensifying with “duo” (A2), page 176
- Moderating positive adjectives with “hai” (A2), page 178
- Special verbs with “hen” (A2), page 296
- Adjectives with “name” and “zheme”
- Expressing “much more” in comparisons
- Positive adjectives with “-ji le”

Expressing "or" in statements (A2)

In English, "or" can be used to connect words when offering or considering choices ("do you want chicken or beef?"). It can also be used as an "or" *statement* ("it doesn't matter if we eat chicken or beef"), in Chinese, this is what 或者 (huòzhě) is used for.

Structure

While 还是 (háishì) is used for "or" in questions[1], 或者 (huòzhě) is used for "or" in **statements.**

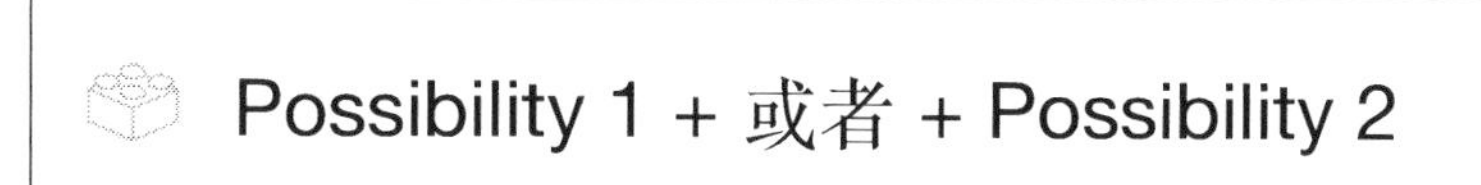

Examples

- 我喝 咖啡 或者 茶 ，都行。
  Wǒ hē kāfēi huòzhě chá , dōu xíng.
  I drink coffee or tea. Either is OK.
- 星期六 或者 星期天 ，都可以。
  Xīngqīliù huòzhě Xīngqītiān , dōu kěyǐ.
  Saturday or Sunday are both OK.
- 今天晚上我想吃 披萨 或者 寿司 。
  Jīntiān wǎnshang wǒ xiǎng chī pīsà huòzhě shòusī .
  Tonight I would like to eat pizza or sushi.
- 周末的时候，我喜欢在家 做饭 或者 看电影 。
  Zhōumò de shíhou, wǒ xǐhuan zài jiā zuòfàn huòzhě kàn diànyǐng .
  During the weekend, I like to cook or watch movies at home.
- 你去 或者 她去 ，都可以。
  Nǐ qù huòzhě tā qù , dōu kěyǐ.
  You go or she goes, either way is fine.

---

1. Offering choices with "haishi" (A1), page 24

- 下班以后 我去你家 或者 你来我家 ，都可以。
  Xiàbān yǐhòu wǒ qù nǐ jiā huòzhě nǐ lái wǒ jiā , dōu kěyǐ.
  After work I will go to your house, or you can come to my house, either way is fine.
- 下个月我打算去 杭州 或者 苏州 旅行。
  Xià gè yuè wǒ dǎsuàn qù Hángzhōu huòzhě Sūzhōu lǚxíng.
  Next month I plan to go to Hangzhou or Suzhou to travel.
- 我们可以 坐飞机 或者 坐高铁 去。
  Wǒmen kěyǐ zuò fēijī huòzhě zuò gāotiě qù.
  We can go by plane or by high-speed train.
- 晚饭以后我和家人 聊天 或者 看电视 。
  Wǎnfàn yǐhòu wǒ hé jiārén liáotiān huòzhě kàn diànshì .
  After dinner I chat with or watch TV with my family.
- 你可以用 手机 或者 电脑 上网。
  Nǐ kěyǐ yòng shǒujī huòzhě diànnǎo shàngwǎng.
  You can use either a cell phone or computer to go online.

Similar to

- Offering choices with “haishi” (A1), page 24
- Comparing “haishi” and “huozhe”
- Expressing “otherwise” with “yaobu”
- Providing two options with double “huozhe”

The filler word "neige" (A2)

In conversation, you may find yourself at a loss for words, unable to find the correct phrase you are looking for, or simply needing time to gather your thoughts. When you experience this feeling, in English, you may say "umm" or "uhhh" or another filler word. In Chinese, the word for this is 那个 (nèige). (The word 那个 can be pronounced both "nàge" and "nèige," but for this usage, "nèige" is normally used.)

Structure

In English, words like "ummm" and "uh" are used as filler words when you're thinking about what to say. In Chinese, 那个 (nèige) is also used for this purpose. To English speakers not fortunate enough to be fluent in Mandarin this may raise an eyebrow because it can sound a bit "racist," but it's very common in Mandarin and you'll hear it quite often around Chinese speakers.

(那个……) (那个……) + [anything] + (那个……)

那个 (nèige) can be inserted into sentences wherever you need to pause for thought.

Examples

- 那个……我不跟你们一起去了，可以吗？
  Nèige … wǒ bù gēn nǐmen yīqǐ qù le, kěyǐ ma?
  So, ummm… I won't go with you guys, OK?
- 我想吃那个……那个……湖南菜。
  Wǒ xiǎng chī nèige … nèige … Húnán cài.
  I want to eat that… ummm, you know… Hunan cuisine.
- 那个……我明天不来了。
  Nèige … wǒ míngtiān bù lái le.
  Ummm… I'm not coming tomorrow.
- 那个……这样做不好吧？
  Nèige … zhèyàng zuò bù hǎo ba?
  Ummm, it's not good to do it this way?

- 那个 …… 你可以做我的女朋友吗？
  Nèige … nǐ kěyǐ zuò wǒ de nǚpéngyou ma?
  Like… could you be my girlfriend?
- 那个 …… 不好意思，我要走了。
  Nèige … bù hǎoyìsi, wǒ yào zǒu le.
  Ummmm… sorry, but I've gotta go.
- 她很漂亮，就像 那个 …… 明星一样。
  Tā hěn piàoliang, jiù xiàng nèige … míngxīng yīyàng.
  She's very pretty, just like, you know, a celebrity.
- 我想看看你买的 那个 …… 那个 …… iPhone。
  Wǒ xiǎng kànkan nǐ mǎi de nèige … nèige … iPhone.
  I'd like to take a look at your, ummm, you know… iPhone you bought.
- 那个 …… 我要去开会了。
  Nèige … wǒ yào qù kāihuì le.
  Ummm… I have to attend a meeting.
- 昨天 那个 …… 那个 …… 小笼包真好吃。
  Zuótiān nèige … nèige … xiǎolóngbāo zhēn hǎochī.
  Yesterday the, you know, steamed soup dumplings were so delicious.

Two words for "but" (A2)

Using "but" in Chinese is really simple to learn. It involves the two words 可是 (kěshì) and 但是 (dànshì). Make no "buts" about it; you'll understand it in no time!

Structure

There are two main words for "but" in Chinese: 可是 (kěshì) and 但是 (dànshì). These are largely the same. The small difference is that 但是 (dànshì) is slightly more formal, whereas 可是 (kěshì) is just a bit more informal and a tad weaker in tone. You really don't need to worry about which one is the right one to use though, since they can be used interchangeably.

Statement, 可是 / 但是 + [Contrary Statement]

Examples

Usually 可是 (kěshì) and 但是 (dànshì) precede a new phrase within a sentence:

- 我喜欢他，可是他不喜欢我。
  Wǒ xǐhuan tā, kěshì tā bù xǐhuan wǒ.
  I like him, but he doesn't like me.
- 我很想去，但是我太忙了。
  Wǒ hěn xiǎng qù, dànshì wǒ tài máng le.
  I really want to go, but I am too busy.
- 中文很有意思，但是也很难。
  Zhōngwén hěn yǒuyìsi, dànshì yě hěn nán.
  Chinese is very interesting, but it is also very hard.
- 我喜欢这件衬衫，可是太贵了。
  Wǒ xǐhuan zhè jiàn chènshān, kěshì tài guì le.
  I like this shirt, but it is too expensive.
- 老板昨天给他打电话，可是他没接。
  Lǎobǎn zuótiān gěi tā dǎ diànhuà, kěshì tā méi jiē.
  The boss gave him a call yesterday, but he didn't answer.

- iPhone 很好，但是 我没钱买。
  iPhone hěn hǎo, dànshì wǒ méi qián mǎi.
  The iPhone is great, but I don't have the money to buy it.
- 你们可以在这里看书，可是 不可以说话。
  Nǐ kěyǐ zài zhèlǐ kàn shū, kěshì bù kěyǐ shuōhuà.
  You can read books here, but you can't talk.
- 你可以吃，但是 不可以吃太多。
  Nǐ kěyǐ chī, dànshì bù kěyǐ chī tài duō.
  You can eat, but you can't eat too much.
- 他说五点来见我，但是 他没来。
  Tā shuō wǔ diǎn lái jiàn wǒ, dànshì tā méi lái.
  He said he would come to see me at five, but he didn't.
- 这个地方很漂亮，但是 人太多了。
  Zhège dìfang hěn piàoliang, dànshì rén tài duō le.
  This place is beautiful, but there are too many people.

Note: In informal spoken Chinese, 可是 (kěshì) can be shortened to 可 (kě), and 但是 (dànshì) can be shortened to 但 (dàn).

Similar to

- A softer "but"
- Expressing "although" with "suiran" and "danshi"

Using "gen" to mean "with" (A2)

Using 跟 (gēn) to express "with" is so simple and helpful, after studying it briefly, it will always be *with* you! 跟 (gēn) is a very common word that will help complete many other sentence structures.

Structure

The preposition 跟 (gēn) is commonly used to express "with." Just remember that the "with" phrase comes *before the verb*.

Subj. + 跟 + Person + Verb + Obj.

The word 一起 (yīqǐ) is used a lot with 跟 (gēn), expressing the idea of "doing something *together with* somebody." It may seem kind of redundant, but it's totally normal in Chinese to use both.

Also, for most of the examples below, 跟 (gēn) is interchangeable with 和 (hé), which you may remember, also means "and," just like 跟 (gēn) does.

Subj. + 跟 + Person + 一起 + Verb + Obj.

Certain Chinese verbs use 跟 (gēn) a lot, so be on the lookout for them (examples below)!

Examples

- 我昨天跟朋友去海滩了。
  Wǒ zuótiān gēn péngyou qù hǎitān le.
  I went to the beach with friends yesterday.
- 不要跟我说话！
  Bùyào gēn wǒ shuōhuà!
  Don't talk to me!
- 我明天要跟新客户见面。
  Wǒ míngtiān yào gēn xīn kèhù jiànmiàn.
  I'm going to meet new clients tomorrow.

- 你什么时候 跟 你女朋友 结婚 ?
  Nǐ shénme shíhou gēn nǐ nǚpéngyou jiéhūn ?
  When are you gonna marry your girlfriend?
- 你喜欢 跟 你父母 聊天 吗?
  Nǐ xǐhuan gēn nǐ fùmǔ liáotiān ma?
  Do you like to talk with your parents?
- 你想 跟 我 一起去 吗?
  Nǐ xiǎng gēn wǒ yīqǐ qù ma?
  Do you want to go with me?
- 请你们 跟 老师 一起读 。
  Qǐng nǐmen gēn lǎoshī yīqǐ dú .
  Please read together with the teacher.
- 下周谁 跟 老板 一起出差 ?
  Xià zhōu shéi gēn lǎobǎn yīqǐ chūchāi ?
  Who is going on a business trip together with the boss next week?
- 结婚以后，你想 跟 父母 一起住 吗?
  Jiéhūn yǐhòu, nǐ xiǎng gēn fùmǔ yīqǐ zhù ma?
  Do you want live together with your parents after you get married?
- 今年中秋节你会 跟 家人 一起过 吗?
  Jīnnián Zhōngqiūjié nǐ huì gēn jiārén yīqǐ guò ma?
  Are you going to spend this Mid-Autumn Festival with your family?

Note: One of the most common beginner mistakes is to fail to use 跟 (gēn) with 见面 (jiànmiàn), "to meet." It might help to think of 见面 (jiànmiàn) as "to meet *with* (somebody)," the "with" cluing you into the fact that you need a 跟 (gēn) in there. The verbs 结婚 (jiéhūn), "to marry," and 聊天 (liáotiān), "to chat" are used with 跟 (gēn) in the exact same way.

Check out the examples below:

✘ 我要 见面 你。
Wǒ yào jiànmiàn nǐ.

✔ 我要 跟 你 见面 。
Wǒ yào gēn nǐ jiànmiàn .
I want to meet with you.

✘ 我昨天 见面 他了。

Wǒ zuótiān jiànmiàn tā le.

✔ 我昨天 跟 他 见面 了。

Wǒ zuótiān gēn tā jiànmiàn le.

I met with him yesterday.

✘ 你什么时候 见面 她?

Nǐ shénme shíhou jiànmiàn tā?

✔ 你什么时候 跟 她 见面 ?

Nǐ shénme shíhou gēn tā jiànmiàn ?

When are you going to meet with her?

✘ 明天我要 见面 我男朋友的家人。

Míngtiān wǒ yào jiànmiàn wǒ nánpéngyou de jiārén.

✔ 明天我要 跟 我男朋友的家人 见面 。

Míngtiān wǒ yào gēn wǒ nánpéngyou de jiārén jiànmiàn .

Tomorrow I am going to meet my boyfriend's family.

✘ 你有没有 见面 过 Obama?

Nǐ yǒu méiyǒu jiànmiàn guo Obama?

✔ 你有没有 跟 Obama 见过面 ?

Nǐ yǒu méiyǒu gēn Obama jiàn guo miàn ?

Have you ever met Obama?

Later on you'll learn more about why this is the case, but for now just memorize the correct pattern.

Where 和 (hé) and 跟 (gēn) Differ

We mentioned earlier that 跟 (gēn) is essentially interchangeable with 和 (hé). There's at least one common usage where this is not the case, though:

✘ 和 我读。

Hé wǒ dú.

✔ 跟 我读。

Gēn wǒ dú.

Read after me.

The reason is that although 跟 (gēn) and 和 (hé) can both mean "and" or "with," the word 跟 (gēn) also has a sense of "to follow" embedded in it. There's a before/after aspect.

The following sentences are both correct, because they're simultaneous rather than before/after:

✔ 和 我 一起 读。
Hé wǒ yīqǐ dú.

✔ 跟 我 一起 读。
Gēn wǒ yīqǐ dú.
Read with me.

Because of this slight difference between 跟 (gēn) and 和 (hé), it's recommended to start out using 跟 (gēn) to mean "with."

Similar to

- Expressing "together" with "yiqi" (A2), page 278
- Using "dui" with verbs
- Using "xiang"
- Verbs preceded by "gei"
- Comparing "gen" and "dui"

After a specific time with "yihou" (A2)

Just as 以前 (yǐqián) can be used[1] to describe the events *before* a specific time, 以后 (yǐhòu) can be used to describe the events *after* a specific time.

Structure

This grammar structure is similar to the English "after such-and-such, something happens." It's quite simple, all you have to do is put the "after" after the time words or time phrase.

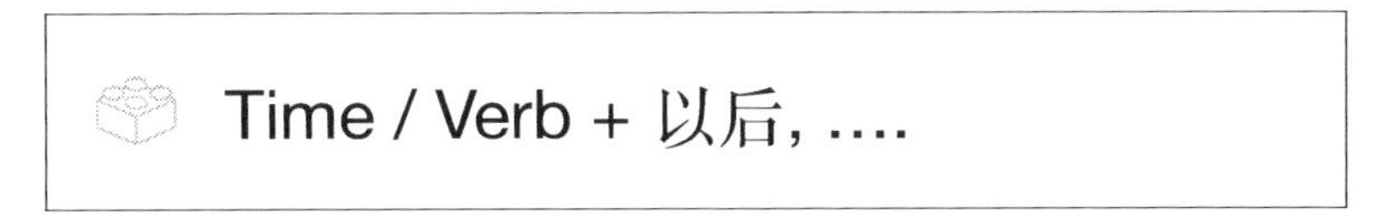

The time can be a time or date, or an action or event. It may or may not be in the future.

Examples

- 下午三点 以后 ，我不在家。
  Xiàwǔ sāndiǎn yǐhòu, wǒ bù zài jiā.
  After three p.m., I will not be at home.
- 来中国 以后 ，她认识了她的老公。
  Lái Zhōngguó yǐhòu, tā rènshi le tā de lǎogōng.
  After coming to China, she met her husband.
- 她 一个月 以后 开始上班。
  Tā yī gè yuè yǐhòu kāishǐ shàngbān.
  After one month, she will start working.
- 吃完午饭 以后 ，我们要开会。
  Chī wán wǔfàn yǐhòu, wǒmen yào kāihuì.
  We are going to have a meeting after we finish lunch.
- 几年 以后 ，我们公司会更大。
  Jǐ nián yǐhòu, wǒmen gōngsī huì gèng dà.
  In a few years, our company will be even bigger.

---

1. Before a specific time with "yiqian" (A2), page 201

- 老板 半个小时 以后 回来。
  Lǎobǎn bàn gè xiǎoshí yǐhòu huílái.
  After half an hour, the boss will return.
- 下班 以后 你想跟我们一起去打球吗?
  Xiàbān yǐhòu, nǐ xiǎng gēn wǒmen yīqǐ qù dǎqiú ma?
  After we get off work, would you like to go play ball with us?
- 老板 来 了 以后，大家都不说话了。
  Lǎobǎn lái le yǐhòu, dàjiā dōu bù shuōhuà le.
  After the boss came, everyone stopped talking.
- 你 到家 以后 给我打电话。
  Nǐ dào jiā yǐhòu gěi wǒ dǎ diànhuà.
  After you get home, call me.
- 结婚 以后 爸爸不喝酒了。
  Jiéhūn yǐhòu bàba bù hējiǔ le.
  After he got married, dad stopped drinking.

Note that this use of 以后 (yǐhòu) is often shortened to 后 (hòu).

Similar to

- Before a specific time with "yiqian" (A2), page 201
- In the future in general with "yihou" (A2), page 209

- Comparing "yihou" and "de shihou"
- Comparing "yihou" and "houlai"
- Comparing "yihou" and "zhihou"

Before a specific time with "yiqian" (A2)

As well as talking about the past in general[1], you can use 以前 (yǐqián) to talk about things that happened *before* a specific time.

Structure

Time / Verb + 以前, ...

The time can be a specific time, or an action (technically, "*when* the action was done").

Examples

- 吃饭 以前 ，你洗手了吗?
  Chīfàn yǐqián, nǐ xǐ shǒu le ma?
  Did you wash your hands before eating?
- 睡觉 以前 ，不要吃东西。
  Shuìjiào yǐqián, bùyào chī dōngxi.
  Don't eat anything before you go to sleep.
- 两年 以前 ，你认识他吗?
  Liǎng nián yǐqián, nǐ rènshi tā ma?
  Did you know him two years ago?
- 星期五 以前 ，你要做完这些工作。
  Xīngqīwǔ yǐqián, nǐ yào zuò wán zhèxiē gōngzuò.
  You need to finish this work before Friday.
- 上大学 以前 ，你来过上海吗?
  Shàng dàxué yǐqián, nǐ lái guo shànghǎi ma?
  Before you went to college, did you ever come to Shanghai?
- 结婚 以前 ，你应该先买房子。
  Jiéhūn yǐqián, nǐ yīnggāi xiān mǎi fángzi.
  Before getting married, you should first buy a house.

---

1. Expressing "before" in general with "yiqian" (A2), page 203

- 二十年 以前 ，这里是一个公园。
  Èrshí nián yǐqián, zhèlǐ shì yī gè gōngyuán.
  Twenty years ago, this was a park.
- 几个月 以前 ，他们分手了。
  Jǐ gè yuè yǐqián, tāmen fēnshǒu le.
  They broke up a few months ago.
- 毕业 以前 ，我要找到工作。
  Bìyè yǐqián, wǒ yào zhǎodào gōngzuò.
  I need to find a job before graduation.
- 当总统 以前 ，Obama 没有白头发。
  Dāng zǒngtǒng yǐqián, Obama méiyǒu bái tóufa.
  Before he became the president, Obama didn't have white hair.

Note that this use of 以前 (yǐqián) can also be shortened to 前 (qián).

Similar to

- Structure of times (basic) (A1), page 42
- Expressing “before” in general with “yiqian” (A2), page 203
- Expressing “when” with “de shihou” (A2), page 207
- Structure of times (advanced) (A2), page 218
- Before and after with “zhiqian” and “zhihou”
- Expressing “when” with “shi”

Expressing “before” in general with “yiqian” (A2)

To talk about things that previously occurred, you can use the word 以前 (yǐqián). You can use this structure to talk about actions that happened at some unspecified time in the past.

Structure

One way to use 以前 (yǐqián) is to start the sentence with it. This is like starting off a sentence in English with “before...” or “in the past...”

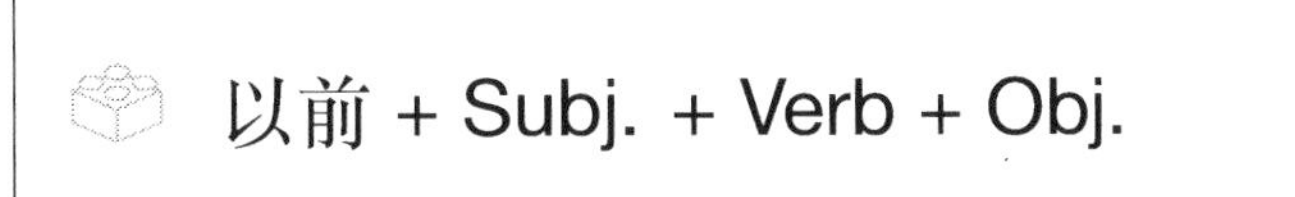

You can also move 以前 (yǐqián) to right after the subject, and it's also correct.

Subj. + 以前 + Verb + Obj.

Examples

- 以前 我不会说中文。
  Yǐqián wǒ bù huì shuō Zhōngwén.
  Before, I could not speak Chinese.
- 你 以前 住在哪儿?
  Nǐ yǐqián zhù zài nǎr?
  Before, where did you live?
- 以前 我不认识他。
  Yǐqián wǒ bù rènshi tā.
  Before, I didn't know him.
- 以前 他是我们的客户吗?
  Yǐqián tā shì wǒmen de kèhù ma?
  Was he our client before?

- 以前 他是一个服务员，现在是老板。
  Yǐqián tā shì yī gè fúwùyuán, xiànzài shì lǎobǎn.
  Before, he was a waiter. Now, he is a boss.
- 我父母 以前 都是老师。
  Wǒ fùmǔ yǐqián dōu shì lǎoshī.
  Before, both of my parents were teachers.
- 爸爸 以前 很喜欢抽烟。
  Bàba yǐqián hěn xǐhuan chōuyān.
  Before, dad really liked smoking.
- 姐姐 以前 有一个很有钱的男朋友。
  Jiějie yǐqián yǒu yī gè hěn yǒuqián de nánpéngyou.
  My older sister had a very rich boyfriend before.
- 他们 以前 没有钱，可是很快乐。
  Tāmen yǐqián méiyǒu qián, kěshì hěn kuàilè.
  They didn't have much money before, but they were happy.
- 我男朋友 以前 在美国工作，现在在中国工作。
  Wǒ nánpéngyou yǐqián zài Měiguó gōngzuò, xiànzài zài Zhōngguó gōngzuò.
  Before, my boyfriend worked in the USA. Now, he works in China.

Similar to

- Before a specific time with “yiqian” (A2), page 201
- In the future in general with “yihou” (A2), page 209

Expressing "just now" with "gangcai" (A2)

In order to say that something "just now" occurred, use the time noun 刚才 (gāngcái). It can be placed in front of the verb or the subject of a statement.

Structure

This grammar structure is pretty straightforward. Similar to the English "just now," you can put 刚才 (gāngcái) right before the verb in a sentence. It can also come before or after the subject.

刚才 + Verb

Examples

- 你刚才说什么了?
  Nǐ gāngcái shuō shénme le?
  What did you just say?
- 刚才谁来了?
  Gāngcái shéi lái le?
  Who came just now?
- 刚才你去哪儿了?
  Gāngcái nǐ qù nǎr le?
  Where did you go just now?
- 刚才我去洗手间了。
  Gāngcái wǒ qù xǐshǒujiān le.
  I just went to the restroom.
- 老板刚才生气了。
  Lǎobǎn gāngcái shēngqì le.
  The boss just got angry.
- 你们刚才在看什么?
  Nǐmen gāngcái zài kàn shénme?
  What were you looking at just now?

- 不好意思，我 刚才 出去 了。
  Bù hǎoyìsi, wǒ gāngcái chūqù le.
  I'm sorry, I just now stepped out.
- 宝宝 刚才 哭 了。
  Bǎobao gāngcái kū le.
  The baby just cried.
- 他们 刚才 去 开会 了。
  Tāmen gāngcái qù kāihuì le.
  They just went to a meeting.
- 刚才 有人 找 你。
  Gāngcái yǒu rén zhǎo nǐ.
  Just now, there was someone looking for you.

Note that for all of those cases, we're talking about something that happened *just now*, as in, within the past 5 minutes or so. If you're talking about something that "just happened" yesterday or last week, don't use 刚才 (gāngcái), use 刚 (gāng)[1].

Similar to

- Expressing "just" with "gang" (A2), page 149
- Comparing "gang" and "gangcai"

1. Expressing "just" with "gang" (A2), page 149

Expressing "when" with "de shihou" (A2)

In English, if we are reflecting on a past time, we often say, "*when* I was a child" or "*when* I was in school." In Chinese, this can also be expressed by using 的时候 (de shíhou).

Structure

To talk about events that happened *at* or *during* a particular time, 的时候 (de shíhou) is often used. This is simply attached to the word or phrase indicating the time:

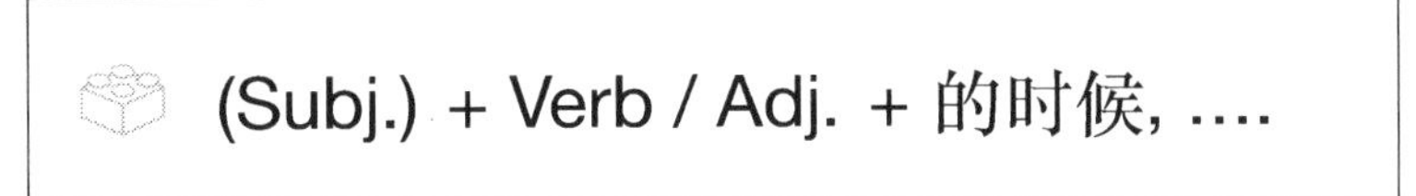

As time words can appear before or after the subject[1], you can also place the "Time + 的时候 (de shíhou)" after the subject:

Examples

- 你 不在 的时候 ，我会想你。
  Nǐ bù zài de shíhou , wǒ huì xiǎng nǐ.
  When you are not here, I'll miss you.
- 我 上大学 的时候 ，有很多朋友。
  Wǒ shàng dàxué de shíhou , yǒu hěn duō péngyou.
  When I was in college, I had a lot of friends.
- 上课 的时候 不要吃东西。
  Shàngkè de shíhou bùyào chī dōngxi.
  Don't eat when you are in class.
- 老板 工作 的时候 喜欢喝咖啡。
  Lǎobǎn gōngzuò de shíhou xǐhuan hē kāfēi.
  When the boss works, he likes to drink coffee.

---

1. Time words and word order (A2), page 211

- 我 生气 的时候 ，请你不要笑。
  Wǒ shēngqì de shíhou , qǐng nǐ bùyào xiào.
  Please don't laugh when I'm angry.
- 妈妈 不在家 的时候 ，我自己做饭。
  Māma bù zài jiā de shíhou , wǒ zìjǐ zuòfàn.
  When mom is not home, I cook for myself.
- 开会 的时候 不要聊天。
  Kāihuì de shíhou bùyào liáotiān.
  Don't chat when you are in a meeting.
- 吃东西 的时候 不要说话。
  Chī dōngxi de shíhou bùyào shuōhuà.
  Don't talk when eating.
- 你 开车 的时候 会打电话吗?
  Nǐ kāichē de shíhou huì dǎ diànhuà ma?
  Do you talk on the phone when you're driving?
- 走路 的时候 不要玩手机。
  Zǒulù de shíhou bùyào wán shǒujī.
  Don't play with your phone while walking.

Similar to

- After a specific time with “yihou” (A2), page 199
- Simultaneous tasks with “yibian” (A2), page 158
- Comparing “yihou” and “de shihou”
- Expressing “when” with “shi”

In the future in general with "yihou" (A2)

Similar to talking about things in the past, talking about things in the future is very straight forward. You can use the simple but useful 以后 (yǐhòu), which also means "later."

Structure

To talk about things happening at some unspecified time in the future, you can use 以后 (yǐhòu). The structure is:

以后 + Subj. + Verb + Obj.

You can also move 以后 (yǐhòu) to right after the subject, and it's also correct.

Subj. + 以后 + Verb + Obj.

This can be used to talk about actions in the future, or to talk about events that happened *after other events* in a story.

Examples

In the examples below, the translation "in the future" is used, because using "later" for 以后 (yǐhòu) either sounds weird, or makes it sound like it's going to happen really soon (just a little later), rather than at some indefinite point in the future, which is what is meant.

- 以后 你们会想我吗?
  Yǐhòu nǐmen huì xiǎng wǒ ma?
  In the future, will you miss me?
- 以后 你想来中国吗?
  Yǐhòu nǐ xiǎng lái Zhōngguó ma?
  In the future, do you want to come to China?
- 我 以后 不喝酒了。
  Wǒ yǐhòu bù hējiǔ le.
  I will not drink alcohol in the future.

- 我们 以后 不在这里工作了。
  Wǒmen yǐhòu bù zài zhèlǐ gōngzuò le.
  We will not work here in the future.
- 你儿子 以后 想做什么?
  Nǐ érzi yǐhòu xiǎng zuò shénme?
  In the future, what does your son want to do?
- 以后 你们想去哪儿工作?
  Yǐhòu nǐmen xiǎng qù nǎr gōngzuò?
  In the future, where would you like to work?
- 以后 我们会有一些新的同事。
  Yǐhòu wǒmen huì yǒu yīxiē xīn de tóngshì.
  We will have some new co-workers in the future.
- 以后 你可以住在这里。
  Yǐhòu nǐ kěyǐ zhù zài zhèlǐ.
  In the future, you can live here.
- 他们 以后 会结婚吗?
  Tāmen yǐhòu huì jiéhūn ma?
  Will they get married in the future?
- 你 以后 不要跟他见面了。
  Nǐ yǐhòu bùyào gēn tā jiànmiàn le.
  In the future, stop seeing him.

Similar to

- After a specific time with “yihou” (A2), page 199
- Expressing “before” in general with “yiqian” (A2), page 203
- Expressing “when” with “de shihou” (A2), page 207
- Before and after with “zhiqian” and “zhihou”
- Comparing “yihou” and “houlai”
- Comparing “yihou” and “zhihou”
- Expressing “when” with “shi”
- Sequencing past events with “houlai”
- Expressing future with “jiang”

Time words and word order (A2)

Remembering where to put the time words, such as "yesterday," "tomorrow," "this week," etc. in a sentence is really important in order to speak Chinese correctly. In Chinese you get two equally correct choices.

Structure

Time words can appear in one of two positions in the sentence in Chinese: either at the beginning of the sentence (before the subject), or directly after the subject. The structures are:

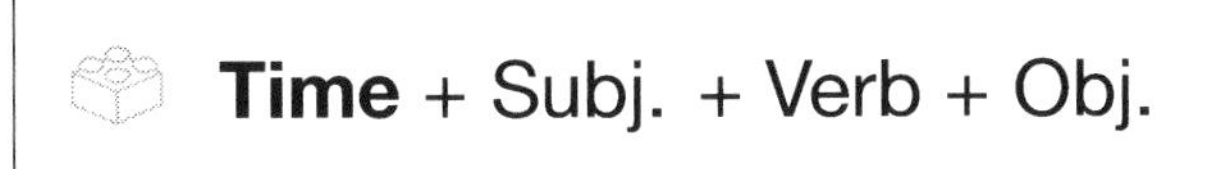

Subj. + **Time** + Verb + Obj.

So if you start speaking with "time first" English word order, you can carry on and get away with it. If, however, you're saving the time word for the *end* of the sentence, you can be pretty sure that it doesn't sound at all natural to your Chinese audience.

Examples

- 昨天 我 去了酒吧。
  Zuótiān wǒ qù le jiǔbā.
  Yesterday I went to the bar.
- 我 昨天 去了酒吧。
  Wǒ zuótiān qù le jiǔbā.
  I went to the bar yesterday.
- 下个星期 他 要回国。
  Xià gè xīngqī tā yào huí guó.
  Next week he is going back to his country.
- 他 下个星期 要回国。
  Tā xià gè xīngqī yào huí guó.
  He is going back to his country next week.

- 明年 我 要开一个公司。
  Míngnián wǒ yào kāi yī gè gōngsī.
  Next year I want to open a company.
- 我 明年 要开一个公司。
  Wǒ míngnián yào kāi yī gè gōngsī.
  I want to open a company next year.
- 下个月 我们 结婚吧?
  Xià gè yuè wǒmen jiéhūn ba?
  Next month shall we get married?
- 我们 下个月 结婚吧?
  Wǒmen xià gè yuè jiéhūn ba?
  Shall we get married next month?
- 现在 你 能来我办公室吗?
  Xiànzài nǐ néng lái wǒ bàngōngshì ma?
  Now you can come to my office?
- 你 现在 能来我办公室吗?
  Nǐ xiànzài néng lái wǒ bàngōngshì ma?
  Can you come to my office now?

Similar to

- Basic sentence order (A1), page 88
- Wanting to do something with “yao” (A1), page 77

Approximating with sequential numbers (A2)

Expressing approximate numbers in Chinese is quite simple, and this article introduces one of the most basic ways to do so.

Structure

An easy way to express approximate numbers is to use two sequential numbers in a row.

This is similar to saying "x or y" or "about x" in English.

Examples

- 一两 天
  yī liǎng tiān
  one or two days
- 三四 个人
  sān sì gè rén
  three or four people
- 老板昨天喝了 七八 瓶胡萝卜汁。
  Lǎobǎn zuótiān hē le qī bā píng húluóbo zhī.
  The boss drank 7 or 8 bottles of carrot juice yesterday.
- 这个词我们学过 两三 次了。
  Zhège cí wǒmen xué guo liǎng sān cì le.
  We've studied this word two or three times now.
- 我等了你 三四 个小时。
  Wǒ děng le nǐ sān sì gè xiǎoshí.
  I waited for you for three or four hours.
- 他们 七八 年没见面了。
  Tāmen qī bā nián méi jiànmiàn le.
  They haven't seen each other for seven or eight years.

- 要做完这个工作需要 一两 个月。
  Yào zuò wán zhège gōngzuò xūyào yī liǎng gè yuè.
  To complete this work, you need one to two months.
- 他们家的孩子 五六 岁了吧。
  Tāmen jiā de háizi wǔ liù suì le ba.
  Their child is about five or six years old.
- 这件衣服只要 七八十 块钱。
  Zhè jiàn yīfu zhǐ yào qī bā shí kuài qián.
  This clothing only costs seventy to eighty kuai.
- 这几本书花了我 两三百 。
  Zhè jǐ běn shū huā le wǒ liǎng sān bǎi.
  These few books cost me two or three hundred kuai.

Similar to

- Structure of numbers (A1), page 36
- Big numbers in Chinese (A2), page 215
- Counting money (A2), page 319
- Measure words for counting (A2), page 328

- Indicating a number in excess

Big numbers in Chinese (A2)

The manner in which large numbers are broken down in Chinese is a little different from English. Unlike in English, where large numbers are broken down by the number of *thousands* they have, Chinese forms numbers between 10,000 and 100,000,000 based off of how many *tens* of thousands they have (with another set of rules for numbers 100,000,000 onwards that will be explained later). While the structure can be difficult to grasp for some learners, there are some easy ways to remember how to form these big numbers.

Different Units

Mandarin has two units that English doesn't have (or at least, it has unique words for these units, whereas English describes them with combinations of other units). These are:

- 万 (wàn): ten thousand
- 亿 (yì): hundred million

Ten Thousand - 万 (wàn)

万 (wàn) comes up the most often and is the largest stumbling block for most people learning Mandarin numbers. In English, numbers are usually broken up into chunks of three digits. Because of 万 (wàn), it's easier to break numbers up into groups of four in Mandarin. In English, we split "twelve thousand" numerically into "12,000" (chunks of three digits). Split it the Chinese way, "1,2000," and the Chinese reading "一万两千" (one *wan* and two "thousand" = yīwàn liǎngqiān) makes more sense.

One way to remember how to write out numbers 10,000 through 99,999 in Chinese characters is that in Chinese, the comma is (mentally) moved one digit to the left. For example, 11,000 could be thought of in tens of thousands as "1,1000," with 万 (wàn) replacing the comma, and then what's left written as 一千 (yīqiān): 一万一千 (yīwàn yīqiān).

Typical split	Chinese split	Characters	Pinyin
10,000	1,0000	一万	yīwàn
12,000	1,2000	一万二	yīwàn èr
13,200	1,3200	一万三千两百	yīwàn sānqiān liǎngbǎi
56,700	5,6700	五万六千七百	wǔwàn liùqiān qībǎi

One Hundred Million - 亿 (yì)

After 99,999,999, there is yet another new numerical unit, 亿 (yì), which is used to express "hundred million." A number like 1,101,110,000 would be written out as "十一亿一百一十一万 (shíyī yì yībǎi yīshí-yī wàn)." Again, an easier way to translate between the two methods is to write the number out in English, move the comma one digit to the left, and then insert the appropriate characters in their respective places, replacing the commas.

Mandarin Number Structure

Numerals	Characters	Pinyin	English
1,000,000,000	十亿	shí yì	Billion
100,000,000	亿	yì	Hundred million
10,000,000	千万	qiān wàn	Ten million
1,000,000	百万	bǎi wàn	Million
100,000	十万	shí wàn	Hundred thousand
10,000	万	wàn	Ten thousand
1,000	千	qiān	Thousand
100	百	bǎi	Hundred
10	十	shí	Ten
1	一	yī	One

A Shortcut

One more simple way to remember how to correctly write out large numbers is to pick one or two numbers and just memorize them. One million, for example, is 一百万 (yībǎi wàn). If you can memorize that, then going to 一千万 (yīqiān wàn) is way easier and faster, since you don't have to count all those zeroes.

The recommended shortcuts are:

- 一百万 *frequently a useful number to know*

  yībǎi wàn

  1 million

- 十四亿 *this just happens to be the population of China*

  shísì yì

  1.4 billion

Examples

- 五 万 两千一百五十二

  wǔ wàn liǎngqiān yībǎi wǔshí-èr

  52,152

- 二百九十一 万 四千六百八十

  èrbǎi jiǔshí-yī wàn sìqiān liùbǎi bāshí

  2,914,680

- 七百八十九 万 零二百九十八

  qībǎi bāshí-jiǔ wàn líng èrbǎi jiǔshí-bā

  7,890,298

- 两千七百二十一 万 四千八百九十六

  liǎngqiān qībǎi èrshí-yī wàn sìqiān bābǎi jiǔshí-liù

  27,214,896

- 五千三百七十九 万 八千两百五十

  wǔqiān sānbǎi qīshí-jiǔ wàn bāqiān liǎngbǎi wǔshí

  53,798,250

- 四 亿 一千四百二十九 万 四千一百八十二

  sì yì yīqiān sìbǎi èrshí-jiǔ wàn sìqiān yībǎi bāshí-èr

  414,294,182

- 十三 亿 两千六百八十 万

  shísān yì liǎngqiān liùbǎi bāshí wàn

  1,326,800,000

- 两百五十一 亿 五千八百三十六 万 七千二百

  liǎngbǎi wǔshí-yī yì wǔqiān bābǎi sānshí-liù wàn qīqiān èrbǎi

  25,158,367,200

Similar to

- Structure of numbers (A1), page 36

Structure of times (advanced) (A2)

If you already know the basics of how to tell time in Chinese[1], you may want to get a little more specific or sophisticated, using words like 分 (fēn) and 刻 (kè).

Minutes Past the Hour

Minutes are marked with 分 (fēn) (short for 分钟 (fēnzhōng)). The way to include them in the time depends on whether they're minutes *past* or *to* the hour.

Minutes *past* the hour are expressed after 点 (diǎn) in the same way as half and quarter hours.

Minutes Less Than 10

Structure

Examples

- 一 点 四十 分
  yī diǎn sìshí fēn
  1:40
- 两 点 十 分
  liǎng diǎn shí fēn
  2:10
- 三 点 二十 分
  sān diǎn èrshí fēn
  3:20
- 七 点 十五 分
  qī diǎn shíwǔ fēn
  7:15
- 九 点 五十 分
  jiǔ diǎn wǔshí fēn
  9:50

1. Structure of times (basic) (A1), page 42

Minutes Greater Than 10

Structure

In Chinese, when the minute is under 10, the word 零 (líng) is often used after 点 (diǎn). For example, 2:07 would be said as “两点零七分” (liǎng diǎn líng qī fēn). However, note that when speaking, it is very common for most Chinese people take out the “分 (fēn)” at the end of the time.

Examples

Quarter Hours

In Chinese, quarter hours are only expressed on the 1st quarter x:15, and the third quarter x:45. Like half hours, they also come after the word 点 (diǎn). We use the word 刻 (kè) to express “quarter hour.”

Structure

Examples

- 九点一刻
  jiǔ diǎn yī kè
  9:15
- 十二点一刻
  shí'èr diǎn yī kè
  12:15
- 六点三刻
  liù diǎn sān kè
  6:45

You can totally just use 十五分 (shíwǔ fēn) for "15 minutes (past)" or 四十五分 (sìshí-wǔ fēn) for "45 minutes (past)" if you're lazy, though. It also works!

Minutes to the Hour

When expressing how many minutes it will be till the next full hour, you put 差 (chā) in front of the time expression.

Structure

Minutes *to* the hour use this structure:

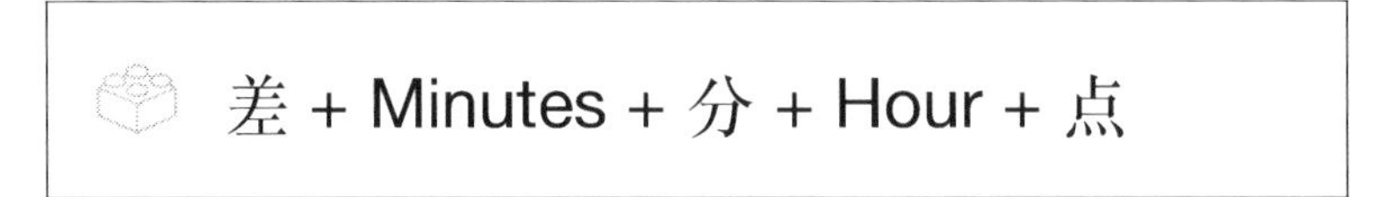

or

Examples

- 差五分三点
  chā wǔ fēn sān diǎn
  five minutes til 3 o'clock
- 十二点差三分
  shí'èr diǎn chā sān fēn
  three minutes til 12 o'clock
- 差五分八点半
  chā wǔ fēn bā diǎn bàn
  five minutes til 8:30
- 十点差两分
  shí diǎn chā liǎng fēn
  two minutes til 10:00

Similar to

- Structure of times (basic) (A1), page 42

Using "ji" to mean "several" (A2)

One of the definitions of the common character 几 (jǐ) is "several," "a couple" or "a few." It's an uncertain number that is at least more than one, and probably less than five, but definitely less than ten.

几 (jǐ) as "a Few"

The simplest way to use 几 (jǐ) to mean "a few" is to use it directly with a measure word.

Structure

几 + Measure Word + Noun

Examples

- 桌子上有 几 本书。
  Zhuōzi shàng yǒu jǐ běn shū.
  There are a few books on the table.
- 只有 几 个人去过那个地方。
  Zhǐyǒu jǐ gè rén qù guo nàge dìfang.
  Only a few people have been to that place.
- 从上海到东京坐飞机只要 几 个小时。
  Cóng Shànghǎi dào Dōngjīng zuò fēijī zhǐ yào jǐ gè xiǎoshí.
  Flying from Shanghai to Tokyo only takes a few hours.
- 我每天都要喝 几 杯咖啡。
  Wǒ měi tiān dōu yào hē jǐ bēi kāfēi.
  Every day I have to drink a couple cups of coffee.
- 老板今天开了 几 个重要的会。
  Lǎobǎn jīntiān kāi le jǐ gè zhòngyào de huì.
  The boss had a few important meetings today.

几 (jǐ) as "a Few Tens"

It is similar to how in English we can say, "a few dozen" or "a couple dozen," though in this case instead of "twelves of something" we are saying "tens of something."

Structure

 几 + 十 + Measure Word + Noun

Examples

- 他只想学 几十 个汉字。
  Tā zhǐ xiǎng xué jǐ shí gè Hànzì.
  He only wants to study a few dozen Chinese characters.
- 我们公司有 几十 个员工。
  Wǒmen gōngsī yǒu jǐ shí gè yuángōng.
  Our company has a few dozen employees.
- 他写过 几十 本书，我都喜欢。
  Tā xiě guo jǐ shí běn shū, wǒ dōu xǐhuan.
  He wrote a few dozen books. I like them all.
- 这个年轻的演员演了 几十 部电影。我都喜欢。
  Zhège niánqīng de yǎnyuán yǎn le jǐ shí bù diànyǐng. Wǒ dōu xǐhuan.
  This young actor has acted in dozens of movies. I like them all.
- 老板在国外有 几十 套房子。
  Lǎobǎn zài guówài yǒu jǐ shí tào fángzi.
  The boss has a few dozen houses abroad.

几 (jǐ) as "a Few Hundred / Thousand / Ten Thousand"

In Chinese we can put 几 (jǐ) together with 百 (bǎi), 千 (qiān), or 万 (wàn), just like how in English we might say, "a few hundred" or a "few thousand."

Structure

 几 + 百 / 千 / 万 + Measure Word + Noun

Examples

- 妈妈每个月都给我 几百 块钱。
  Māma měi gè yuè dōu gěi wǒ jǐ bǎi kuài qián.
  Mom gives me a couple hundred dollars every month.
- 这个月我们卖了 几千 本书。
  Zhège yuè wǒmen mài le jǐ qiān běn shū.
  We sold a couple thousand books this month.
- 几百 家外国公司参加了这个大会。
  Jǐ bǎi jiā wàiguó gōngsī cānjiā le zhège dàhuì.
  Several hundred foreign companies attended this conference.
- 这篇文章有 几万 个字，太长了。
  Zhè piān wénzhāng yǒu jǐ wàn gè zì, tài cháng le.
  This article has tens of thousands of characters. It's too long.
- 我认识一个朋友，她有 几百 双鞋。
  Wǒ rènshi yī gè péngyou, tā yǒu jǐ bǎi shuāng xié.
  I have a friend that has a couple hundred pairs of shoes.

好几 (hǎojǐ) as "Quite a Few"

You can think of 好几 (hǎojǐ) as meaning "quite a few," usually in the range of five to ten.

Structure

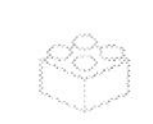

好几 + Measure Word + Noun

Examples

- 他读了 好几 遍。
  Tā dú le hǎojǐ biàn.
  He's read quite a few times.
- 我有 好几 个室友。
  Wǒ yǒu hǎojǐ gè shìyǒu.
  I have quite a few roommates.

- 我奶奶有 好几 个孩子。
  Wǒ nǎinai yǒu hǎojǐ gè háizi.
  My grandma has quite a few children.
- 他吃了 好几 碗米饭。
  Tā chī le hǎojǐ wǎn mǐfàn.
  He ate quite a few bowls of rice.
- 我们去过 好几 次北京。
  Wǒmen qù guo hǎojǐ cì Běijīng.
  We've been to Beijing quite a few times.

Similar to

- Expressing "some" with "yixie" (A2), page 315
- Using "youde" to mean "some" (A2), page 317
- Indicating a number in excess

Change of state with "le" (A2)

Also known as: 了2, change-of-state 了, sentence 了 and modal 了.

了 (le) has many uses. You probably first learned 了 (le) as a particle that tells you an action is completed[1], which is also known as "了1." However, this article is not about that use of 了 (le); instead, it is about indicating a *change of state* (了2). In other words, there is now a new situation, or there is about to be a new situation. This whole "change of state" idea can take numerous forms, and this page includes some helpful examples.

Structure

When used in this way, 了 (le) is placed at the end of the sentence to indicate a new situation.

[New Situation] + 了

Examples

- 下雨了。 *It wasn't raining, but now it is.*
  Xià yǔ le.
  It's raining.
- 妈妈老了。 *We aren't used to thinking of her as old, but she is now.*
  Māma lǎo le.
  Mom is old.
- 你胖了。 *You used to not be fat.*
  Nǐ pàng le.
  You've gotten fat.
- 家里没有牛奶了。 *We had milk before.*
  Jiālǐ méiyǒu niúnǎi le.
  We don't have any milk at home.
- 爸爸今年 50 岁了。 *Seems like just a year ago he was only 49!*
  Bàba jīnnián wǔshí suì le.
  Dad is 50 years old this year.

---

1. Expressing completion with "le" (A2), page 236

- 手机没电 了 。 *It was working fine until now.*
  Shǒujī méi diàn le .
  The cell phone ran out of power.
- 宝宝会说话 了 。 *He couldn't before.*
  Bǎobao huì shuōhuà le .
  The baby can speak.
- 你哥哥有女朋友 了 吗? *He didn't have one before.*
  Nǐ gēge yǒu nǚpéngyou le ma?
  Does your older brother have a girlfriend?
- 我男朋友找到新工作 了 。 *A big change for sure.*
  Wǒ nánpéngyou zhǎodào xīn gōngzuò le .
  My boyfriend found a new job.
- 你老婆怀孕 了 吗? *I know you guys have been trying...*
  Nǐ lǎopo huáiyùn le ma?
  Is your wife pregnant?

Too General?

The whole "change of state" concept might seem very general, and it is. It's vague, and it also takes some getting used to. You should expect it to take a while to get used to this use of 了 (le).

Because it's a little vague and confusing, most learners find it useful to break this "change of state" 了 (le) down into more specific usages, such as using it to mean "now"[1], "already"[2], or "not anymore"[3]. Although these are all "flavors" of the "change of state" 了 (le), identifying them as specific cases can make it much easier to get used to using 了 (le) in this way.

---

1. Expressing "now" with "le" (A2), page 234
2. Expressing "already" with just "le" (A2), page 230
3. Expressing "not anymore" with "le" (A2), page 232

Conceding with "ba" (A2)

The particle 吧 (ba) can also be used to *concede* a point. That is, 吧 (ba) can be used to accept or agree with something that you're not particularly happy about, the way we might use "all right" or "fine then" in English.

Structure

Similar to other uses of 吧 (ba), this usage is also simply placed on the end of a sentence or statement.

Examples

To understand what someone is conceding to, it's best to present this usage as a number of super short dialogs which provide a little context.

In this first one, B has to accept that his luxury goods shopping dreams have been shattered.

A: 太贵了！

Tài guì le!

That's too expensive!

B: 好吧，我们可以看看别的。

Hǎo ba, wǒmen kěyǐ kànkan biéde.

All right, we can take a look at something else.

Now B must accept inconvenient schedule changes.

A: 下午我不在家，你可以晚上来吗?

Xiàwǔ wǒ bù zài jiā, nǐ kěyǐ wǎnshang lái ma?

This afternoon I won't be home. Can you come by this evening?

B: 行吧。

Xíng ba.

All right.

B is now conceding that going out in this crazy rain doesn't make sense.

A: 雨太大了，明天再去买吧。

Yǔ tài dà le, míngtiān zài qù mǎi ba.

It's raining heavily. Let's go buy it tomorrow.

B: 好 吧 ，但是明天一定要买到。

Hǎo ba , dànshì míngtiān yídìng yào mǎidào.

Fine, but tomorrow we definitely have to buy it.

Now B is agreeing to let more guys into his secret club.

A: 可以带朋友吗?

Kěyǐ dài péngyou ma ?

Can I bring friends?

B: 行 吧 ，但是不能带女孩。

Xíng ba , dànshì bù néng dài nǚhái.

All right, but you can't bring girls.

Now B is having a friend cancel plans on him. Not a good day for B!

A: 我今天不太舒服，你可以自己去吗?

Wǒ jīntiān bù tài shūfu, nǐ kěyǐ zìjǐ qù ma?

I'm not feeling well today. Can you go by yourself?

B: 好 吧 ，那你好好休息。

Hǎo ba , nà nǐ hǎohǎo xiūxi.

All right, rest well then.

Similar to

- Suggestions with “ba” (A1), page 52
- Softening speech with “ba” (A2), page 243
- Reviewing options with “ba”

Expressing "already" with just "le" (A2)

You understand the word 已经 (yǐjīng)[1] to mean "already" in Chinese, and it is followed with a 了 (le). However, sometimes, that feeling of "already" can also be expressed with 了 (le) alone if it is used in response to a preceding question or statement.

Structure

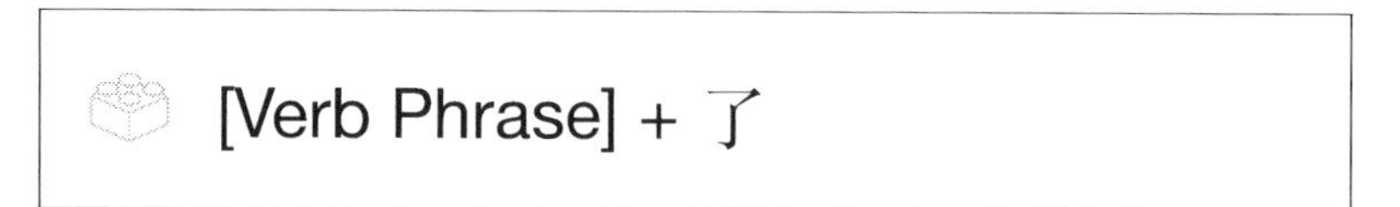
[Verb Phrase] + 了

Examples

When "already" is implied using this structure, it is usually (if not always) in response to a preceding question or statement. Therefore, the following examples are in dialogue format.

A: 老板呢?

Lǎobǎn ne?

Where is the boss?

B: 他走 了 。

Tā zǒu le.

He (already) left.

A: 孩子还在上大学吗?

Háizi hái zài shàng dàxué ma?

Are your kids still in college?

B: 他们工作 了 。

Tāmen gōngzuò le.

They (already) work.

This expression emphasizes that they're not students anymore, and have already entered the workforce.

A: 用我的车吧?

Yòng wǒ de chē ba?

How about using my car?

1. Expressing "already" with "yijing" (A2), page 138

B: 谢谢，我们有车 了 。

Xièxie, wǒmen yǒu chē le .

Thanks. We (already) have a car.

A: 你要不要告诉他？

Nǐ yào bu yào gàosu tā?

Are you going to tell him?

B: 他知道 了 。

Tā zhīdào le .

He (already) knows.

A: 你应该问老师。

Nǐ yīnggāi wèn lǎoshī.

You should ask the teacher.

B: 我问 了 。

Wǒ wèn le .

I (already) asked.

Similar to

- Expressing "already" with "yijing" (A2), page 138

Expressing "not anymore" with "le" (A2)

In a negative sentence, the sentence-final 了 (le)[1] can take on the meaning of "(not) anymore" or "no longer." The word 已经 (yǐjīng), which means "already,"[2] may nor may not accompany it.

Structure

已经 (yǐjīng) is optional for this pattern, but either 不 (bù) or 没有 (méiyǒu) will be needed to make the verb negative. The sentence-final 了 (le)[1] is, of course, required.

> (已经 +) 不 / 没 (有) + [Verb Phrase] + 了

Examples

- 没有纸了。
  Méiyǒu zhǐ le.
  There's no paper anymore.

  in other words, "we're out of paper"
- 手机没有电了。
  Shǒujī méiyǒu diàn le.
  My cell phone has run out of power.
- 他没有家了。
  Tā méiyǒu jiā le.
  He doesn't have his home anymore.
- 我们都没有钱了。
  Wǒmen dōu méiyǒu qián le.
  We all don't have any more money.
- 你不喜欢我了吗?
  Nǐ bù xǐhuan wǒ le ma?
  You don't like me anymore?

---

1. Change of state with "le" (A2), page 226
2. Expressing "already" with just "le" (A2), page 230

- 我 不 想吃 了 。
  Wǒ bù xiǎng chī le.
  I don't want to eat anymore.
- 你们 不 能喝 了 。
  Nǐmen bù néng hē le.
  You can't drink anymore.
- 我 已经不 住这里 了 。
  Wǒ yǐjīng bù zhù zhèlǐ le.
  I don't live here anymore.
- 他 已经不 在这儿工作 了 。
  Tā yǐjīng bù zài zhèr gōngzuò le.
  He doesn't work here anymore.
- 他们 已经不 在一起 了 。
  Tāmen yǐjīng bù zài yīqǐ le.
  They are no longer together.

Expressing “now” with “le” (A2)

现在 (xiànzài) isn’t the only way to express “now.” You’ll notice that in many common expressions, 了 (le) is used in place of the word for “now.”

Structure

This pattern is actually the same as change of state with “le”[1], but the examples below are somewhat idiomatic and can also easily be confused with a direct translation of “now” in Chinese, so they get special treatment here.

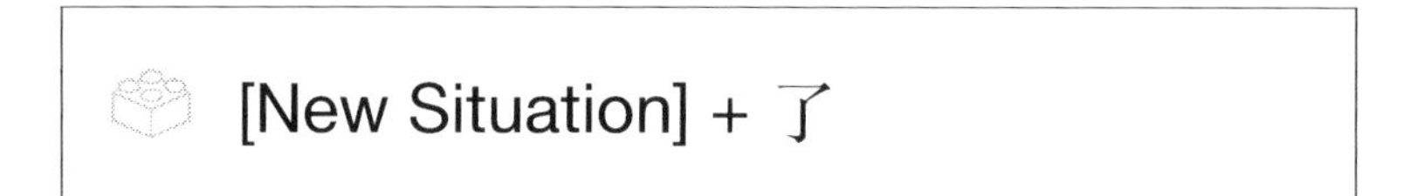

Examples

- 知道了。
  Zhīdào le.
  Got it. / I see.
  This is something I didn’t know before now
- 懂了。
  Dǒng le.
  Now I understand.
- 吃饭了！
  Chīfàn le!
  Time to eat!
- 我走了。
  Wǒ zǒu le.
  I'm leaving now.
- 他来了。
  Tā lái le.
  He's coming over now. / He's on the way.
  This can also mean “He’s here now.” Be careful!
- 上课了！
  Shàngkè le!
  Class begins now!

1. Change of state with “le” (A2), page 226

- 我去睡觉 了 。
  Wǒ qù shuìjiào le.
  I'm going to bed now.
- 快点儿，开会 了 ！
  Kuài diǎnr, kāihuì le!
  Hurry up, it's time for the meeting now!
- 该你 了 。
  Gāi nǐ le.
  It's your turn now.
- 电影开始 了 ！
  Diànyǐng kāishǐ le!
  The movie is starting now!

Expressing completion with "le" (A2)

Also known as: 了1, verb 了, completed action 了 and perfective aspect 了.

The particle 了 (le) has a lot of uses. One of the most common is to express the completion of an action. This is called aspect, which is not the same as tense. Tense is about *when an action happens*: past, present or future. Aspect is about *whether the action is complete* in a certain time frame.

Basic Pattern

To indicate completeness with 了 (le), the structure is:

Subj. + Verb + 了 + Obj.

Notice that 了 (le) goes directly after the verb. This 了 (le) is called **verb 了 (le)** or **了 1**.

Examples

- 你今天早上吃了什么?
  Nǐ jīntiān zǎoshang chī le shénme?
  What did you eat this morning?
- 他买了一个新手机。
  Tā mǎi le yī gè xīn shǒujī.
  He bought a new cell phone.
- 昨天晚上我看见了UFO。
  Zuótiān wǎnshang wǒ kànjiàn le UFO.
  I saw a UFO last night.
- 我学了两年中文。
  Wǒ xué le liǎng nián Zhōngwén.
  I studied Chinese for two years.
- 今年夏天我跟我男朋友去了台湾。
  Jīnnián xiàtiān wǒ gēn wǒ nánpéngyou qù le Táiwān.
  I went to Taiwan with my boyfriend this summer.

The examples above indicate a completed action, but they might also seem very similar to a "past tense" in English. To illustrate that 了 (le) can also indicate that one action is completed before another, see the following examples:

- 你到 了 告诉我。 *future action*
  Nǐ dào le gàosu wǒ.
  When you have arrived, tell me.
- 老板走 了 以后，你们可以走。 *future action*
  Lǎobǎn zǒu le yǐhòu, nǐmen kěyǐ zǒu.
  After the boss has left, you may leave.
- 你找到 了 以后，给我打电话。 *future action*
  Nǐ zhǎodào le yǐhòu, gěi wǒ dǎ diànhuà.
  After you have found it, give me a call.
- 你们吃 了 饭以后，可以出去。 *future action*
  Nǐmen chī le fàn yǐhòu, kěyǐ chūqù.
  After you have eaten your food, you can go out.
- 下 了 课以后，我要问老师一些问题。 *future action*
  Xià le kè yǐhòu, wǒ yào wèn lǎoshī yīxiē wèntí.
  After class is over, I need to ask the teacher a few questions.

As you can see, 了 (le) can appear in sentences about the future as well as the past. What's important is whether or not the action has been *completed*, no matter what time frame we're talking about. This also means that this 了 (le) isn't used with habitual or continuous actions.

Similar to

- Expressing experiences with "guo" (A2), page 238
- Time words and word order (A2), page 211
- Using "guo" with "le" (A2), page 249

Expressing experiences with "guo" (A2)

The aspect particle 过 (guo) is used to indicate that an **action has been experienced** in the past.

Basic Usage

Structure

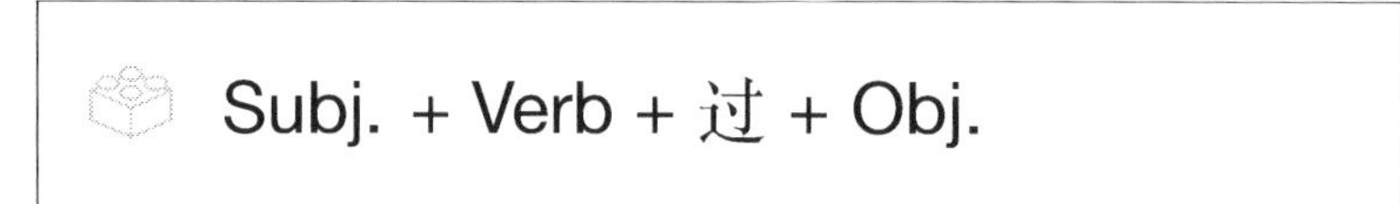

Subj. + Verb + 过 + Obj.

What this expresses is that the verb *has been* done at least once before, without specifying a particular time. 过 (guo) is used to talk about whether something has *ever* happened - whether it *has been experienced*.

Examples

In English, if you're asking a question and really trying to figure out if someone has *ever* done something before, we tend to use the words "ever" and "before." In Chinese, 过 (guo) alone expresses this, without the need for additional words.

- 你学 过 中文吗?
  Nǐ xué guo Zhōngwén ma?
  Have you ever studied Chinese?
- 你见 过 那个人吗?
  Nǐ jiàn guo nàge rén ma?
  Have you seen that person before?
- 我们来 过 这个地方。
  Wǒmen lái guo zhège dìfang.
  We've been to this place before.
- 我也吃 过 日本菜。
  Wǒ yě chī guo Rìběn cài.
  I've also eaten Japanese food before.
- 你看 过 这个电影吗?
  Nǐ kàn guo zhège diànyǐng ma?
  Have you seen this movie?

Negating a 过 (guo) Sentence

Because 过 (guo) is used to talk about past actions, it should be negated with 没[1] (méi).

Structure

Subj. + 没 + Verb + 过 + Obj.

Examples

Note that when you translate these examples into English, "have *never*" [done something] is often more natural, indicating that someone *lacks the **experience** of having done something*, rather than just "have not" [done something].

- 我没想过这个问题。
  Wǒ méi xiǎng guo zhège wèntí.
  I've never thought about this question before.
- 我没学过这个词。
  Wǒ méi xué guo zhège cí.
  I have never studied this word before.
- 妈妈没买过很贵的衣服。
  Māma méi mǎi guo hěn guì de yīfu.
  Mom has never bought any expensive clothes before.
- 我们都没坐过飞机。
  Wǒmen dōu méi zuò guo fēijī.
  None of us has ever been on a airplane before.
- 你们没见过美女吗?
  Nǐmen méi jiàn guo měinǚ ma?
  Have you never seen beautiful girls before?

To emphasize "never" even more, you can also use the word 从来 (cónglái)[2].

1. Negation of past actions with "meiyou" (A1), page 81
2. Expressing "never" with "conglai" (A2), page 276

Using 过 (guo) with 了 (le)

You'll sometimes see 过 (guo) used together with 了 (le). This can be a little confusing, as it doesn't seem to be following the rules laid out above. For more on this special usage of 过 (guo), see the article on using 过 (guo) with 了 (le)[1].

Similar to

- Expressing completion with "le" (A2), page 236
- Taiwanese "you"

1. Using "guo" with "le" (A2), page 249

Sentence-final interjection "a" (A2)

The interjection 啊 (a) is often added to the end of sentences to add a tone of urgency, exclamation or excitement. However, the exact meaning often depends on context.

啊 (a) Expressing Exclamation

When used like this, 啊 (a) is placed at the end of a statement and has a tone of exclamation, excitement or enthusiasm. (In a lot of cases, the only English "translation" you can offer is an exclamation point.)

Examples

- 对啊！
  Duì a!
  You're right!
  Banging fist on table...
- 这里好漂亮啊！
  Zhèlǐ hǎo piàoliang a!
  This place is so pretty!
- 你家真大啊！
  Nǐ jiā zhēn dà a!
  Your house is so big.
- 学中文真难啊！
  Xué Zhōngwén zhēn nán a!
  Learning Chinese is so hard!
- 好香啊！什么东西?
  Hǎo xiāng a! Shénme dōngxi?
  It smells great! What is it?

啊 (a) Expressing Certainty or Urgency

啊 (a) can also add a sense of certainty or urgency to a statement, sometimes with the feeling of an order.

Examples

- 是啊，我也觉得！
  Shì a, wǒ yě juéde!
  Definitely, I think so too!

- 行 啊 ！
  Xíng a!
  All right!
- 可以 啊 ！
  Kěyǐ a!
  It's fine!
- 小心 啊 ！
  Xiǎoxīn a!
  Be careful!
- 吃 啊 ！
  Chī a!
  Eat some!

啊 (a) Used in Questions

Finally, it can be used with questions, again with a sense of urgency or concern for the listener.

Examples

- 你走不走 啊 ？
  Nǐ zǒu bu zǒu a?
  Are you going or what?
- 你吃不吃 啊 ？
  Nǐ chī bu chī a?
  Are you eating or not?
- 谁说的 啊 ？
  Shéi shuō de a?
  Who said so?
- 你傻 啊 ？
  Nǐ shǎ a?
  What are you, stupid?
- 看什么 啊 ？没见过漂亮姑娘 啊 ？
  Kàn shénme a? Méi jiàn guo piàoliang gūniang a?
  What are you looking at? Have you never seen a pretty girl before?

Softening speech with "ba" (A2)

The particle 吧 (ba) can be used to soften the feel of a sentence. This could be to make it more polite, gentler and less forceful, or to turn a command into a suggestion.

Structure

Examples

- 这不太好 吧 。
  Zhè bù tài hǎo ba.
  This isn't so good.
- 算了 吧 。
  Suàn le ba.
  Let's forget it.
- 应该是 吧 。
  Yīnggāi shì ba.
  It should be.
- 钱太少了 吧 。
  Qián tài shǎo le ba.
  It's too little money.
- 再等一等 吧 。
  Zài děng yī děng ba.
  Wait a little longer.
- 太晚了，不要走了 吧 。
  Tài wǎn le, bùyào zǒu le ba.
  It's too late now, don't leave.
- 你们早点来 吧 。
  Nǐmen zǎo diǎn lái ba.
  Come a little earlier.

- 快点 吧 ，要迟到了。
  Kuài diǎn ba, yào chídào le.
  Please hurry, we're going to be late.
- 太贵了 吧 ，我不买了。
  Tài guì le ba, wǒ bù mǎi le.
  It's too expensive. I'm not buying it.
- 那个地方太远了 吧 ，我不想去。
  Nàge dìfang tài yuǎn le ba ， wǒ bù xiǎng qù.
  That place is too far away. I don't want to go.

Similar to

- Suggestions with "ba" (A1), page 52
- Conceding with "ba" (A2), page 228
- Reduplication of verbs (A2), page 290

- Softening the tone of questions with "ne"

Structural particle "de" (A2)

The structural particle "de" has three written forms in modern Chinese, each with its own uses:

- 的 (de), most often used for modifying nouns
- 得 (de), most often used with complements
- 地 (de), most often used with adverbial phrases

There is also a modal particle 的 (de), not covered in this grammar point.

的 (de) Before Nouns

Before nouns, 的 (de) is used to mark **possession** or **modification**. One way to think about 的 (de) is that it works like apostrophe-"s" in English. Think of this one as the "possessive *de*" or "noun-modifying *de*."

- 小李 的 房子
  Xiǎo Lǐ de fángzi
  Xiao Li's house

This comparison works very well for possession, as it shows how English and Chinese handle possession in a similar way. Just remember that Chinese uses this "possession" far more widely than English. Modifying, describing qualities, and assigning attributes are all handled in the same way as possession, by using 的 (de).

Another way to use 的 (de) is as an attributive. It's just a way of connecting adjectives or other words with a noun. It gives us more information about the noun, and the 的 (de) makes it clear that the extra information is connected to the noun. Here's an example:

- 红色 的 自行车
  hóngsè de zìxíngchē
  red bicycle

Here 的 (de) is used to modify "bicycle" with the color "red." It attributes the color "red" to the "bicycle."

Structure

Although certainly not complete for all uses, this simple structure should help as a general guideline:

Examples

- 我 的 手机
  wǒ de shǒujī
  my cell phone
- 我们 的 老师
  wǒmen de lǎoshī
  our teacher
- 漂亮 的 衣服
  piàoliang de yīfu
  beautiful clothes
- 热闹 的 酒吧
  rènao de jiǔbā
  a boisterous bar
- 我女朋友 的 公司
  wǒ nǚpéngyou de gōngsī
  my girlfriend's company

For you nerdier learners, 的 (de) is known to the Chinese as 白勺的 (bái-sháo de) as it's composed of the characters 白 (bái) and 勺 (sháo).

得 (de) After Verbs

This *de* is probably the trickiest to crack for English speakers as it has no obvious equivalent in English. 得 (de) is used to construct various kinds of complements and is usually associated with verbs. You can think of it as the "complement *de*."

Structure

Although certainly not complete for all uses, this simple structure should help:

Examples

- 做 得 很好
  zuò de hěn hǎo
  do very well

- 说 得 太快
  shuō de tài kuài
  speak too fast
- 玩 得 很开心
  wán de hěn kāixīn
  play very happily
- 开 得 很快
  kāi de hěn kuài
  drive very fast
- 住 得 很舒服
  zhù de hěn shūfu
  live very comfortably

For you nerdier learners, 得 (de) is known as 双人得 (shuāngrén de), as the character component 彳 is often referred to as 双人 (shuāngrén), or the "double person" component.

Not an Adverb?

You might be wondering how the examples using 得 (de) above are different from adverbs. That's actually a really good question, but it's one that you should defer until later in your studies. Complements are a bit tricky, and you'll be learning a lot more about them at the intermediate level, so be patient!

地 (de) Before Verbs

地 (de) is used to turn adjectives into adverbs, and can be thought of as equivalent to the suffix *-ly* in English. You could call it the "adverb *de*" or "adverbial *de*," since it precedes verbs like adverbs do.

Structure

Although not complete for all uses, this simple structure should help:

Note that it's the "adjective + 地 (de)" structure that makes the adjective into an "adverb phrase" (called an adverbial). If it's a straight-up adverb you're using (instead of an adjective), then you don't need 地 (de) at all.

This pattern is also the least common of the three; you'll be using 的 (de) and 得 (de) a lot more in everyday communication than this one.

Examples

- 生气 地 说
  shēngqì de shuō
  angrily say
- 开心 地 笑
  kāixīn de xiào
  happily laugh
- 慢慢 地 走
  mànmàn de zǒu
  slowly walk
- 伤心 地 哭
  shāngxīn de kū
  sadly cry
- 认真 地 听
  rènzhēn de tīng
  carefully listen

Again, you don't have to know this, but this 地 (de) is known in Chinese as 土也地 (tǔ-yě de), as it's composed of the 土 (tǔ) component on the left with a 也 (yě) on the right.

Using All Three "de"s

This example is naturally going to be a little more difficult than the ones above, since we're cramming all three usages into one sentence, but you may find this useful.

- 今天 的 作业你做 得 不好，因为你没认真 地 听课。
  Jīntiān de zuòyè nǐ zuò de bù hǎo, yīnwèi nǐ méi rènzhēn de tīngkè.
  You didn't do today's homework well because you didn't listen attentively in class.

Using "guo" with "le" (A2)

You might be familiar with using 过 (guo) to indicate that an **action has been experienced** in the past[1], but then also see it used together with 了 (le)[2]. What's going on here? If you're already familiar with the basic usage of both 了 (le) and 过 (guo), then a special explanation of how they sometimes work together is now in order.

Basic Pattern

Structure

Verb + 过 + 了

You'll notice that this pattern is often used for everyday behaviors. It's used for actions like "eating" and "brushing one's teeth" and "taking a shower."

Examples

- 她吃过了。
  Tā chī guo le.
  She has eaten (already).
- 牙刷过了。
  Yá shuā guo le.
  I've brushed my teeth (already).
- 洗过了。
  Xǐ guo le.
  I've showered (already).
- 我们看过了。
  Wǒmen kàn guo le.
  We've seen it (already).
- 他们见过了。
  Tāmen jiàn guo le.
  They've met (already).

---

1. Expressing experiences with "guo" (A2), page 238
2. Expressing completion with "le" (A2), page 236

The Pattern with an Object

For the examples above, you could have inserted an object to modify the basic pattern, getting this:

Verb + 过 + Obj. + 了

The object has been inserted in the sentences below:

- 你吃过饭了吗?
  Nǐ chī guo fàn le ma?
  Have you eaten (already)?
- 我刷过牙了。
  Wǒ shuā guo yá le.
  I have brushed my teeth (already).
- 他洗过澡了。
  Tā xǐ guo zǎo le.
  He has showered (already).
- 我给他打过电话了。
  Wǒ gěi tā dǎ guo diànhuà le.
  I called him (already).
- 客户看过合同了吗?
  Kèhù kàn guo hétong le ma?
  Has the client read the contract (already)?

What 过 (guo) Does

You would be right to point out that 过 (guo) is mainly used to call attention to the fact that someone *has had an* ***experience.*** This is the basic pattern pointed out in the article on the basic usage of the aspectual particle 过[1] (guo). In the examples above, though, it's not any "once-in-a-lifetime" *experiences* being expressed, it's more just the information that these actions are *done*. Here, 过 (guo) and 了 (le) work together to emphasize that an action is *already done.* This is why the translations on the side add the word "already" in parentheses at the end; this is the feeling the sentences give you. In fact, to emphasize

1. Expressing experiences with "guo" (A2), page 238

the idea of *already done* even further, you could add the word for "already," 已经 (yǐjīng), before the verbs in the examples below, and it also works just fine:

- 她 已经 吃 过 饭 了。
  Tā yǐjīng chī guo fàn le.
  She has already eaten (a meal).
- 我 已经 刷 过 牙 了。
  Wǒ yǐjīng shuā guo yá le.
  I have already brushed my teeth.
- 他 已经 洗 过 澡 了。
  Tā yǐjīng xǐ guo zǎo le.
  He has already had a shower.

When to Use 过 (guo) with 了 (le)

So when would you use the sentences above? You'd be emphasizing that the action has *already* occurred (so it doesn't need to be done again), so it would probably be something like this:

For the eating example:

A: 她想吃饭吗?
Tā xiǎng chīfàn ma?
Does she want to eat?

B: 她 已经 吃 过 饭 了。
Tā yǐjīng chī guo fàn le.
She has already eaten.

For the tooth brushing example:

A: 别忘记刷牙。
Bié wàngjì shuā yá.
Don't forget to brush your teeth.

B: 我 已经 刷 过 牙 了。
Wǒ yǐjīng shuā guo yá le.
I have already brushed my teeth.

For the taking a shower example:

A: 他应该洗澡。

Tā yīnggāi xǐzǎo.

He should take a shower.

B: 他 已经 洗 过了 。

Tā yǐjīng xǐ guo le.

He has already showered.

Basic comparisons with "bi" (A2)

Also known as: 比字句 (bǐ zì jù).

One of the most common words when comparing things in Chinese is to use 比 (bǐ). 比 (bǐ) has similarities to the English word "than," but it requires a word order that's not so intuitive, so you'll want to practice it quite a bit.

Basic Usage

You could think of 比 (bǐ) as meaning "than," except that it sits between the two things being compared. The word order will take a little getting used to, but aside from that, the pattern is quite easy.

Structure

To say that one thing is more *adjective* than another, the structure is:

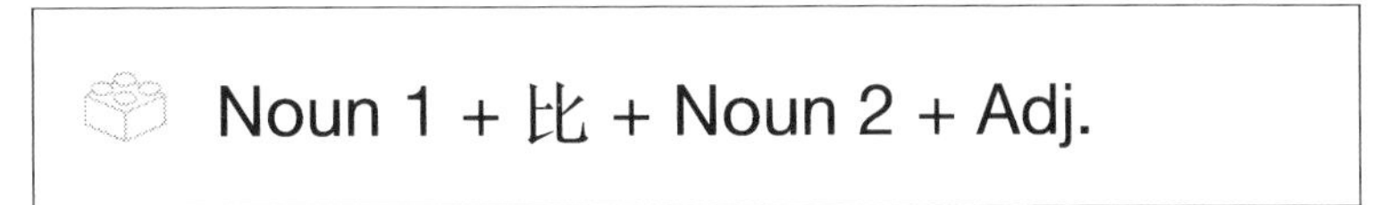

The noun that's placed first is the one that comes out on top in the comparison. So in the sentence:

- 小李 比 小张 高 。
  Xiǎo Lǐ bǐ Xiǎo Zhāng gāo .
  Xiao Li is taller than Xiao Zhang.

小李 (Xiǎo Lǐ) is taller. The same situation could be described as

- 小张 比 小李 矮 。
  Xiǎo Zhāng bǐ Xiǎo Lǐ ǎi .
  Xiao Zhang is shorter than Xiao Li.

Examples

- 他 比 老师 聪明 。
  Tā bǐ lǎoshī cōngming .
  He is smarter than the teacher.
- 上海 比 纽约 大 吗?
  Shànghǎi bǐ Niǔyuē dà ma?
  Is Shanghai bigger than New York?

- 她 比 她妈妈 漂亮 。

  Tā bǐ tā māma piàoliang .

  She is prettier than her mother.

- 星巴克的咖啡 比 这里的咖啡 贵 。

  Xīngbākè de kāfēi bǐ zhèlǐ de kāfēi guì .

  The coffee at Starbucks is more expensive than the coffee here.

- 地铁 比 公交车 方便 。

  Dìtiě bǐ gōngjiāochē fāngbiàn .

  The subway is more convenient than the bus.

Common Errors

Try not to make these mistakes:

The adjective used in the comparison should be positive, not negative.

✘ 我 比 你 不聪明 。

Wǒ bǐ nǐ bù cōngming .

✔ 你 比 我 聪明 。

Nǐ bǐ wǒ cōngming .

You are smarter than me.

比 (bǐ) is not used with 一样 (yīyàng). 比 (bǐ) is used when two things are *not* the same.

✘ 我 比 你 一样 聪明。

Wǒ bǐ nǐ yīyàng cōngming.

✔ 我 跟 你 一样 聪明。

Wǒ gēn nǐ yīyàng cōngming.

I am as smart as you.

Pattern Using 比 (bǐ) and 更 (gèng)

This is a slight upgrade of the basic 比 (bǐ) comparison pattern, adding in 更 (gèng) before the adjective[1]. 更 (gèng) means "even more," so the idea is that while one thing is already quite [adjective], this other thing is ***even more*** [adjective]. Pretty simple!

1. Expressing "even more" with "geng" (A2), page 147

Structure

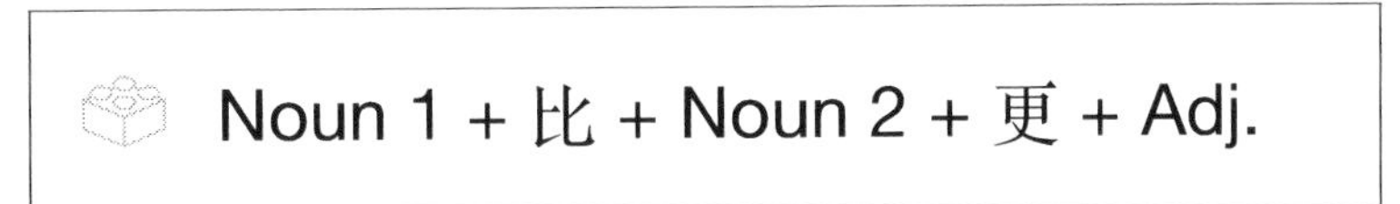

The only new thing here is the addition of 更 (gèng) before the adjective.

- 小李 比 小张 更高 。
  Xiǎo Lǐ bǐ Xiǎo Zhāng gèng gāo .
  Xiao Li is even taller than Xiao Zhang.

The implication is that while Xiao Zhang is *tall*, 小李 (Xiǎo Lǐ) is *even taller*.

Examples

- 我哥哥 比 我 更高 。
  Wǒ gēge bǐ wǒ gèng gāo .
  My big brother is even taller than me.
- 你男朋友 比 我男朋友 更帅 。
  Nǐ nánpéngyou bǐ wǒ nánpéngyou gèng shuài .
  Your boyfriend is even more handsome than mine.
- 这里的冬天 比 纽约的冬天 更冷 。
  Zhèlǐ de dōngtiān bǐ Niǔyuē de dōngtiān gèng lěng .
  The winter here is even colder than it is in New York.
- 中文语法 比 汉字 更好玩 。
  Zhōngwén yǔfǎ bǐ Hànzì gèng hǎowán .
  Chinese grammar is even more fun than Chinese characters.
- 你的问题 比 我的问题 更麻烦 。
  Nǐ de wèntí bǐ wǒ de wèntí gèng máfan .
  Your problem is even more troublesome than mine.

Similar to

- Basic comparisons with “meiyou” (A2), page 258
- Basic comparisons with “yiyang” (A2), page 162
- Expressing “much more” in comparisons

Expressing "from... to..." with "cong... dao..." (A2)

从⋯⋯到⋯⋯(cóng... dào...) is used in the same way as "from... to..." is used in English, and can be used both for times and places.

Used for Times

To express from one time to another, the following structure is used:

Structure

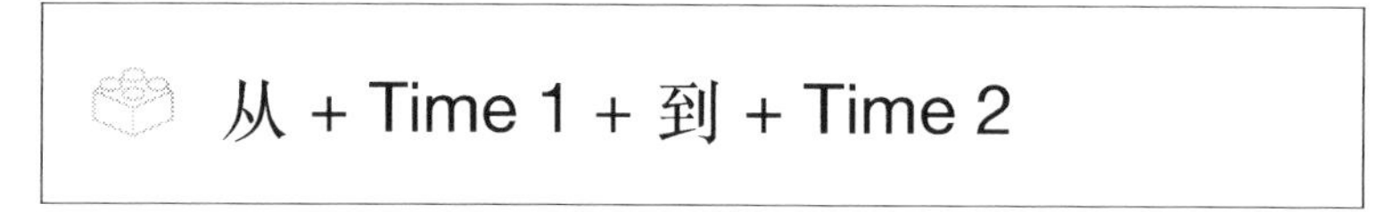

The "time" here does not necessarily have to be a standard time word; it can be any event or action.

Examples

- 从 2004 年 到 2008 年
  cóng èr-líng-líng-sì nián dào èr-líng-líng-bā nián
  from 2004 to 2008
- 从 一号 到 五号都在下雨。
  Cóng yī hào dào wǔ hào dōu zài xiàyǔ.
  From the first to the fifth, it's been raining non-stop.
- 老板 从 周二 到 周五都要出差。
  Lǎobǎn cóng Zhōuèr dào Zhōuwǔ dōu yào chūchāi.
  From Tuesday until Friday the boss will go on a business trip.
- 她 从 18 岁 到 现在都一个人住。
  Tā cóng shíbā suì dào xiànzài dōu yīgèrén zhù.
  She's lived alone since she was 18 until now.
- 你不能 从 早 到 晚不吃东西。
  Nǐ bù néng cóng zǎo dào wǎn bù chī dōngxi.
  You can't eat nothing from morning to night.

Remember that there are two options for the word order of time words[1].

1. Time words and word order (A2), page 211

Used for Places

The same structure can also be used to express "from" one place "to" another.

Structure

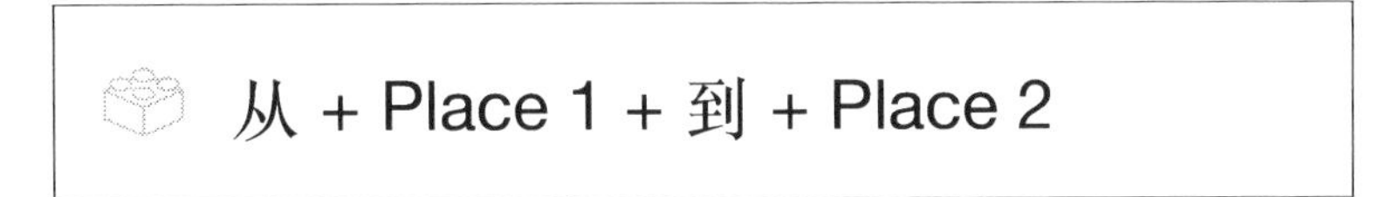

Examples

- 从 南京西路 到 南京东路
  cóng Nánjīng Xī Lù dào Nánjīng Dōng Lù
  from West Nanjing Road to East Nanjing Road
- 从 酒店 到 机场不太远。
  Cóng jiǔdiàn dào jīchǎng bù tài yuǎn.
  From the hotel to the airport is not too far.
- 从 上海 到 北京要几个小时。
  Cóng Shànghǎi dào Běijīng yào jǐ gè xiǎoshí.
  From Shanghai to Beijing it takes a few hours.
- 从 你家 到 机场可以坐地铁吗?
  Cóng nǐ jiā dào jīchǎng kěyǐ zuò dìtiě ma?
  From your place to the airport, can I take the subway?
- 从 这里 到 我们公司，你会看见很多美女。
  Cóng zhèlǐ dào wǒmen gōngsī, nǐ huì kànjiàn hěn duō měinǚ.
  From here to our company, you'll see many beautiful girls.

Similar to

- Expressing distance with "li" (A2), page 173
- Using "dao" to mean "to go to" (A2), page 298
- Comparing "li" and "cong"
- Expressing "ever since" with "zicong"

Basic comparisons with "meiyou" (A2)

In Chinese, there is another way to make comparisons. You can use 没有 (méiyǒu)[1] to express that something is "not as" *adjective* as something else. (Yes, that's the same 没有 (méiyǒu) that means "not have," used here in a different way.)

Basic Usage

As well as with 比 (bǐ)[2], you can also use 没有 (méiyǒu) to make basic comparisons. You could think of 没有 (méiyǒu) as the opposite of 比 (bǐ) - it works in the same way, but rather than expressing "more… than…" it expresses "not as… as…":

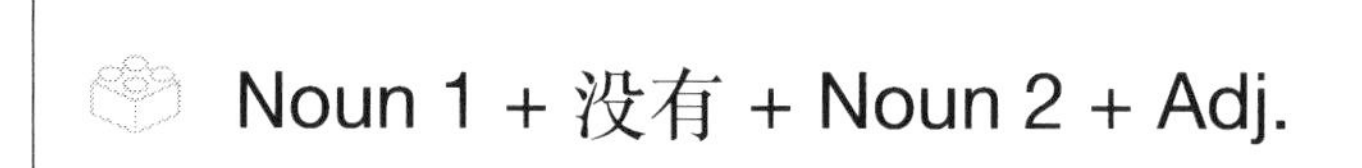

In this structure, the noun that's placed first is *less* "adjective" than the second noun, making 没有 (méiyǒu) the *opposite* of 比 (bǐ)[2] for comparison purposes. So in the sentence:

- 小张 没有 小李高。
  Xiǎo Zhāng méiyǒu Xiǎo Lǐ gāo.
  Xiao Zhang is not as tall as Xiao Li.

小李 (Xiǎo Lǐ) is taller. The same situation could be described as:

- 小李 没有 小张矮。
  Xiǎo Lǐ méiyǒu Xiǎo Zhāng ǎi.
  Xiao Li is not as short as Xiao Zhang.

Examples

- 这个地方 没有 上海好玩。
  Zhège dìfang méiyǒu Shànghǎi hǎowán.
  This place is not as fun as Shanghai.

- 火车 没有 飞机快。
  Huǒchē méiyǒu fēijī kuài.
  Trains are not as fast as airplanes.

---

1. Negation of "you" with "mei" (A1), page 12
2. Basic comparisons with "bi" (A2), page 253

- 他 没有 他弟弟聪明。
  Tā méiyǒu tā dìdi cōngming.
  He's not as smart as his younger brother.
- Clinton 没有 Obama 帅。
  Clinton méiyǒu Obama shuài.
  Clinton is not as handsome as Obama.
- 马云 没有 Bill Gates 有钱。
  Mǎyún méiyǒu Bill Gates yǒuqián.
  Jack Ma is not as rich as Bill Gates.
- 你们公司 没有 我们公司大。
  Nǐmen gōngsī méiyǒu wǒmen gōngsī dà.
  Your company is not as big as ours.
- 拼音 没有 汉字难。
  Pīnyīn méiyǒu Hànzì nán.
  Pinyin is not as difficult as Chinese characters.
- 坐公交车 没有 坐地铁方便。
  Zuò gōngjiāochē méiyǒu zuò dìtiě fāngbiàn.
  Taking the bus is not as convenient as taking the metro.
- 小米手机 没有 iPhone 贵。
  Xiǎomǐ shǒujī méiyǒu iPhone guì.
  The Xiaomi phone is not as expensive as the iPhone.
- 爸爸做的菜 没有 妈妈做的菜好吃。
  Bàba zuò de cài méiyǒu māma zuò de cài hǎochī.
  The food dad cooks is not as tasty as the food mom cooks.

Similar to

- Negation of "you" with "mei" (A1), page 12
- Basic comparisons with "bi" (A2), page 253
- Basic comparisons with "yiyang" (A2), page 162
- Comparing "bu" and "mei" (A2), page 358
- Expressing "age difference" with "da and xiao"
- Expressing "compared with" with "gen"

Directional verbs "lai" and "qu" (A2)

来 (lái) and 去 (qù) are both words that help to express direction from the perspective of the speaker. 来 (lái) means "come" (towards the speaker), while 去 (qù) means "go" (away from the speaker). For example, if you are in China, a local person might ask you: "When did you come to China?" using 来 (lái). Another example is if you want to go from China to Japan, your friends might ask you: "When are you going to Japan?" using 去 (qù).

Seems really easy, right? Well, learn them well now, because you'll get a lot of mileage out of these words in future grammar patterns.

Basic Usage

Structure

Examples

For the examples below, keep in mind that if the speaker uses 去 (qù), then she is not at the place mentioned *now*. If the speaker uses 来 (lái), she must already be at the place mentioned. Just stay consistent with this, and you're good.

- 妈妈要 去 超市。
  Māma yào qù chāoshì.
  Mom will go to the supermarket.
- 老板今天 来 公司吗?
  Lǎobǎn jīntiān lái gōngsī ma?
  Is the boss coming into the office today?
- 你现在 来 南京路吧。
  Nǐ xiànzài lái Nánjīng Lù ba.
  Come to Nanjing Road now.
- 你不想 来 我们公司工作吗?
  Nǐ bù xiǎng lái wǒmen gōngsī gōngzuò ma?
  Do you not want to come to work for our company?

- 去年她 去 美国工作了几个月。
  Qùnián tā qù Měiguó gōngzuò le jǐ gè yuè.
  Last year she went to work in the USA for a few months.
- 你们想 去 Starbucks 还是 Costa?
  Nǐmen xiǎng qù Starbucks háishì Costa?
  Would you like to go to Starbucks or Costa?
- 周末我喜欢 去 朋友家。
  Zhōumò wǒ xǐhuan qù péngyou jiā.
  I like to go to my friends' places on the weekends.
- 爸爸明天 去 北京出差。
  Bàba míngtiān qù Běijīng chūchāi.
  Dad will go to Beijing on a business trip tomorrow.
- 我今天不上班，你们可以 来 我家吃饭。
  Wǒ jīntiān bù shàngbān, nǐmen kěyǐ lái wǒ jiā chīfàn.
  I don't have to go to work today. You can come to my home to eat dinner.

Advanced Usage

来 (lái) and 去 (qù) can both be paired with other simple verbs to demonstrate the direction an action has taken. For example, 进来 (jìnlái, "come in"), 进去 (jìnqù, "go in"), 出来 (chūlái, "come out"), 出去 (chūqù, "go out"), 回来 (huílái, "come back"), 回去 (huíqù, "go back"), etc.

When you start tacking these two-character verbs onto the ends of other verbs, they are called direction complements, and are covered in detail in a more advanced article.

Auxiliary verb "yao" and its multiple meanings (A2)

You probably already know the basic meaning of 要 (yào)[1] as "to want." It is actually a quite versatile word, though, and can also take on the meanings of "to need" as well as "will (do something)." In every case, context is crucial for figuring out which meaning someone is trying to express.

要 (yào) as "Want"

This structure could be used when ordering food at a restaurant or a shop. Here, it's being used for saying that you want *something.*

Structure

Examples

- 你 要 什么?
  Nǐ yào shénme?
  What do you want?
- 我 要 一杯水。
  Wǒ yào yī bēi shuǐ.
  I want a cup of water.
- 你们都 要 冰可乐吗?
  Nǐmen dōu yào bīng kělè ma?
  Do you all want coke with ice?
- 你 要 茶还是咖啡?
  Nǐ yào chá háishì kāfēi?
  Do you want tea or coffee?
- 我们 要 三碗米饭。
  Wǒmen yào sān wǎn mǐfàn.
  We want three bowls of rice.

1. Wanting to do something with "yao" (A1), page 77

要 (yào) as "Want to"

In Chinese, 要 (yào) can mean "want to" (similar to 想 (xiǎng)[1]), but its tone is quite firm. So it's used for saying that you want ***to do** something*.

Structure

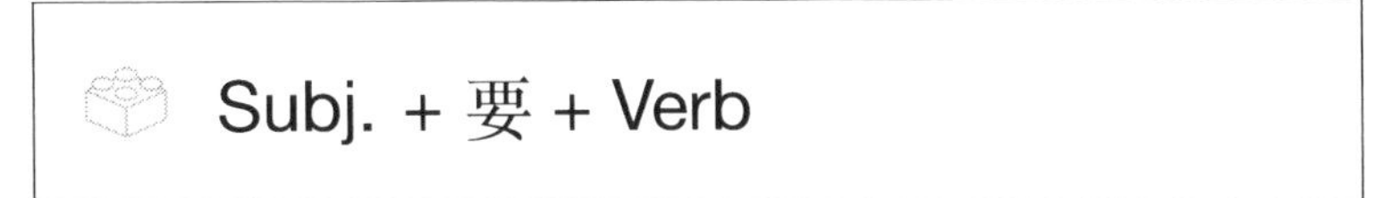

Examples

- 你 要 喝什么酒?
  Nǐ yào hē shénme jiǔ?
  What kind of wine do you want to drink?
- 爸爸 要 买一个新手机。
  Bàba yào mǎi yī gè xīn shǒujī.
  Dad wants to buy a new cell phone.
- 我 要 跟你一起去。
  Wǒ yào gēn nǐ yīqǐ qù.
  I want to go with you.
- 她 要 去大城市找工作。
  Tā yào qù dà chéngshì zhǎo gōngzuò.
  She wants to go to a big city to find a job.
- 周末你们 要 一起看电影吗?
  Zhōumò nǐmen yào yīqǐ kàn diànyǐng ma?
  Do you want to go see a movie together this weekend?

要 (yào) as "Need to"

If you crank the urgency of "to want" up a few notches, you get "to need." The two meanings overlap, creating a fuzzy, "needy" gray area.

---

1. Expressing "would like to" with "xiang" (A2), page 270

Structure

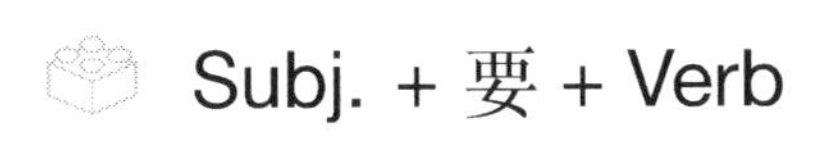

Examples

- 你 要 早点睡觉。
  Nǐ yào zǎo diǎn shuìjiào.
  You need to go to bed earlier.
- 我们明天 要 上班。
  Wǒmen míngtiān yào shàngbān.
  We need to work tomorrow.
  logically, most people don't really WANT to work
- 老板今天 要 见一个新客户。
  Lǎobǎn jīntiān yào jiàn yī gè xīn kèhù.
  Today the boss needs to see a new client.
- 老师太累了， 要 好好休息。
  Lǎoshī tài lèi le, yào hǎohǎo xiūxi.
  The teacher is too tired. She needs to rest well.
- 明天下雨，你 要 带伞。
  Míngtiān xiàyǔ, nǐ yào dài sǎn.
  It's going to rain tomorrow; you need to bring an umbrella.

要 (yào) as "Going to"

This use of 要 (yào) is like "going to" (similar to 会[1] (huì)).

Structure

Again, no change to the structure here, but it often includes a mention of a time *when* something is *going to happen*.

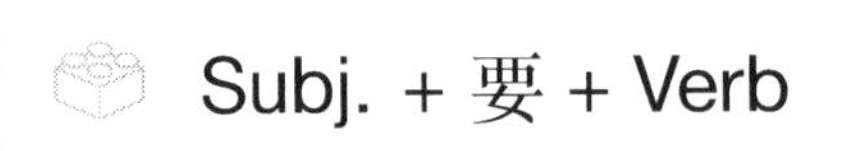

1. Expressing "will" with "hui" (A2), page 268

If you want to know more about the related pattern "要…… 了" (yào... le), please see the "kuai... le" pattern[1].

Examples

- 星期五我们 要 开会。
  Xīngqīwǔ wǒmen yào kāihuì.
  We are going to have a meeting on Friday.
- 12 点我 要 去吃饭。
  Shí'èr diǎn wǒ yào qù chīfàn.
  I am going to go eat at 12 o'clock.
- 老板下周 要 出差吗?
  Lǎobǎn xià zhōu yào chūchāi ma?
  Is the boss going on a business trip next week?
- 他们明年 要 结婚了。
  Tāmen míngnián yào jiéhūn le.
  They are going to get married next year.
- 今年你 要 回家过年吗?
  Jīnnián nǐ yào huíjiā guònián ma?
  Are you going to return home this year to celebrate the Chinese New Year?

Context, Context, Context

You may have noticed that the meanings can easily overlap. To figure out what is intended, you need to use context. How urgent is the situation? is it likely to be something the speaker really *wants* to do? is it something that's totally *going to* happen, regardless of anyone's preference? Most often, a little background knowledge and some common sense are all you need to figure it out.

Similar to

- Wanting to do something with "yao" (A1), page 77
- Expressing "about to happen" with "le" (A2), page 347

- Expressing "about to" with "jiuyao"
- Expressing "don't need to" with "buyong"
- Expressing determination with "feiyao"

---

1. Expressing "about to happen" with "le" (A2), page 347

Expressing "should" with "yinggai" (A2)

应该 (yīnggāi) translates to the English word "should," and is an essential word to know for your conversaitonal Chinese. You *should* definitely get comfortable using 应该 (yīnggāi) right away!

Basic Usage

Structure

The auxiliary verb 应该 (yīnggāi) is the most common way to express "should" in Chinese. The structure is:

Subj. + 应该 + Verb + Obj.

Examples

- 在中国，你 应该 喝白酒。
  Zài Zhōngguó, nǐ yīnggāi hē báijiǔ.
  In China, you should drink baijiu.
- 我 应该 给你多少钱？
  Wǒ yīnggāi gěi nǐ duōshao qián?
  How much money should I give you?
- 感冒的时候 应该 喝热水。
  Gǎnmào de shíhou yīnggāi hē rè shuǐ.
  You should drink hot water when you have a cold.
- 明天你 应该 八点半来公司。
  Míngtiān nǐ yīnggāi bādiǎn bàn lái gōngsī.
  You should come to the office tomorrow at 8:30.
- 他太累了，应该 回家休息。
  Tā tài lèi le, yīnggāi huíjiā xiūxi.
  He's too tired. He should go home and rest.

Negate 应该 (yīnggāi) with 不 (bù)

Structure

Add the negative adverb 不[1] (bù) before 应该 (yīnggāi) to negate it.

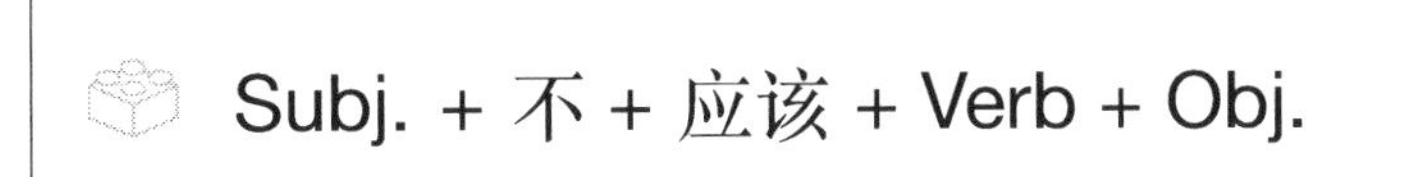

Examples

- 你 不应该 告诉他。
  Nǐ bù yīnggāi gàosu tā.
  You should not tell him.
- 他 不应该 打人。
  Tā bù yīnggāi dǎ rén.
  He should not hit people.
- 我们 不应该 迟到。
  Wǒmen bù yīnggāi chídào.
  We shouldn't be late.
- 你们 不应该 笑她。
  Nǐmen bù yīnggāi xiào tā.
  You shouldn't laugh at her.
- 你们 不应该 拿别人的东西。
  Nǐmen bù yīnggāi ná biérén de dōngxi.
  You should not take other people's stuff.

Similar to

- Wanting to do something with “yao” (A1), page 77
- Expressing “would like to” with “xiang” (A2), page 270
- Expressing “had better” with “haishi”
- Expressing “had better” with “zuihao”
- Expressing “must” with “dei”

---

1. Standard negation with “bu” (A1), page 85

Expressing "will" with "hui" (A2)

会 (huì) has multiple uses, but in this context, it is being used to express the possibility of an action happening in the future.

Basic Usage

Structure

As well as expressing a learned skill[1], 会 (huì) can also be used to indicate that something *will* happen or that someone *will* do something.

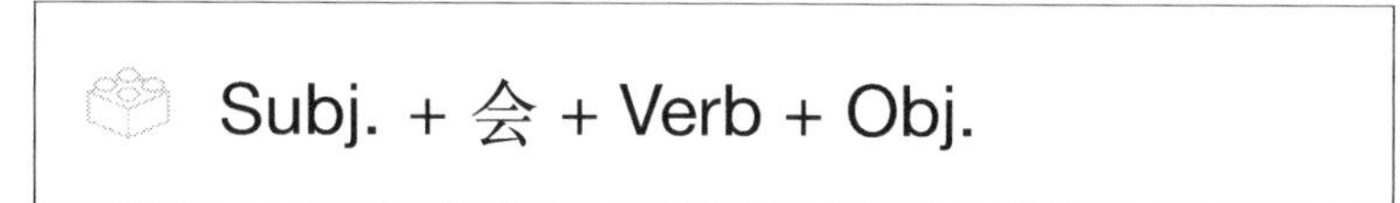

Examples

- 明天你 会 来吗？
  Míngtiān nǐ huì lái ma?
  Will you come tomorrow?
- 他 会 来看你吗？
  Tā huì lái kàn nǐ ma?
  Will he come to see you?
- 明天 会 下雨吗？
  Míngtiān huì xiàyǔ ma?
  Will it rain tomorrow?
- 我出去一下，很快 会 回来。
  Wǒ chūqù yīxià, hěnkuài huì huílái.
  I'm going out for a little while. I'll come back very soon.
- 老板 会 同意吗？
  Lǎobǎn huì tóngyì ma?
  Will the boss agree?
- 你女儿 会 听你的话。
  Nǐ nǚér huì tīng nǐ de huà.
  Your daughter will listen to you.

---

1. Expressing a learned skill with "hui" (A1), page 69

- 下班以后，我 会 给你打电话。
  Xiàbān yǐhòu, wǒ huì gěi nǐ dǎ diànhuà.
  After getting off work, I will give you a call.

Negating 会 (huì) with 不 (bù)

Nothing new here. You remember everyone's favorite Negative Nelly 不 (bù)[1], right?

Structure

Subj. + 不 + 会 + Verb + Obj.

Examples

- 我们 不会 告诉你。
  Wǒmen bù huì gàosu nǐ.
  We won't tell you.
- 他 不会 跟你结婚。
  Tā bù huì gēn nǐ jiéhūn.
  He won't marry you.
- 今晚我 不会 在外面吃饭。
  Jīnwǎn wǒ bù huì zài wàimiàn chīfàn.
  Tonight I will not eat out.

Similar to

- Expressing a learned skill with "hui" (A1), page 69
- Wanting to do something with "yao" (A1), page 77
- Auxiliary verb "yao" and its multiple meanings (A2), page 262
- In the future in general with "yihou" (A2), page 209
- Expressing future with "jiang"

---

1. Standard negation with "bu" (A1), page 85

Expressing "would like to" with "xiang" (A2)

If you want to express something that you "would like to do," 想 (xiǎng) will be a very helpful auxiliary verb to know. Although similar to 要 (yào), 想 (xiǎng) will give you another more tactful option when you want to articulate a desire.

Basic Usage

Structure

The verb 想 (xiǎng) can be used to express "would like to." In this case it's an auxiliary verb. The structure is:

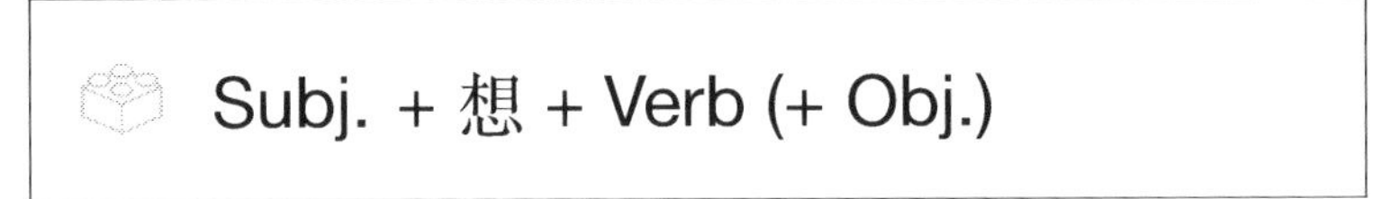

Examples

- 你想去吗?
  Nǐ xiǎng qù ma?
  Would you like to go?
- 我想吃面。
  Wǒ xiǎng chī miàn.
  I would like to eat noodles.
- 你想喝水吗?
  Nǐ xiǎng hē shuǐ ma?
  Would you like to drink some water?
- 我们想看电视。
  Wǒmen xiǎng kàn diànshì.
  We would like to watch TV.
- 他想买一个大房子。
  Tā xiǎng mǎi yī gè dà fángzi.
  He would like to buy a big apartment.

Negate 想 (xiǎng) with 不 (bù)

No surprises here: use 不 (bù) to negate[1] 想 (xiǎng).

Structure

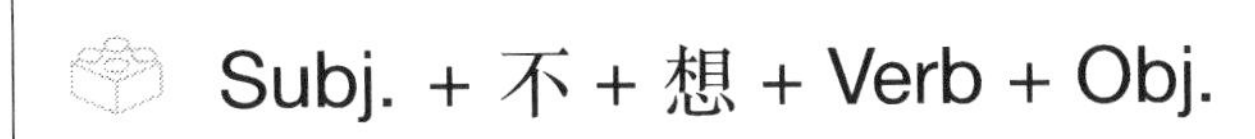

Subj. + 不 + 想 + Verb + Obj.

Examples

- 他们 不想 去酒吧。
  Tāmen bù xiǎng qù jiǔbā.
  They wouldn't like to go to the bar.
- 你 不想 认识这个美女吗?
  Nǐ bù xiǎng rènshi zhège měinǚ ma?
  Would you not like to know this beautiful lady?
- 我 不想 回家。
  Wǒ bù xiǎng huíjiā.
  I wouldn't like to return home.
- 那个地方很近，我 不想 开车。
  Nàge dìfang hěn jìn, wǒ bù xiǎng kāichē.
  That place is so close. I would not like to drive.
- 他 不想 花父母的钱。
  Tā bù xiǎng huā fùmǔ de qián.
  He would not like to spend his parents' money.

Similar to

- Wanting to do something with “yao” (A1), page 77
- Comparing “yao” and “xiang” (A2), page 367
- Expressing “should” with “yinggai” (A2), page 266
- Expressing “must” with “dei”

---

1. Standard negation with “bu” (A1), page 85

Actions in a row (A2)

Linking actions together in a sentence is very straightforward and to the point. Because of this, there is no new word or phrase needed!

Structure

In Chinese, it's very easy to describe two actions in a row. Simply place one verb phrase after another, in this structure:

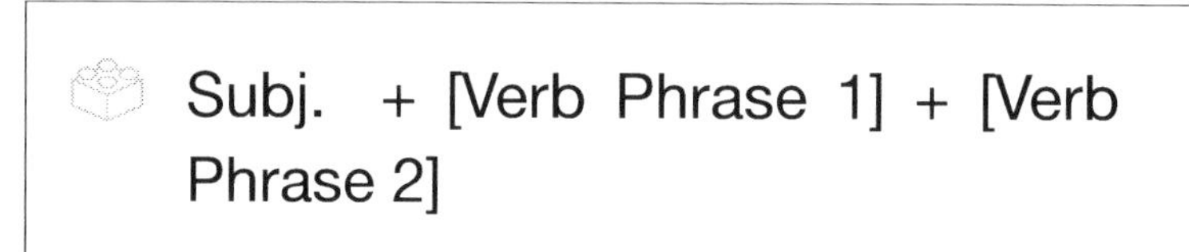

No connecting word is needed. A common mistake in the early stages of learning Chinese is to try and link verbs with 和 (hé). This is incorrect; 和 (hé) is for linking nouns[1]. Just use one verb phrase after another and the sequence of events is clear.

Examples

- 我要回家吃饭。
  Wǒ yào huí jiā chī fàn.
  I want to go home and eat.
- 你要去超市买东西吗?
  Nǐ yào qù chāoshì mǎi dōngxi ma?
  Are you going to the supermarket to buy things?
- 他不想去图书馆看书。
  Tā bù xiǎng qù túshūguǎn kàn shū.
  He doesn't want to go to the library and read.
- 你打电话告诉他了吗?
  Nǐ dǎ diànhuà gàosu tā le ma?
  Did you call and tell him?
- 我们要坐飞机去美国。
  Wǒmen yào zuò fēijī qù Měiguó.
  We are going to take an airplane to go to the USA.

1. Expressing "and" with "he" (A1), page 22

- 你们可以 上 网 买 机票吗?
  Nǐmen kěyǐ shàng wǎng mǎi jīpiào ma?
  Can you use the Internet to buy airplane tickets?
- 老板下周 去 北京 开 会。
  Lǎobǎn xià zhōu qù Běijīng kāi huì.
  Next week the boss will go to Beijing to have a meeting.
- 中国人都要 回 家 过 年。
  Zhōngguó rén dōu yào huí jiā guò nián.
  Chinese people all go back home for Chinese New Year.
- 周末我喜欢自己 买 菜 做 饭。
  Zhōumò wǒ xǐhuan zìjǐ mǎi cài zuò fàn.
  I like to buy food to cook for myself on the weekend.
- 早上我先 刷 牙 洗 脸，再吃早饭。
  Zǎoshang wǒ xiān shuā yá xǐ liǎn, zài chī zǎofàn.
  In the morning, I first brush my teeth and wash my face, and then I eat breakfast.

Note that the English translations of these sentences use the word "and," but there is no equivalent to it in Chinese.

Similar to

- Basic sentence order (A1), page 88
- Events in quick succession with "yi… jiu…"

Expressing “difficult” with “nan” (A2)

难 (nán) is an adjective that means “difficult.” When something is “hard to do” (as in difficult), the word 难 (nán) can be used before the verb.

难 (nán) with General Verbs

Just as 好 (hǎo) can be used to indicate that it's easy to do something[1], 难 (nán) can be attached to verbs (with a few special exceptions), to indicate that something is *hard to do*.

Structure

The structure is:

Examples

- 这句话很 难懂 。
  Zhè jù huà hěn nán dǒng.
  This sentence is hard to understand.
- 汉语很 难学 。
  Hànyǔ hěn nán xué.
  Mandarin is hard to learn.
- 中国菜很 难做 。
  Zhōngguó cài hěn nán zuò.
  Chinese food is hard to make.
- 这个东西现在很 难买 。
  Zhège dōngxi xiànzài hěn nán mǎi.
  This thing is really difficult to purchase now.
- 这个汉字很 难写 。
  Zhège Hànzì hěn nán xiě.
  This character is very difficult to write.

1. Using “hao” to mean “easy” (A2), page 301

难 (nán) with Sense Verbs

难 (nán) can also be attached to "sense verbs" (e.g. look, taste, smell, etc.) to indicate that something offers a "bad sensory experience."

Structure

The structure is:

Examples

- 你做的菜很 难吃 。
  Nǐ zuò de cài hěn nánchī.
  The dishes you cook taste bad.
- 这里的咖啡很 难喝 。
  Zhè lǐ de kāfēi hěn nánhē.
  The coffee here tastes bad.
- 这首歌很 难听 。
  Zhè shǒu gē hěn nántīng.
  This song is terrible (hard to listen to).
- 这种花很 难闻 。
  Zhè zhǒng huā hěn nánwén.
  This kind of flower smells bad.
- 这件衣服很 难看 吗?
  Zhè jiàn yīfu hěn nánkàn ma?
  Is this article of clothing ugly?

Warning! If you're trying to say that a particular dish is "difficult to eat," don't use 难吃 (nánchī)! The word 难吃 (nánchī) *only* means "bad-tasting" and *not* "difficult to eat."

Similar to

- Using "hao" to mean "easy" (A2), page 301
- Expressing "hard to avoid" with "nanmian"
- Expressing difficulty with "hao (bu) rongyi"

Expressing "never" with "conglai" (A2)

Although it can also work in the positive, 从来 (cónglái) is usually used when you want to express that you ***never** do something* (as a habit, or as a rule), or that you *have **never** done something* (it's not a part of your life experience). In either usage, 从来 (cónglái) may be shortened to just 从 (cóng) in casual speech.

"To Never Do" with 从来 (cónglái) + 不 (bù)

When you follow 从来 (cónglái) with 不 (bù), you are expressing that you ***never** do something* (as a habit, or as a rule). It's often used as a way to refuse something, as in "I never drink."

Structure

The structure is:

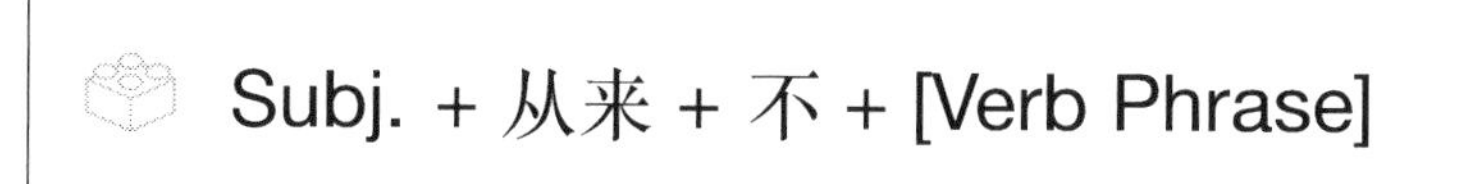

Keep in mind that 从来 (cónglái) may be shortened to just 从 (cóng) in casual speech.

Examples

- 她从来不喝酒。
  Tā cónglái bù hējiǔ.
  She never drinks.
- 我女朋友从不给我打电话。 *来 has been omitted here.*
  Wǒ nǚpéngyou cóng bù gěi wǒ dǎ diànhuà.
  My girlfriend never calls me.
- 这个人很奇怪，他从来不笑。
  Zhège rén hěn qíguài, tā cónglái bù xiào.
  This person is very strange. He never laughs.
- 你父母从来不打你吗? *"hit" can mean "spank"*
  Nǐ fùmǔ cónglái bù dǎ nǐ ma?
  Your parents never hit you?
- 他从不关心别人。 *来 has been omitted here.*
  Tā cóng bù guānxīn biérén.
  He never cares about other people.

"To Have Never Done" with 从来 (cónglái) + 没有 (méiyǒu)

Use 从来 (cónglái) with 没 (méi) or 没有 (méiyǒu) (and 过 (guo) after the verb) to indicate that you *have **never** done something* (it's not a part of your life experience). You're talking about the past now, because you're talking about what you haven't done before, so 没有 (méiyǒu) is appropriate. 过 (guo) also makes sense, because you're making a statement about your life experience.

Structure

The structure is:

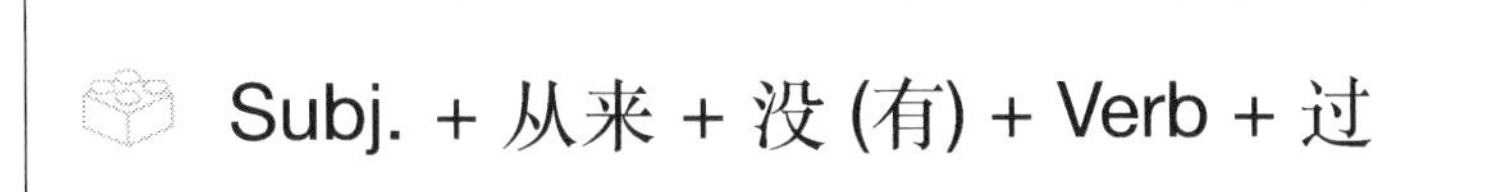

Again, 从来 (cónglái) may be shortened to just 从 (cóng) in casual speech. Note that you can have an object or other information after the verb, but the 过 (guo) needs to come immediately after the verb.

Examples

- 你 从来没有 想 过 这个问题吗?
  Nǐ cónglái méiyǒu xiǎng guo zhège wèntí ma?
  Have you never thought about this question?
- 她 从来没 见 过 她妈妈。
  Tā cónglái méi jiàn guo tā māma.
  She has never met her mother.
- 我 从没 学 过 这个词。 *来 has been omitted here.*
  Wǒ cóngméi xué guo zhège cí.
  I have never before studied this word.
- 你们 从来没有 听说 过 这个地方吗?
  Nǐmen cónglái méiyǒu tīngshuō guo zhège dìfang ma?
  Have you never heard about this place before?
- 很多中国人 从来没 出 过 国。
  Hěn duō Zhōngguó rén cónglái méi chū guo guó.
  A lot of Chinese people have never been abroad.

Expressing "together" with "yiqi" (A2)

If you want to express that you are doing something *together* with someone else, 一起 (yīqǐ) is your word!

Note: The pinyin for 一起 is written "yīqǐ" but pronounced "yìqǐ" due to a tone change rule.

Structure

一起 (yīqǐ) is the easiest way to express an action being done together with other people.

> Subj. + 一起 + Verb + Obj.

The subject must be plural - a plural noun or two or more nouns linked with a conjunction. You can't do things together on your own, after all.

Examples

- 我们 一起 吃晚饭吧。
  Wǒmen yīqǐ chī wǎnfàn ba.
  Let's eat dinner together.
- 早上我和老公 一起 去上班。
  Zǎoshang wǒ hé lǎogōng yīqǐ qù shàngbān.
  In the morning, I go to work together with my husband.
- 周末我们 一起 去看电影，好吗？
  Zhōumò wǒmen yīqǐ qù kàn diànyǐng, hǎo ma?
  Let's go to the movies this weekend, shall we?
- 这两个公司 一起 做这个产品。
  Zhè liǎng gè gōngsī yīqǐ zuò zhège chǎnpǐn.
  These two businesses made this product together.
- 下班以后，你们 一起 来我家吧。
  Xiàbān yǐhòu, nǐmen yīqǐ lái wǒ jiā ba.
  After work, why don't you all come to my home together?

- 下个月我和妈妈 一起 去旅行。
  Xià gè yuè wǒ hé māma yīqǐ qù lǚxíng.
  Next month I'll go on a trip together with mom.
- 你们有没有 一起 玩过这个游戏?
  Nǐmen yǒu méiyǒu yīqǐ wán guo zhège yóuxì?
  Have you all ever played this game together?
- 他想和他太太 一起 学中文。
  Tā xiǎng hé tā tàitai yīqǐ xué Zhōngwén.
  He wants to study Chinese together with his wife.
- 结婚以后，你和父母会 一起 住吗?
  Jiéhūn yǐhòu, nǐ hé fùmǔ huì yīqǐ zhù ma?
  Will you live together with your parents after you get married?
- 今天晚上老板要和我们 一起 加班。
  Jīntiān wǎnshang, lǎobǎn yào hé wǒmen yīqǐ jiābān.
  Tonight the boss is going to to work overtime together with us.

Similar to

- Using “gen” to mean “with” (A2), page 195

Expressing duration with "le" (A2)

Whether you need to express how long you lived somewhere, how long you studied astrophysics, or how long you worked as a mime, you'll need to use 了 (le) to express that time duration.

Basic Usage

Structure

Saying *how long* you did something *for* in Chinese can seem tricky, as there is no preposition as in English. Instead it's all about word order:

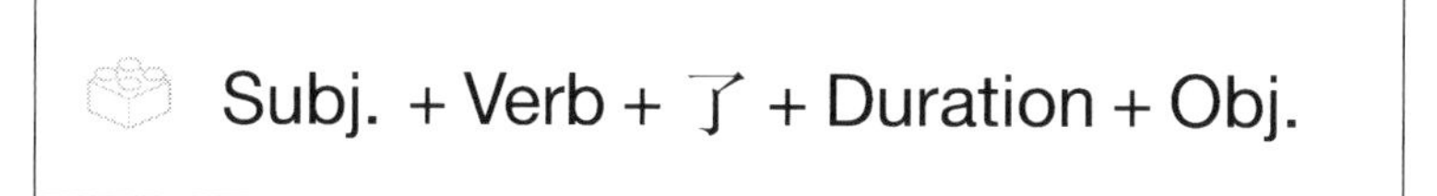

So 了 (le) is placed after the verb (to indicate that the action is completed[1]), followed by the duration. This is how you talk about the duration of completed actions.

Examples

- 他学了 一年 中文。
  Tā xué le yī nián Zhōngwén.
  He studied Chinese for a year.
- 我看了 一个晚上 书。
  Wǒ kàn le yī gè wǎnshang shū.
  I read books all evening.
- 妈妈看了 一天 电视。
  Māma kàn le yī tiān diànshì.
  Mom watched TV all day.
- 他在 Google 做了 八年 经理。
  Tā zài Google zuò le bā nián jīnglǐ.
  He worked as a manager at Google for eight years.
- 我们坐了 十五个小时 飞机去美国。
  Wǒmen zuò le shíwǔ gè xiǎoshí fēijī qù Měiguó.
  We took a fifteen hour flight to the United States.

---

1. Expressing completion with "le" (A2), page 236

To Express "Definitely Concluded"

Structure

Note that the previous pattern can be used to express the duration of completed actions *which are no longer in progress*, although strictly speaking, it's not entirely clear if the actions are still ongoing or not. To indicate that the actions are definitely concluded (not ongoing), a time word[1] may be inserted into the sentence to indicate that you're talking about an event in the past:

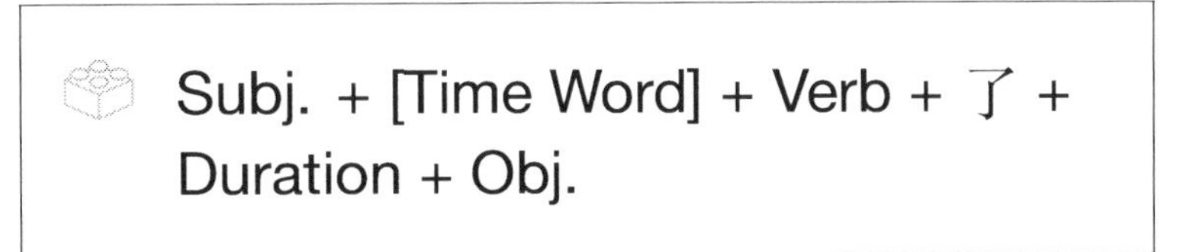

Examples

- 昨天他写了 一天 作业。
  Zuótiān tā xiě le yī tiān zuòyè.
  He did his homework all day yesterday.
- 我刚才打了 半个小时 电话。
  Wǒ gāngcái dǎ le bàn gè xiǎoshí diànhuà.
  I was on the phone for half an hour.
- 他今天喝了 一个晚上 酒。
  Tā jīntiān hē le yī gè wǎnshang jiǔ.
  He drank alcohol all night.
- 我昨天玩了 一个下午 游戏。
  Wǒ zuótiān wán le yī gè xiàwǔ yóuxì.
  Yesterday, I played games all afternoon.
- 上个周末我和老公开了 三个小时 车回老家。
  Shàng gè zhōumò wǒ hé lǎogōng kāi le sān gè xiǎoshí chē huí lǎojiā.
  Last weekend, my husband and I drove three hours to our hometown.

To indicate that the action is *definitely still in progress*, use a slightly different pattern[2].

---

1. Time words and word order (A2), page 211
2. Expressing ongoing duration with double "le" (A2), page 283

Similar to

- Expressing ongoing duration with double “le” (A2), page 283
- Expressing duration of inaction

Expressing ongoing duration with double "le" (A2)

The 了 (le) particle is used in many different ways. In this article, we will explore how to use the double 了 (le) to express the duration of an activity that is ongoing.

Ongoing Duration with Simple Verbs

Expressing *how long* you did something in the past[1] is one thing, but what if the action is still ongoing?

A clarifying example (in English) is appropriate:

- I lived in Shanghai for 5 years. (concluded, not ongoing)
- I have lived in Shanghai for 5 years. (mostly likely ongoing)
- I have been living in Shanghai for 5 years. (definitely ongoing)

This article is about expressing the third situation above, the one which is *definitely ongoing*.

Structure

Subj. + Verb + 了 + Duration + 了

The first 了 (le) is placed after the verb (to indicate that the action is completed), followed by the duration, followed by an additional 了 (le) which tells us that the action has not concluded and is ongoing. You can think of the second 了 (le) as communicating the meaning of "up until now."

Examples

- 你睡了一天了。
  Nǐ shuì le yī tiān le.
  You have been sleeping for the whole day.
- 他在北京住了两年了。
  Tā zài Běijīng zhù le liǎng nián le.
  He has been living in Beijing for two years.

1. Expressing duration with "le" (A2), page 280

- 这个会，他们开 了 两个小时 了 。
  Zhège huì, tāmen kāi le liǎng gè xiǎoshí le.
  They've been holding this meeting for the past two hours.
- 我在这儿等 了 半个小时 了 。
  Wǒ zài zhèr děng le bàn gè xiǎoshí le.
  I have been waiting here for half an hour.
- 他们在酒吧待 了 一个晚上 了 。
  Tāmen zài jiǔbā dāi le yī gè wǎnshang le.
  They have been staying at the bar for the whole evening.

When the Verb Takes an Object

Structure

Note that in the examples above, the verbs have no objects. When the verb has an object, the verb is often repeated:

> Subj. + Verb + Obj. + Verb + 了 + Duration + 了

Examples

- 我学中文学 了 一年 了 。
  Wǒ xué Zhōngwén xué le yī nián le.
  I have been learning Chinese for a year.
- 他打电话打 了 一个多小时 了 。
  Tā dǎ diànhuà dǎ le yī gè duō xiǎoshí le.
  He has been on the phone for more than an hour.
- 老板打游戏打 了 一个上午 了 。
  Lǎobǎn dǎ yóuxì dǎ le yī gè shàngwǔ le.
  The boss has been playing video games all morning.
- 你洗澡洗 了 差不多一个小时 了 。
  Nǐ xǐzǎo xǐ le chàbuduō yī gè xiǎoshí le.
  You have been showering for almost an hour.

- 妈妈看电视看 了 一晚上 了 。
  Māma kàn diànshì kàn le yī wǎnshang le.
  Mom has been watching TV all evening.

Similar to

- Expressing duration with "le" (A2), page 280
- Expressing duration of inaction

Inability with "mei banfa" (A2)

If you are trying to express that something is impossible, you can use the phrase 没办法 (méi bànfǎ). 没办法 (méi bànfǎ) essentially means "there is no way," and whule it works just fine by itself, it can also come before verbs.

Structure

One easy way to express inability is to place the phrase 没办法 (méi bànfǎ) before the verb.

Subj. + 没办法 + Verb + Obj.

Examples

- 今天太忙了，中午 没办法 出去吃饭。
  Jīntiān tài máng le, zhōngwǔ méi bànfǎ chūqù chīfàn.
  It's too busy today. There's no way to go out for lunch.
- 他没带手机，没办法 给我打电话。
  Tā méi dài shǒujī, méi bànfǎ gěi wǒ dǎ diànhuà.
  He didn't bring his phone, so he has no way to give me a call.
- 没有水，我们 没办法 洗衣服。
  Méiyǒu shuǐ, wǒmen méi bànfǎ xǐ yīfu.
  There's no water. There's no way for us to wash clothes.
- 这里太吵了，我 没办法 工作。
  Zhèlǐ tài chǎo le, wǒ méi bànfǎ gōngzuò.
  It's too noisy here. I can't work.
- 他不开门，所以她 没办法 进去。
  Tā bù kāimén, suǒyǐ tā méi bànfǎ jìnqù.
  He didn't open the door, so she has no way to enter.
- 你不会说中文，没办法 在我们公司工作。
  Nǐ bù huì shuō Zhōngwén, méi bànfǎ zài wǒmen gōngsī gōngzuò.
  You can't speak Chinese, so there is no way for you to work for our company.

- 事情太多了，我今天 没办法 做完。
  Shìqing tài duō le, wǒ jīntiān méi bànfǎ zuò wán.
  There's too much to do. I have no way to finish today.
- 老板不同意，我 没办法 帮你。
  Lǎobǎn bù tóngyì , wǒ méi bànfǎ bāng nǐ.
  The boss didn't agree, so I have no way to help you.
- 这里没有 wifi，我 没办法 上网。
  Zhèlǐ méiyǒu wifi，wǒ méi bànfǎ shàngwǎng.
  There is no wifi here, so I have no way of going online.
- 他很笨，我 没办法 跟他一起工作。
  Tā hěn bèn, wǒ méi bànfǎ gēn tā yīqǐ gōngzuò.
  He's really dumb. There is no way I can work with him.

Similar to

- Negation of “you” with “mei” (A1), page 12

Indicating location with "zai" before verbs (A2)

If you need to include the place where an action takes place, you can use 在 (zài). Just pay close attention to word order[1], as this is one case in which Chinese word order is quite different from English.

Structure

To indicate the location that a verb takes place in, 在 (zài), followed by a location, comes before the verb.

Notice that the location is placed *before* the verb in Chinese, whereas in English it appears *afterwards*.

Examples

- 我在上海上大学。
  Wǒ zài Shànghǎi shàng dàxué.
  I went to college in Shanghai.
- 你一直在这家公司工作吗?
  Nǐ yīzhí zài zhè jiā gōngsī gōngzuò ma?
  Have you always been working in this company?
- 我周末想在家睡觉。
  Wǒ zhōumò xiǎng zài jiā shuìjiào.
  On the weekend, I want to sleep at home.
- 不要在床上吃东西。
  Bù yào zài chuáng shàng chī dōngxi.
  Don't eat food on the bed.
- 你想在哪儿开生日派对?
  Nǐ xiǎng zài nǎr kāi shēngrì pàiduì?
  Where do you want to have the birthday party?

---

1. Basic sentence order (A1), page 88

- 他喜欢 在 厕所里 抽烟。
  Tā xǐhuan zài cèsuǒ lǐ chōuyān.
  He likes to smoke in the bathroom.
- 很多人 在 地铁上 吃早饭。
  Hěn duō rén zài dìtiě shàng chī zǎofàn.
  Many people eat breakfast on the subway.
- 现在我们 在 KTV 唱歌。
  Xiànzài wǒmen zài KTV chànggē.
  Now we're singing songs at karaoke.
- 老板 在 会议室 见客户。
  Lǎobǎn zài huìyìshì jiàn kèhù.
  The boss is seeing the client in the meeting room.
- 你 在 外面 吃过晚饭了吗?
  Nǐ zài wàimiàn chī guo wǎnfàn le ma?
  Did you eat dinner outside?

Remember: in English we usually put the location at the end of a sentence. In Chinese, we put the location after the subject but *before* the verb.

Getting More Specific with Locations

Rather than just using 在 (zài) to mean "at" a location, you might want to use it to mean "in," "on," or "under" a specific location. To do this, you'll need to add an extra word after the location. Learn about expressing location with "zai… shang / xia / li"[1].

Similar to

- Basic sentence order (A1), page 88
- Expressing existence in a place with "zai" (A1), page 54
- Expressing location with "zai… shang / xia / li" (A2), page 355
- Special cases of "zai" following verbs (A2), page 293
- Time words and word order (A2), page 211
- Using "dao" to mean "to go to" (A2), page 298

1. Expressing location with "zai… shang / xia / li" (A2), page 355

Reduplication of verbs (A2)

One of the fun things about Chinese is that when speaking, you can repeat a verb to express "a little bit" or "briefly." This is called reduplication. It creates a casual tone, and a sense that whatever the action is, it's not going to take long.

Reduplication with the AA Pattern

Structure

In Chinese, verbs can be reduplicated to indicate that they happen briefly or "a little bit."

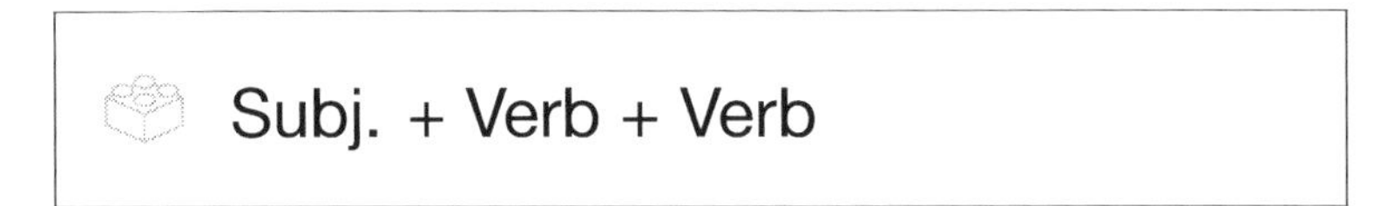

Chinese grammar books frequently refer to the reduplication of a single-character word as a "AA" pattern. Note that for this pattern, the second verb's tone changes to the neutral tone.

Examples

- 你 看看 。
  Nǐ kànkan.
  Take a little look.
- 我 试试 。
  Wǒ shìshi.
  I'll give it a try.
- 说说 你的想法。
  Shuōshuo nǐ de xiǎngfǎ.
  Talk a little bit about your ideas.
- 出去 玩玩 吧！
  Chūqù wánwan ba!
  Go out and have fun!
- 我想出去 走走 。
  Wǒ xiǎng chūqù zǒuzou.
  I want to go out and walk for a bit.

Reduplication with 一 (yī)

Structure

Another way to reduplicate verbs is to insert 一 (yī), in the following structure:

> Verb + 一 + Verb

Examples

- 别生气了，笑一笑！
  Bié shēngqì le, xiào yī xiào!
  Don't be mad, gimme a smile!
- 你去问一问他们厕所在哪里。
  Nǐ qù wèn yī wèn tāmen cèsuǒ zài nǎlǐ.
  Go and ask them where the bathroom is.
- 我可以用一用你的电脑吗?
  Wǒ kěyǐ yòng yī yòng nǐ de diànnǎo ma?
  Can I use your computer for a little bit?
- 你现在有时间吗? 我们聊一聊吧。
  Nǐ xiànzài yǒu shíjiān ma? Wǒmen liáo yī liáo ba.
  Do you have a second? Let's chat for a bit.
- 你想尝一尝我做的菜吗?
  Nǐ xiǎng cháng yī cháng wǒ zuò de cài ma?
  Do you want to taste the food that I cooked?

Using this kind of structure lightens the mood and seriousness of the question. It also adds variety to sentence structure. Because these phrases are used colloquially, there is not set rule to which verbs this can be applied to. There are some verbs that are often reduplicated and some verbs that sound weird when reduplicated. With practice and exposure, you will learn which ones are often used.

ABAB Reduplication with Two-Syllable Verbs

In the examples above, all verbs are only one syllable. Those verbs get reduplicated a lot, so those examples are quite useful. Occasionally, though, two-syllable verbs get reduplicated as well. When this happens, it's important to use the "ABAB" pattern for verbs (meaning the entire word is repeated), and not the "AABB" pattern you use for adjectives (where each character is repeated individually).

Examples

- 考虑考虑

  kǎolǜ kǎolǜ

  think it over

  In addition to "在" you need a "上" to indicate the location "in the subway."

- 讨论讨论

  tǎolùn tǎolùn

  discuss it

- 商量商量

  shāngliang shāngliang

  talk it over

- 打听打听

  dǎting dǎting

  inquire about it

Similar to

- Softening speech with "ba" (A2), page 243
- Verbing briefly with "yixia" (A2), page 304
- Reduplication of adjectives

Special cases of "zai" following verbs (A2)

When used to indicate locations of actions, 在 (zài) is usually placed after the subject and before the verb[1]. There are certain cases, however, when 在 (zài) goes after the verb.

Structure

This pattern is used regularly with special types of verbs, including: 住 (zhù), 放 (fàng), 坐 (zuò), and 站 (zhàn). These are verbs that imply movement or location. Technically, the structure is called a location complement, but it can be understood without going into that much detail. Just remember that for verbs implying *movement* or *location* like the ones above, the default sentence order[2] changes and you get this structure:

Subj. + [Special Verb] + 在 + Location

Examples

- 你住 在 上海 吗?
  Nǐ zhù zài Shànghǎi ma?
  Do you live in Shanghai?
- 他坐 在 老板的旁边 。
  Tā zuò zài lǎobǎn de pángbiān .
  He sits next to the boss.
- 你应该站 在 我后面 。
  Nǐ yīnggāi zhàn zài wǒ hòumiàn .
  You should stand behind me.
- 不要坐 在 我的床上 。
  Bùyào zuò zài wǒ de chuáng shàng .
  Don't sit on my bed.

---

1. Indicating location with "zai" before verbs (A2), page 288
2. Expressing existence in a place with "zai" (A1), page 54

- 你的衣服不可以放在这里。
  Nǐ de yīfu bù kěyǐ fàng zài zhèlǐ.
  You can't put your clothes here.
- 不要站在路中间。
  Bùyào zhàn zài lù zhōngjiān.
  Don't stand in the middle of the road.
- 不要坐在地上。
  Bùyào zuò zài dì shàng.
  Don't sit on the ground.
- 那本书我放在桌子上了。
  Nà běn shū wǒ fàng zài zhuōzi shàng le.
  I placed that book on the table.
- 不要走在草地上。
  Búyào zǒu zài cǎodì shàng.
  Don't walk on the grass.
- 周末我不想待在家里。
  Zhōumò wǒ bù xiǎng dāi zài jiā lǐ.
  I don't want to stay at home on weekends.

Remember that this is an *exception to the normal rule*. A common mistake is to over apply this and produce incorrect sentences. Note the incorrect and correct versions below.

✘ 我工作在上海。
Wǒ gōngzuò zài Shànghǎi.

✔ 我在上海工作。
Wǒ zài Shànghǎi gōngzuò.
I work in Shanghai.

✘ 我学习在图书馆。
Wǒ xuéxí zài túshūguǎn.

✔ 我在图书馆学习。
Wǒ zài túshūguǎn xuéxí.
I study in the library.

Similar to

- Expressing existence in a place with “zai” (A1), page 54
- Expressing location with “zai… shang / xia / li” (A2), page 355
- Indicating location with “zai” before verbs (A2), page 288
- Idiomatic phrases with “zai”

Special verbs with "hen" (A2)

Using 很 (hěn) to intensify verbs that express thoughts or feeling is really easy.

Structure

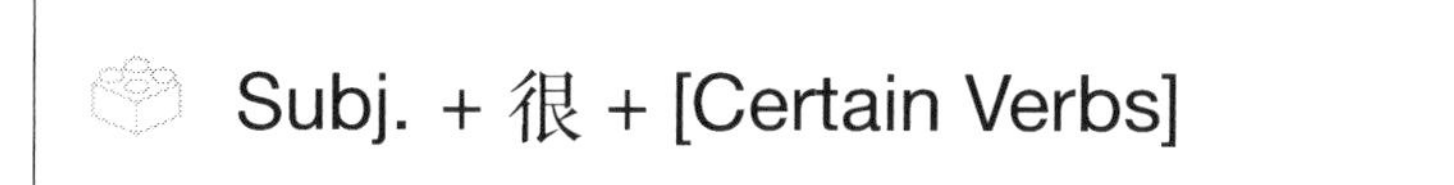

Certain "psychological verbs" related to feelings or emotional sates can be modified with 很 (hěn) to increase their intensity. This is similar to using "really" or "very much" in English. Remember that this only applies to psychological verbs, such as:

- 想 (xiǎng) to think; to want; to miss
- 喜欢 (xǐhuan) to like
- 小心 (xiǎoxīn) to be careful
- 怕 (pà) to fear; to be afraid of
- 了解 (liǎojiě) to know a lot about
- 讨厌 (tǎoyàn) to hate
- 担心 (dānxīn) to worry about
- 希望 (xīwàng) to hope

Examples

- 我很想你。
  Wǒ hěn xiǎng nǐ.
  I really miss you.
- 他很喜欢你。
  Tā hěn xǐhuan nǐ.
  He really likes you.
- 你应该很小心。
  Nǐ yīnggāi hěn xiǎoxīn.
  You should be very careful.

- 我很怕晚上一个人在家。
  Wǒ hěn pà wǎnshang yīgèrén zài jiā.
  I fear staying home alone at night.
- 你应该很了解自己的孩子。
  Nǐ yīnggāi hěn liǎojiě zìjǐ de háizi.
  You should know a lot about your child.
- 外国人很讨厌中国的公共厕所。
  Wàiguó rén hěn tǎoyàn Zhōngguó de gōnggòng cèsuǒ.
  Foreigners really hate public toilets in China.
- 你两天没回家，妈妈很担心你。
  Nǐ liǎng tiān méi huíjiā, māma hěn dānxīn nǐ.
  You haven't gone home in two days. Mom is really worried about you.
- 父母都很希望我能上一个好大学。
  Fùmǔ dōu hěn xīwàng wǒ néng shàng yī gè hǎo dàxué.
  Both of my parents really hope that I can go to a good college.

Did you ever notice that some Chinese people with less-than-perfect English will use the phrase "very like?" Now you know why!

Similar to

- Expressing "excessively" with "tai" (A1), page 94
- Simple "noun + adjective" sentences (A1), page 96
- Positive adjectives with "-ji le"

Using "dao" to mean "to go to" (A2)

A simple and direct way to indicate that you or someone is going to a specific place or has arrived at a specific place is to use the verb 到 (dào).

到 (dào) for Arriving in a Place

Structure

The verb 到 (dào) is used to talk about arriving in places.

Examples

For these examples, it's straightforward to think of 到 (dào) as simply meaning "to arrive."

- 他们已经 到 酒吧了。
  Tāmen yǐjīng dào jiǔbā le.
  They have already arrived at the bar.
- 我刚 到 家。
  Wǒ gāng dào jiā.
  I just got home.
- 你 到 机场了吗?
  Nǐ dào jīchǎng le ma?
  Have you arrived at the airport?
- 我已经 到 火车站了。
  Wǒ yǐjīng dào huǒchēzhàn le.
  I've already arrived at the train station.
- 我们先 到 北京，然后 到 香港。
  Wǒmen xiān dào Běijīng, ránhòu dào Xiānggǎng.
  First we'll arrive in Beijing, then in Hong Kong.

In some examples translating 到 (dào) as "to arrive" doesn't work as well and you might need to expand your understanding of exactly what 到 (dào) means. That's what we'll examine below.

Going to a Place and Performing an Action

Structure

If you are going to a place to do something else, you can first use 到 (dào) to indicate where you're going, then add another verb after that. This has the meaning of "going to the place to do something," and it's one case where the "arrive" translation doesn't really work anymore.

Examples

- 明天我要 到 南京路买衣服。
  Míngtiān wǒ yào dào Nánjīng Lù mǎi yīfu.
  Tomorrow I'll go to Nanjing Road to buy clothes.
- 你们晚上 到 哪儿吃饭啊?
  Nǐmen wǎnshang dào nǎr chīfàn a?
  Where will you all go to eat food this evening?
- 我跟朋友经常 到 KTV 唱歌。
  Wǒ gēn péngyou jīngcháng dào KTV chànggē.
  I often go to Karaoke to sing songs with friends.
- 今年春节我要 到 女朋友家见她的父母。
  Jīnnián Chūnjié wǒ yào dào nǚpéngyou jiā jiàn tā de fùmǔ.
  This Spring Festival I am going to my girlfriend's house to meet her parents.
- 下个月我要 到 美国出差。
  Xià gè yuè wǒ yào dào Měiguó chūchāi.
  Next month I need to go to the USA on a business trip.

You might be wondering: *can I just use 去 (qù) instead of 到 (dào)?* For sentences like this, *yes, you can.* But native speakers will frequently use 到 (dào) in this way, so it's still good to be familiar with this pattern. If you want to sound more native, you should use it too!

到 (dào), 去 (qù), and 走 (zǒu)

Sometimes it can be hard to figure out exactly which word to use in Chinese to mean "go." 到 (dào) is used when you talk about *arriving* at a place, emphasizing the destination. 去 (qù) is used when you are *going to* a place. The exact meaning is "to go," and it emphasizes *getting to* somewhere. 走 (zǒu) is used when talking about "leaving." The emphasis is on getting *away* from a particular place.

Using "hao" to mean "easy" (A2)

Of course 好 (hǎo) means "good." But it can also be used to express that something is "easy to do" or "good to do." And it is quite... *easy to do*! All you need to do is place a 好 (hǎo) before a verb.

General Verbs

Just as 难 (nán) can be used to indicate that it's hard to do something[1], 好 (hǎo) can also come before verbs to indicate that something is *easy to do*.

Structure

The simple form is just:

好 + Verb

If you want to make a sentence out of it:

Examples

- 这个词的意思很 好懂 。
  Zhège cí de yìsi hěn hǎo dǒng.
  The meaning of this word is easy to understand.
- 这个汉字很 好写 。
  Zhège Hànzì hěn hǎo xiě.
  This Chinese character is easy to write.
- 三明治很 好做 。
  Sānmíngzhì hěn hǎo zuò.
  Sandwiches are easy to make.

1. Expressing "difficult" with "nan" (A2), page 274

- 苹果手机现在很 好买 。

  Píngguǒ shǒujī xiànzài hěn hǎo mǎi.

  iPhones are easy to buy now.

- 这个笔很 好用 。

  Zhège bǐ hěn hǎo yòng.

  This pen is easy to use.

Exceptions

好 (hǎo) can also be attached to "sense verbs" (e.g. "look," "taste," "smell," etc.) to indicate that something is **good *to do* (rather than "*easy* to do").**

There's a limited number of these, but some of them are super common, so just memorize them as exceptions:

- 好吃

  hǎochī

  good to taste, good to eat, delicious

- 好喝

  hǎohē

  good to taste, good to drink

- 好看

  hǎokàn

  good to look at, good-looking, attractive

- 好听

  hǎotīng

  good to listen to, pleasant to listen to, good-sounding

- 好闻

  hǎowén

  good to smell, smells good, good-smelling

The word for "fun" in Chinese is also of this form, even though it's not a sense verb:

- 好玩

  hǎowán

  fun

Examples

- 这首歌很 好听 。

  Zhè shǒu gē hěn hǎotīng.

  This song is great.

- 这种茶很 好闻 。

  Zhè zhǒng chá hěn hǎowén.

  This kind of tea smells good.

- 你的新包很 好看 。

  Nǐ de xīn bāo hěn hǎokàn.

  Your new bag looks good.

- 妈妈做的菜很 好吃 。

  Māma zuò de cài hěn hǎochī.

  The food mom makes is delicious.

- 我觉得上海很 好玩 。

  Wǒ juéde Shànghǎi hěn hǎowán.

  I think Shanghai is a lot of fun.

Similar to

- Expressing "difficult" with "nan" (A2), page 274
- Expressing difficulty with "hao (bu) rongyi"
- Expressing purpose with "haorang"

Verbing briefly with "yixia" (A2)

After briefly reading this article, you will know how to use 一下 (yīxià) to express a brief action!

Note: The pinyin for 一下 is written "yīxià" but pronounced "yíxià" due to a tone change rule.

Structure

To express that a verb is carried out briefly or "a little bit," you can add 一下 (yīxià) after it. Sometimes 一下 (yīxià) can soften the tone.

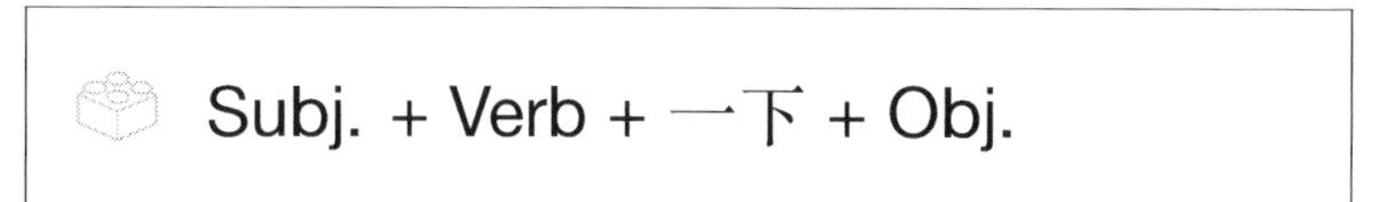

Often, adding 一下 (yīxià) just makes the Chinese feel more natural. This is not something you can get a feel for quickly. You'll want to observe how native speakers use 一下 (yīxià) over a long period of time to really get used to how it is used.

Examples

- 请你等一下。
  Qǐng nǐ děng yīxià.
  Please wait a little bit.
  You get the feeling that it shouldn't be a long wait.
- 你看一下。
  Nǐ kàn yīxià.
  Take a look.
  It should be quick.
- 试一下吧。
  Shì yīxià ba.
  Try it.
  How long can trying it take?
- 我要想一下。
  Wǒ yào xiǎng yīxià.
  I want to think a little.
  You're supposed to believe that I won't need to think about it long.
- 开一下门吧。
  Kāi yīxià mén ba.
  Please open the door.
  How long can it take to open the door?

- 请你说 一下 为什么。
  Qǐng nǐ shuō yīxià wèishénme.
  Please say why.
  I feel it should be a quick explanation.
- 不要生气了，笑 一下 ！
  Bùyào shēngqì le, xiào yīxià!
  Don't be mad, laugh!
  Just one quick laugh!
- 宝宝，亲 一下 爸爸。
  Bǎobao, qīn yīxià bàba.
  Baby, give your dad a kiss.
  If a baby's kiss isn't quick, it's weird for everyone.
- 你可以来 一下 我的办公室吗?
  Nǐ kěyǐ lái yīxià wǒ de bàngōngshì ma?
  Could you please come to my office?
  Just come real quick.
- 你能介绍 一下 自己吗?
  Nǐ néng jièshào yīxià zìjǐ ma?
  Could you introduce yourself briefly?
  Not your life story, just a brief self-introduction.

Similar to

- Reduplication of verbs (A2), page 290

Verbs that take double objects (A2)

There are some common verbs in Chinese that can take two objects. In this article, we will look at how they are used.

Structure

As in English, some verbs in Chinese take two objects. A typical example for English is "to bake someone a cake," and there are countless more. The structure in Chinese is:

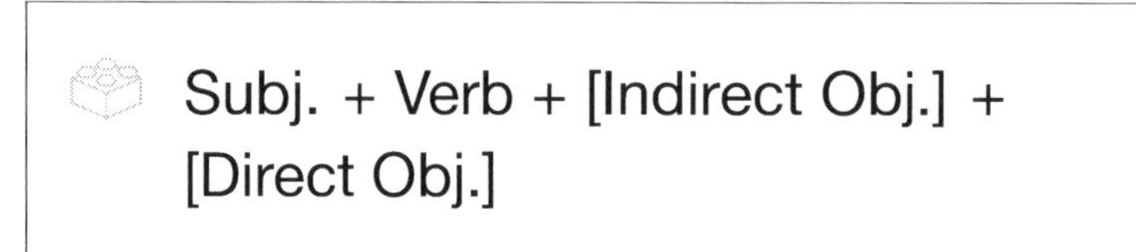

If you don't know what direct and indirect objects are, don't worry - the terms can be thought of as "object 1" and "object 2." The main point is that there are two of them. A simple way to think about it is that the direct object is the thing that the action happens to (e.g. the cake that gets baked) while the indirect object is the recipient of the direct object (e.g. the person the cake is given to).

Examples

- 老师，我可以问你一个问题吗？
  Lǎoshī, wǒ kěyǐ wèn nǐ yī gè wèntí ma?
  Teacher, may I ask you a question?
- 大家都叫他"怪叔叔"。
  Dàjiā dōu jiào tā "guài shūshu."
  Everyone calls him ``Uncle Weirdo."
- 我想告诉你一个好消息。
  Wǒ xiǎng gàosu nǐ yī gè hǎo xiāoxi.
  I want to tell you the good news.
- 他们给了你多少钱？
  Tāmen gěi le nǐ duōshao qián?
  How much money did they give you?

- 他送了女朋友很多花。
  Tā sòng le nǚpéngyou hěn duō huā.
  He gave his girlfriend lots of flowers.
- 我想送给你一本书。
  Wǒ xiǎng sòng gěi nǐ yī běn shū.
  I want to give you a book.
- 爸爸要送给我一个很贵的生日礼物。
  Bàba yào sòng gěi wǒ yī gè hěn guì de shēngrì lǐwù.
  My dad is going to give me a very expensive birthday gift.
- 你可以借我两千块钱吗?
  Nǐ kěyǐ jiè wǒ liǎng qiān kuài qián ma?
  Can you lend me 2000 kuai?
- 老板刚发给我上个月的工资。
  Lǎobǎn gāng fā gěi wǒ shàng gè yuè de gōngzī.
  The boss just gave me my pay for last month.
- 这个人骗了我很多钱。
  Zhège rén piàn le wǒ hěn duō qián.
  This person cheated me out of a lot of money.

Similar to

- Verbs preceded by "gei"

Potential complement "-bu dong" for not understanding (A2)

Chinese learners often have to express that they don't understand something, especially in the beginning when they start learning. One of the ways to express that is to use the 不懂 (bù dǒng) verb complement.

Structure

Yes, 不懂 (bù dǒng) by itself simply means "not understand," and you can use it this way. But you'll find that more often, it follows a verb. When used this way, it is a complement.

The potential complement 不懂 (bù dǒng) is used to talk about things that can't be understood. Note that this is about *potential*: the subject doesn't have the *ability* to understand.

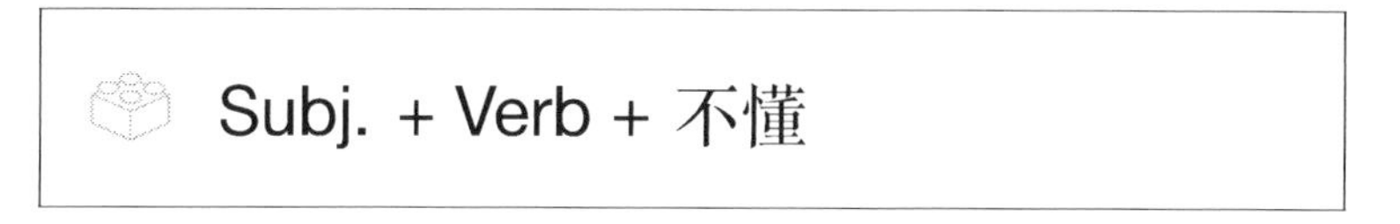

The 不懂 (bù dǒng) may also be swapped out with 不明白 (bù míngbai).

Examples

- 我 看 不懂 这本书。
  Wǒ kàn bu dǒng zhè běn shū.
  I don't understand the book.
- 孩子们 看 不懂 你写的汉字。
  Háizi men kàn bu dǒng nǐ xiě de Hànzì.
  Kids don't understand the characters that you wrote.
- 你 看 不懂 我的邮件吗?
  Nǐ kàn bu dǒng wǒ de yóujiàn ma?
  Do you not understand my emails?
- 老板的中文说得很好，可是他 看 不懂 中文报纸。
  Lǎobǎn de Zhōngwén shuō de hěn hǎo, kěshì tā kàn bu dǒng Zhōngwén bàozhǐ.
  The boss speaks very good Chinese, but he doesn't understand Chinese newspapers.

- 我 听 不懂 上海话。
  Wǒ tīng bu dǒng Shànghǎi-huà.
  I don't understand Shanghai dialect.
- 你们 听 不懂 我的话吗?
  Nǐmen tīng bu dǒng wǒ de huà ma?
  Do you not understand what I say?
- 我 听 不懂 你说的英语。
  Wǒ tīng bu dǒng nǐ shuō de Yīngyǔ.
  I don't understand your English.
- 我们都 听 不懂 你的意思。
  Wǒmen dōu tīng bu dǒng nǐ de yìsi.
  None of us understand what you mean.
- 很多人 读 不懂 这本书。
  Hěn duō rén dú bu dǒng zhè běn shū.
  Many people don't understand this book.
- 这个句子很难，学生们都 读 不懂 。
  Zhège jùzi hěn nán, xuéshengmen dōu dú bu dǒng.
  This sentence is very difficult. None of the students understand.

Similar to

- Potential complement "bu xia"

Result complement "-wan" for finishing (A2)

On its own, 完 (wán) means "to finish" or "to complete." Using it in this grammar structure, it expresses the idea of doing some action to completion.

Structure

As well as with 到 (dào) and 见 (jiàn)[1], you can also form result complements with 完 (wán). This indicates that an action is finished or completed.

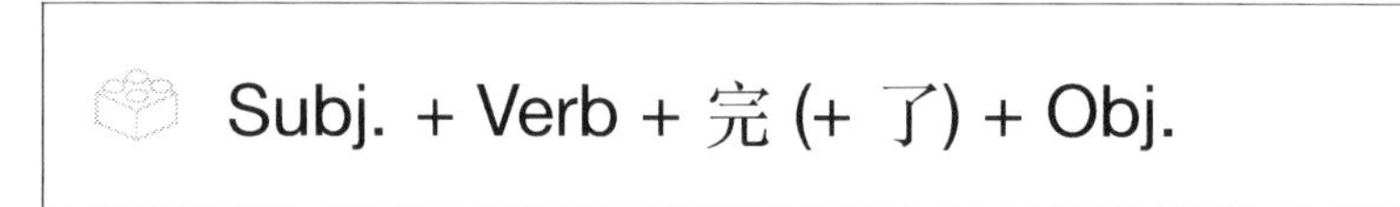

Frequently, you'll also see a 了 (le) at the end, indicating completion[2].

Examples

- 我说完了。
  Wǒ shuō wán le.
  I am finished talking.
- 你吃完了吗?
  Nǐ chī wán le ma?
  Are you done eating?
- 我想看完这个电影。
  Wǒ xiǎng kàn wán zhège diànyǐng.
  I want to finish watching the movie.
- 你做完以后,就可以下班了。
  Nǐ zuò wán yǐhòu, jiù kěyǐ xiàbān le.
  After you finish doing it, you can get off work.
- 你今天可以做完作业吗?
  Nǐ jīntiān kěyǐ zuò wán zuòyè ma?
  Can you finish doing your homework today?

---

1. Result complements "-dao" and "-jian" (A2), page 312
2. Expressing completion with "le" (A2), page 236

- 你什么时候可以看 完 这本书?
  Nǐ shénme shíhou kěyǐ kàn wán zhè běn shū?
  When can you finish reading this book?
- 妈妈洗 完 衣服以后，就去做晚饭了。
  Māma xǐ wán yīfu yǐhòu, jiù qù zuò wǎnfàn le.
  After mom finished washing clothes, she went to cook dinner.
- 做 完 这些作业需要两个小时。
  Zuò wán zhèxiē zuòyè xūyào liǎng gè xiǎoshí.
  To finish your homework you will need two hours.
- 看 完 以后告诉我。
  Kàn wán yǐhòu gàosu wǒ.
  Tell me when you have finished watching.
- 我们学 完 了一百个词。
  Wǒmen xué wán le yībǎi gè cí.
  We have finished learning 100 words.

In English we say "I finished the movie," or "I finished supper," but in Chinese you should explicitly use the verb implied in English along with 完了 (wán le) to emphasize that you completed the action: "watch the movie (till the end)" or "eat (all my) supper."

✗ 我 完 了电影。
Wǒ wán le diànyǐng.

✓ 我看 完 了电影。
Wǒ kàn wán le diànyǐng.
I finished watching the movie.

To tell us that you watched it till the end.

Similar to

- Result complements "-dao" and "-jian" (A2), page 312
- Result complements

Result complements "-dao" and "-jian" (A2)

Two of the most common result complements in Chinese are 到 (dào) and 见 (jiàn). On this page we're only going to be talking about verbs related to the senses ("see," "hear," etc.), and for this usage, the two are interchangeable.

Verbs with 到 (dào) and 见 (jiàn)

Structure

Result complements are a huge topic in Chinese grammar, but you can approach them in stages. The structure you come across the most is a verb with 到 (dào):

Subj. + Verb + 到 + Obj.

What 到 (dào) does is indicate that the outcome of the verb is achieved - what its *result* is. Without a result complement, the sentence would describe only the action itself. To illustrate, 看 (kàn) "to look" is the action of turning your head in a particular direction and focusing your eyes, whereas 看到 (kàndào), "to see," is the result of your brain taking in the visual input. It may sound a little hokey, but it really is possible to "look but not see," and Chinese makes a clear distinction between the action and the result.

The complement 见 (jiàn) is very similar to 到 (dào), and it is used in the same way:

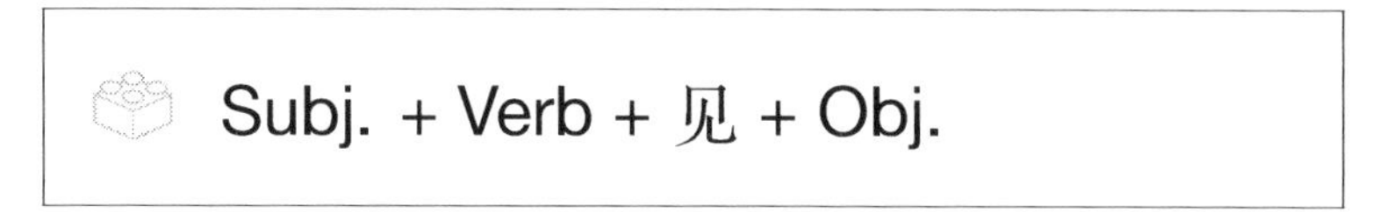
Subj. + Verb + 见 + Obj.

However, there is a difference. 见 (jiàn) is generally *only* used after verbs involving one of the senses, like 听 (tīng) and 看 (kàn), whereas 到 (dào) can be attached to a large variety of verbs, which we will discuss at a higher level later.

Examples

- 你 看 见 那个帅哥了吗?
  Nǐ kàn jiàn nàge shuàigē le ma?

- 你 看 到 那个帅哥了吗?
  Nǐ kàn dào nàge shuàigē le ma?
  Did you see that handsome guy?

- 我 看 见 了。
  Wǒ kàn jiàn le.

We didn't say what "I" saw; you have to infer it from the context.

- 我 看 到 了。
  Wǒ kàn dào le.
  I saw it.

- 你 听 见 了吗?
  Nǐ tīng jiàn le ma?

- 你 听 到 了吗?
  Nǐ tīng dào le ma?
  Did you hear it?

Negative Forms

Structure

This structure can be negated using 没 (méi) on 没有 (méiyǒu). This is because if there is a result, then it already happened. And you need to use 没 (méi) to negate past events[1], not 不 (bù).

Examples

- 你 没 看 到 那个帅哥吗?
  Nǐ méi kàn dào nàge shuàigē ma?

- 你 没 看 见 那个帅哥吗?
  Nǐ méi kàn jiàn nàge shuàigē ma?
  You didn't see that handsome guy?

1. Negation of "you" with "mei" (A1), page 12

- 我 没有 看 到 。
  Wǒ méiyǒu kàn dào.
- 我 没有 看 见 。
  Wǒ méiyǒu kàn jiàn.
  I didn't see it.

We didn't say what "I" didn't see; you have to infer it from the context.

- 你 没 听 到 吗?
  Nǐ méi tīng dào ma?
- 你 没 听 见 吗?
  Nǐ méi tīng jiàn ma?
  You didn't hear it?

Similar to

- Result complement "-wan" for finishing (A2), page 310
- Result complement "-cuo"
- Result complement "-qilai"
- Tricky uses of "dao"
- Further uses of resultative complement "qilai"

Expressing “some” with “yixie” (A2)

In order to express “some” or “a few,” you can use 一些 (yīxiē). To use it in this way, 一些 (yīxiē) is placed before the noun it modifies. 一些 (yīxiē) can modify the subject or the object.

Note: The pinyin for 一些 is written “yīxiē” but pronounced “yìxiē” due to a tone change rule.

Structure

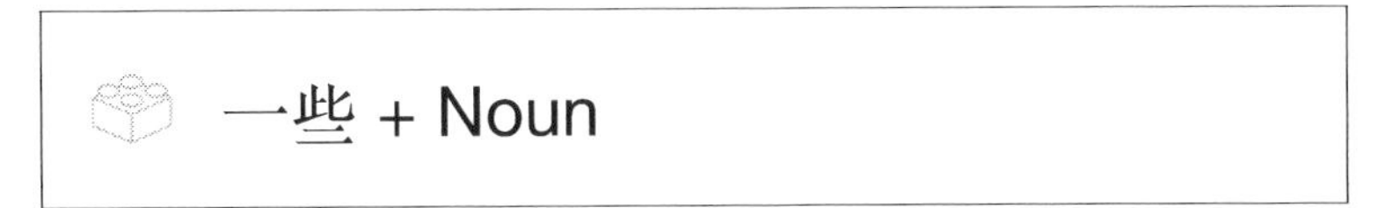

Examples

- 妈妈去超市买了 一些 水果。
  Māma qù chāoshì mǎi le yīxiē shuǐguǒ.
  Mom went to the supermarket and bought some fruit.
- 上个周末他买了 一些 衣服。
  Shàng gè zhōumò tā mǎi le yīxiē yīfu.
  He bought some clothes last weekend.
- 我们很快会见到 一些 新同事。
  Wǒmen hěn kuài huì jiàndào yīxiē xīn tóngshì.
  We're going to meet some new co-workers very soon.
- 你饿不饿？这里有 一些 吃的。
  Nǐ è bu è? Zhèlǐ yǒu yīxiē chīde.
  Are you hungry or not? There is some food here.
- 下课以后，学生们问了 一些 问题。
  Xiàkè yǐhòu, xuéshengmen wèn le yīxiē wèntí.
  After class, the students asked some questions.
- 给我 一些 时间，好吗？
  Gěi wǒ yīxiē shíjiān, hǎo ma?
  Give me some time, OK?

- 他给我带了 一些 书。
  Tā gěi wǒ dài le yīxiē shū.
  He brought me some books.
- 你可以借我 一些 钱吗?
  Nǐ kěyǐ jiè wǒ yīxiē qián ma?
  Can you lend me some money?
- 你想在咖啡里放 一些 糖吗?
  Nǐ xiǎng zài kāfēi lǐ fàng yīxiē táng ma?
  Do you want to put some sugar in your coffee?
- 我在中国的时候，去过 一些 很漂亮的地方。
  Wǒ zài Zhōngguó de shíhou, qù guo yīxiē hěn piàoliang de dìfang.
  When I was in China, I went to some beautiful places.

Similar to

- Expressing “a little too” with “you dian” (A2), page 165
- Measure words with “this” and “that” (A2), page 333
- Using “ji” to mean “several” (A2), page 222
- Using “youde” to mean “some” (A2), page 317

Using "youde" to mean "some" (A2)

To refer to just *certain* members of group, you can use 有的 (yǒude). This usage is normally translated as "some" in English. It is often used multiple times in one sentence to refer to different groups.

Structure

All you need to do is put 有的 (yǒude) before the nouns there are "some of" in the sentence. If there is already some context, you can omit the subject, and the 有的 (yǒude) can just mean "some" instead of "some of something."

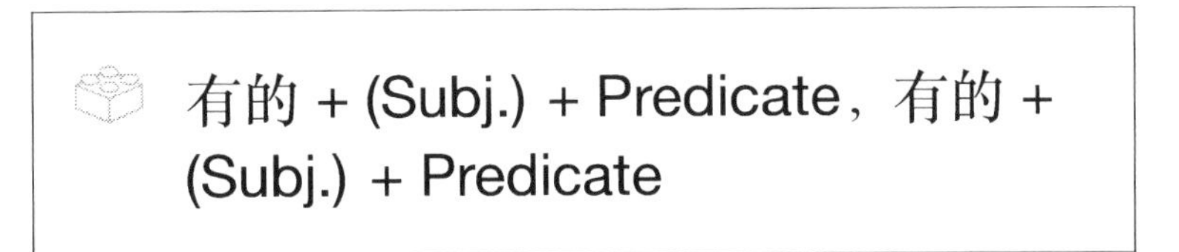

Also, you aren't limited to just two 有的 (yǒude) in the sentence. You can have multiple groups doing different things, and just precede them with a 有的 (yǒude) each time.

Examples

- 外国人 有的 很有钱，有的 没钱。
  Wàiguó rén yǒude hěn yǒuqián, yǒude méi qián.
  Some foreigners are rich, but some aren't.
- 我们公司有一些电脑，有的 是新的，有的 是旧的。
  Wǒmen gōngsī yǒu yīxiē diànnǎo, yǒude shì xīn de, yǒude shì jiù de.
  Our company has some computers. Some are new, and some are old.
- 他写了很多书，有的 卖得很好，有的 卖得不好。
  Tā xiě le hěn duō shū, yǒude mài de hěn hǎo, yǒude mài de bù hǎo.
  He has written a lot of books. Some sell well, but some don't.
- 中国菜 有的 好吃，有的 不好吃。
  Zhōngguó cài yǒude hǎochī, yǒude bù hǎochī.
  Some Chinese foods are tasty, while some aren't.
- 这家店的衣服 有的 贵，有的 便宜。
  Zhè jiā diàn de yīfu yǒude guì, yǒude piányi.
  In this shop, some of the clothes are expensive and some are cheap.

- 他有很多房子，有的 在国内，有的 在国外。

  Tā yǒu hěn duō fángzi, yǒude zài guónèi, yǒude zài guówài.

  He has a lot of houses, some of them are within the country and some are abroad.

- 晚上六点以后，有的 人下班了，有的 人在加班。

  Wǎnshang liùdiǎn yǐhòu, yǒude rén xiàbān le, yǒude rén zài jiābān.

  After six o'clock some people are off work, while some are still working.

- 我的大学老师 有的 很年轻，有的 很老。

  Wǒ de dàxué lǎoshī yǒude hěn niánqīng, yǒude hěn lǎo.

  Some of my college teachers are young, some are old.

- 酒吧里，有的 人在喝酒，有的 人在跳舞，还 有的 人在聊天。

  Jiǔbā lǐ, yǒude rén zài hējiǔ, yǒude rén zài tiàowǔ, hái yǒude rén zài liáotiān.

  In the bar, some people are drinking, some are dancing, and some are chatting.

- 因为工作，我认识了很多人，有的 是大学老师，有的 是 CEO。

  Yīnwèi gōngzuò, wǒ rènshi le hěn duō rén, yǒude shì dàxué lǎoshī, yǒude shì CEO.

  I know a lot of people because of my work. Some are college teachers and some are CEOs.

Similar to

- Expressing "some" with "yixie" (A2), page 315
- Using "ji" to mean "several" (A2), page 222

Counting money (A2)

Cash is king, even though China is now crazy for mobile payments. Either way, though, mastering how to say quantities of money is vital!

Asking "How Much Money" with 多少钱 (duōshao qián)

Before you learn how to count money in Chinese, make sure you know how to ask "how much money" when you go shopping in China.

Structure

Examples

- 多少钱 ?
  Duōshao qián ?
  How much?
- 你的手机 多少钱 ?
  Nǐ de shǒujī duōshao qián ?
  How much was your cell phone?
- 我们的午饭 多少钱 ?
  Wǒmen de wǔfàn duōshao qián ?
  How much is our lunch?
- 这杯咖啡 多少钱 ?
  Zhè bēi kāfēi duōshao qián ?
  How much for this cup of coffee?
- 这件衣服 多少钱 ?
  Zhè jiàn yīfu duōshao qián ?
  How much is this clothing?

Stating Quantities of Money

Structure

Chinese has a specific structure for talking about quantities for money:

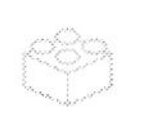

Number + 块 + Number + 毛

Examples

- 两块五毛
  liǎng kuài wǔ máo
  two kuai five mao (2.5)
- 三块八毛
  sān kuài bā máo
  three kuai eight mao (3.8)
- 十块两毛
  shí kuài liǎng máo
  ten kuai two mao (10.2)
- 二十三块八毛
  èrshí-sān kuài bā máo
  Twenty-three kuai eight mao (23.8)
- 五十块五毛
  wǔshí kuài wǔ máo
  fifty kuai five mao (50.5)

Note that "2.5 RMB" reads as 两块五 (liǎng kuài wǔ).

- ✗ 二块五
  èr kuài wǔ
- ✓ 两块五
  liǎng kuài wǔ
  two kuai five mao (2.5)

If the smaller units are only in tens, you can just say the number of tens. So "3.8 RMB" is 三块八 (sān kuài bā). This way of giving the price is normally only used for amounts under 100 RMB.

When the smallest unit is 2, it reads as 二 (èr) instead of 两 (liǎng).

- ✗ 两块两
  liǎng kuài liǎng

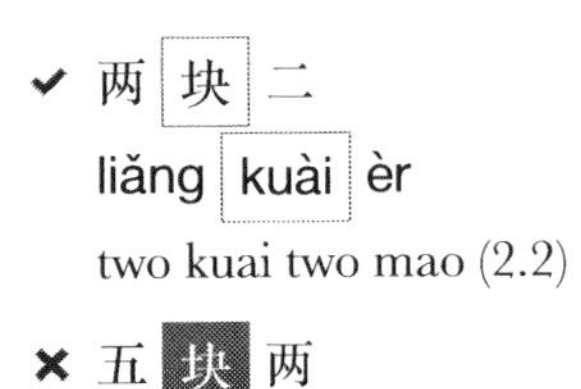

✔ 两 块 二

liǎng kuài èr

two kuai two mao (2.2)

✘ 五 块 两

wǔ kuài liǎng

✔ 五 块 二

wǔ kuài èr

five kuai two mao (5.2)

The first number is the amount of whole RMB (or dollars etc.), and the second is the amount smaller units (e.g. cents). So "3.86 RMB" is

- 三 块 八毛六

  sān kuài bā máo liù

  three kuai eight mao six fen (3.86)

And if there's no smaller unit, e.g. "3 RMB," you can just say:

- 三 块

  sān kuài

  Three kuai

块 (kuài) is the more common, informal way to talk about money. More formally you can use 元 (yuán) in exactly the same way. This is similar to the difference between "dollars" and "bucks" in American English, or "pounds" and "quid" in British English. 块 (kuài) is appropriate in more situations than "bucks" or "quid," though.

Similar to

- Approximating with sequential numbers (A2), page 213
- Indicating a number in excess

Expressing "every" with "mei" (A2)

In this article we will look at the structure for saying "every" in Chinese, which is slightly more involved than just throwing in the word 每 (měi).

Structure

The pronoun 每 (měi) covers the meanings of "each" and "every." It should normally be used with a measure word and used with 都 (dōu)[1] in a complete sentence.

 每 + Measure Word + Noun + 都

Note that there are some words that don't use measure words because they themselves are already measure words. For example: 天 (tiān), 年 (nián), 周 (zhōu), 次 (cì) etc.

Examples

- 每个菜都好吃。
  Měi gè cài dōu hěn hǎochī.
  Every dish is delicious.
- 你每个人都认识吗?
  Nǐ měi gè rén dōu rènshi ma?
  Do you know every person?
- 老板每个月都出差。
  Lǎobǎn měi gè yuè dōu chūchāi.
  The boss goes on business trips every month.
- 他每天都不吃早饭。
  Tā měi tiān dōu bù chī zǎofàn.
  Every morning he skips breakfast.
- 他每年都来中国。
  Tā měi nián dōu lái Zhōngguó.
  He comes to China every year.

1. Emphasizing quantity with "dou" (A2), page 133

- 我每个星期都给妈妈打电话。
  Wǒ měi gè xīngqī dōu gěi māma dǎ diànhuà.
  I give mom a phone call every week.
- 这个班的每个学生都很聪明。
  Zhège bān de měi gè xuéshēng dōu hěn cōngming.
  Each of the students in this class are very smart.
- 老师每天都给我们很多作业。
  Lǎoshī měi tiān dōu gěi wǒmen hěn duō zuòyè.
  Every day the teacher gives us a lot of homework.
- 我们每周都要开会。
  Wǒmen měi zhōu dōu yào kāihuì.
  Every week we need to have a meeting.
- 他们每个周末都去公园。
  Tāmen měi gè zhōumò dōu qù gōngyuán.
  Every weekend they go to the park.

Similar to

- The "all" adverb "dou" (A1), page 15
- Emphasizing quantity with "dou" (A2), page 133
- Measure words for counting (A2), page 328
- Expressing "every time" with "mei" and "dou"
- Measure words for verbs

Expressing "half" with "ban" (A2)

The Chinese word 半 (bàn) means "half." That's simple enough, but what can get slightly tricky is the rules for how it combines with measure words.

Basic Usage

Used Alone

Structure

You'll need to use a measure word (Measure Word) in this structure.

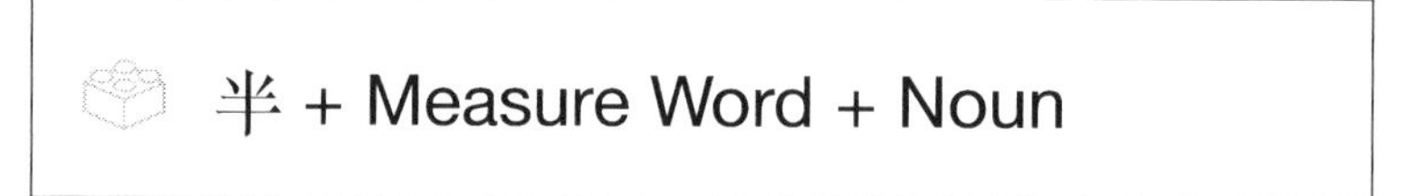

Examples

The measure words are also indicated below.

With a Number

When it's more than just a half, then 半 (bàn) comes after the measure word instead of before. It's the difference between "half an hour" and "an hour and a half."

- 半 个 小时
  bàn gè xiǎoshí
  half an hour
- 一 个 半 小时
  yī gè bàn xiǎoshí
  an hour and a half

The order is actually basically the same as what we do in English (we just don't have so many pesky measure words to keep track of in English!).

Structure

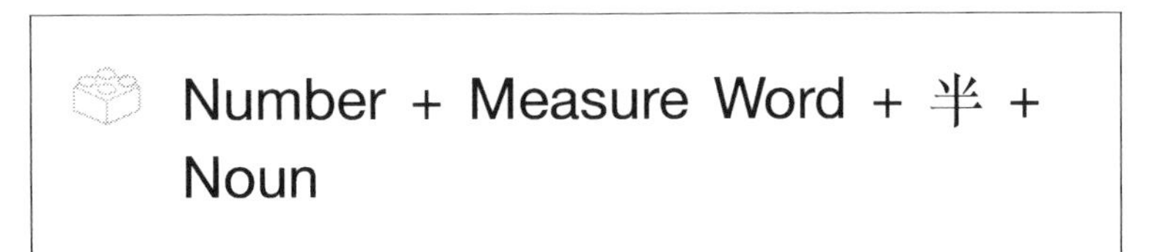

Examples

- 三 个 半 小时
  sān gè bàn xiǎoshí
  three and a half hours
- 两 个 半 月
  liǎng gè bàn yuè
  two and a half months
- 一 斤 半 水果
  yī jīn bàn shuǐguǒ
  one and a half jin of fruit

  One "jin" = 500g
- 一 瓶 半 白酒
  yī píng bàn báijiǔ
  one and a half bottles of wine
- 四 块 半 巧克力
  sì kuài bàn qiǎokèlì
  four and a half pieces of chocolate

Notable Exceptions

There are some words that act as their own measure words, notably the time words 天 (tiān), meaning "day," and 年 (nián), meaning "year."

Used Alone

Structure

Examples

- 半天
  bàn tiān
  half a day
- 半年
  bàn nián
  half a year

Note that you do *not* need to use 个 (gè) here; in fact, it's *wrong* to do so:

- ✗ 半个天
  bàn gè tiān
  half a day
- ✗ 半个年
  bàn gè nián
  half a year

With a Number

天 (tiān) and 年 (nián) aren't the *only* words that take this alternate pattern, but they're the two key ones you need to learn first.

Structure

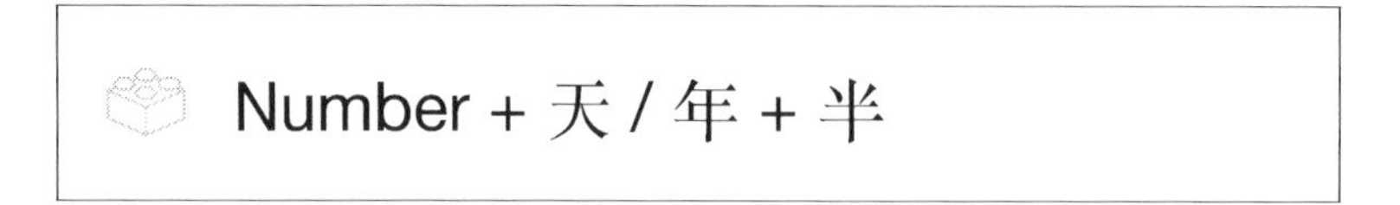

Examples

- 两天半
  liǎng tiān bàn
  two and a half days

- 一 年 半
  yī nián bàn
  a year and a half
- 三 天 半
  sān tiān bàn
  three and a half days
- 四 年 半
  sì nián bàn
  four and a half years

Measure words for counting (A2)

Chinese uses measure words, a type of word called classifiers in linguistics which are common in East Asian languages. Measure words have a number of important uses, but one of the first ways you'll need to use them is for counting. Chinese learners should master them, starting with the measure word 个 (gè).

Structure

Whenever you talk about the quantity of something in Chinese, you need a measure word.

Number + Measure Word + Noun

English does actually have measure words, it's just that most nouns usually don't need them. In English, most nouns are *count nouns* - they specify one instance of something. "An apple," for example. Some nouns are *mass nouns* and refer to something without specifying how much of it there is. Examples are "furniture," "paper," "water," etc. You can't say "a furniture"; you need a measure word: "a *piece* of furniture," "two *sheets* of paper," "three *glasses* of water," and so on.

In Chinese, *all* nouns are *mass nouns* so they all need measure words. Just as in English, different nouns are associated with different measure words (e.g. it wouldn't make sense to talk about "a glass of furniture" unless something went horribly wrong in the factory).

Examples

- 一个人
  yī gè rén
  a person
- 两只猫
  liǎng zhī māo
  two cats
- 三条鱼
  sān tiáo yú
  three fish

- 四 杯 牛奶
  sì bēi niúnǎi
  four glasses of milk
- 五 瓶 水
  wǔ píng shuǐ
  five bottles of water
- 六 块 巧克力
  liù kuài qiǎokèlì
  six pieces of chocolate
- 七 盒 茶叶
  qī hé cháyè
  seven boxes of tea leaves
- 八 台 电脑
  bā tái diànnǎo
  eight computers
- 九 支 玫瑰
  jiǔ zhī méiguī
  nine roses
- 十 个 美女
  shí gè měinǚ
  ten beautiful women

Also remember that there isn't a one-to-one relationship between nouns and measure words. One measure word can be used with several different nouns:

- 一 条 狗
  yī tiáo gǒu
  a dog
- 一 条 河
  yī tiáo hé
  a river
- 一 条 路
  yī tiáo lù
  a road

- 一 条 龙
  yī tiáo lóng
  a dragon
- 一 条 鱼
  yī tiáo yú
  a fish
- 一 条 短信
  yī tiáo duǎnxìn
  a text (message)

And one noun can take different measure words in different situations:

- 一 块 巧克力
  yī kuài qiǎokèlì
  a piece of chocolate
- 一 盒 巧克力
  yī hé qiǎokèlì
  a box of chocolate
- 一 颗 巧克力
  yī kē qiǎokèlì
  a small piece of chocolate

Similar to

- Age with "sui" (A1), page 26
- Measure word "ge" (A1), page 28
- Approximating with sequential numbers (A2), page 213
- Measure words in quantity questions (A2), page 331
- Measure words with "this" and "that" (A2), page 333
- Ordinal numbers with "di" (A2), page 335
- Measure words for verbs

Measure words in quantity questions (A2)

Quantity questions are phrases for asking questions like "how much?" or "how many?" You'll need to use the question word[1] 几 (jǐ) with measure words for this.

Asking About Small Numbers with 几 (jǐ)

Structure

You can use the quantity question word[1] 几 (jǐ) instead of a number to ask about quantity with measure words[2].

> Subj. + Verb + 几 + Measure Word + Noun?

Examples

- 他有 几 个孩子?
  Tā yǒu jǐ gè háizi?
  How many kids does he have?
- 你家有 几 个房间?
  Nǐ jiā yǒu jǐ gè fángjiān?
  How many rooms are there in your house?
- 他们在这里住 几 个星期?
  Tāmen zài zhèlǐ zhù jǐ gè xīngqī?
  How many weeks are they staying here?
- 你带了 几 件衣服?
  Nǐ dài le jǐ jiàn yīfu?
  How many pieces of clothing have you brought?
- 老板每天工作 几 个小时?
  Lǎobǎn měi tiān gōngzuò jǐ gè xiǎoshí?
  How many hours does the boss work every day?

---

1. Placement of question words (A1), page 105
2. Measure words for counting (A2), page 328

Asking About Big Numbers with 多少 (duōshao)

When the number is not certain but you assume it's definitely more than ten, it's better to ask the question with 多少 (duōshao) instead of 几 (jǐ).

Structure

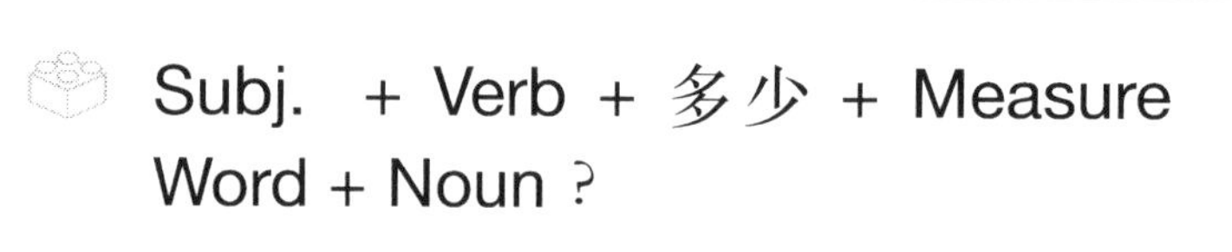

Examples

- 你去过 多少 个国家?
  Nǐ qù guo duōshao gè guójiā?
  How many countries have you been to?
- 你们班有 多少 个学生?
  Nǐmen bān yǒu duōshao gè xuéshēng?
  How many students are there in your class?
- 你大学的时候看了 多少 本书?
  Nǐ dàxué de shíhou kàn le duōshao běn shū?
  How many books did you read when you were in college?
- 他们昨天请了 多少 个朋友?
  Tāmen zuótiān qǐng le duōshao gè péngyou?
  How many friends did they invite yesterday?
- 上海有 多少 个外国公司?
  Shànghǎi yǒu duōshao gè wàiguó gōngsī?
  How many foreign companies are there in Shanghai?

Similar to

- Age with "sui" (A1), page 26
- Measure word "ge" (A1), page 28
- Measure words for counting (A2), page 328
- Measure words with "this" and "that" (A2), page 333
- Measure words for verbs

Measure words with “this” and “that” (A2)

In English, when you refer to “this table” or “that girl” you only need two words: “this” or “that” plus the noun you’re referring to. In Chinese, though, you also need a measure word in the middle between the two. In the very beginning you can get away with using 个 (gè)[1] for everything, but pretty soon you’re going to have to start using other measure words in these simple phrases.

Structure

If you use 这 (zhè) or 那 (nà) before a noun, you also need to include a measure word before the noun.

Examples

Note: In this usage, the tone of 个 (gè) tends to soften, so it’s represented below as a neutral tone.

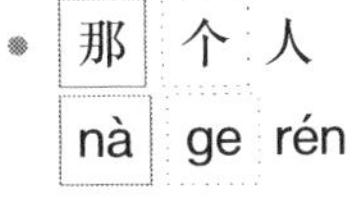

- 那 个 人
  nà ge rén
  that person
- 这 本 书
  zhè běn shū
  this book
- 那 件 事
  nà jiàn shì
  that matter (in the sense of business, affair, or thing)
- 这 瓶 啤酒
  zhè píng píjiǔ
  this bottle of beer
- 那 个 房间
  nà ge fángjiān
  that room

---

1. Measure word “ge” (A1), page 28

- 那 台 电脑
  nà tái diànnǎo
  that new computer
- 这 只 猫
  zhè zhī māo
  that cat
- 那 条 河
  nà tiáo hé
  that river
- 这 件 衣服
  zhè jiàn yīfu
  this piece of clothing

Although we didn't get into it here, the same pattern holds true when you use 哪 (nǎ) to ask "which?"

Similar to

- Measure word "ge" (A1), page 28
- Expressing "some" with "yixie" (A2), page 315
- Measure words for counting (A2), page 328
- Measure words in quantity questions (A2), page 331
- Measure words for verbs

Ordinal numbers with "di" (A2)

Also known as: 序数 (xùshù), ordinals and sequence numbers.

We use ordinal numbers to express things like "number one" or "second," so mastering them in Chinese is important. Fortunately, they are also very easy to learn by just adding the prefix 第 (dì).

Basic Usage

In English, there are four different suffixes for ordinal numbers: *-st*, *-nd*, *-rd* and *-th*. Chinese makes things a lot simpler by using one prefix for all ordinal numbers: 第 (dì). This character is simply placed in front of the number:

Structure

第 + Number

Examples

Chinese	English
第一 dì-yī	The first
第二 dì-èr	The second
第三 dì-sān	The third
第四 dì-sì	The fourth
第五 dì-wǔ	The fifth
第六 dì-liù	The sixth
第七 dì-qī	The seventh
第八 dì-bā	The eighth

第九 dì-jiǔ	The ninth
第十 dì-shí	The tenth

Full Pattern with Measure Words

You can also add in a measure word and a noun to make the structure a bit fuller.

Structure

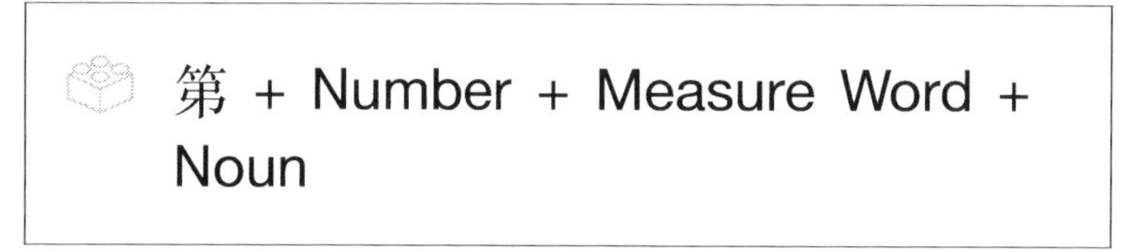

Examples

- 我是 第一 个 到公司的人。
  Wǒ shì dì-yī gè dào gōngsī de rén.
  I'm the first person that came to the office.
- 他要坐早上 第一 班 地铁去上班。
  Tā yào zuò zǎoshang dì-yī bān dìtiě qù shàngbān.
  He needs to take the first train in the morning to go to work.
- 小李是她的 第三 个 男朋友。
  Xiǎo Lǐ shì tā de dì-sān gè nánpéngyou.
  Little Li is her third boyfriend.
- 我的 第一 个 中文老师是美国人。
  Wǒ de dì-yī gè Zhōngwén lǎoshī shì Měiguó rén.
  My first Chinese teacher was American.
- 爸爸的 第一 个 手机是 NOKIA。
  Bàba de dì-yī gè shǒujī shì NOKIA.
  Dad's first cell phone was a Nokia.

- 你的 第一 个 工作是什么？
  Nǐ de dì-yī gè gōngzuò shì shénme?
  What was your first job?
- 到美国的 第二 个 月，我找到了工作。
  Dào Měiguó de dì-èr gè yuè, wǒ zhǎodào le gōngzuò .
  I found a job the second month I was in the USA.
- 第二 行 第五 个 汉字怎么读？
  Dì-èr háng dì-wǔ gè Hànzì zěnme dú?
  How do you read the fifth character from the second line?
- 这次考试，我是我们班 第一 。
  Zhè cì kǎoshì, wǒ shì wǒmen bān dì-yī.
  On this test, I was first in our class.
- 这次比赛，我们班 第一 ，他们班 第二 。
  Zhè cì bǐsài, wǒmen bān dì-yī, tāmen bān dì-èr.
  In this contest, our class is the first, their class is the second.

Note that there are some words that don't use measure words because they themselves are already measure words. For example: 天 (tiān), 年 (nián), 周 (zhōu), 次 (cì), etc.

- 第一 天 ，我们在宾馆里。
  Dì-yī tiān , wǒmen zài bīnguǎn lǐ.
  On the first day, we will be in the hotel.
- 来上海以后的 第二 年 ，他开了这家公司。
  Lái Shànghǎi yǐhòu de dì-èr nián , tā kāi le zhè jiā gōngsī.
  He started this company his second year after coming to Shanghai.
- 下个月的 第一 周 老板要出差。
  Xià gè yuè de dì-yī zhōu , lǎobǎn yào chūchāi.
  The boss needs to go on a business trip the first week of next month.
- 这是我 第一 次 去北京。
  Zhè shì wǒ dì-yī cì qù Běijīng.
  This is my first time going to Beijing.

Exceptions

Note that some nouns can form ordinals without 第 (dì). With these, the number can be used directly. For example, 七楼 (qī lóu) is "the seven*th* floor," even though there is no 第 (dì).

Chinese	English	Example
楼 lóu	floor (of a building)	七楼 qī lóu
层 céng	floor (of a building)	一层 yī céng

Similar to

- Age with "sui" (A1), page 26
- Measure word "ge" (A1), page 28
- Measure words for counting (A2), page 328

Asking why with "zenme" (A2)

Aside from just meaning "how,"[1] 怎么 (zěnme) can also be used to ask "why" or "how come."

Basic Usage

With a Verb

Structure

Similar to the question word 为什么 (wèishénme), questions can also be asked with 怎么 (zěnme).

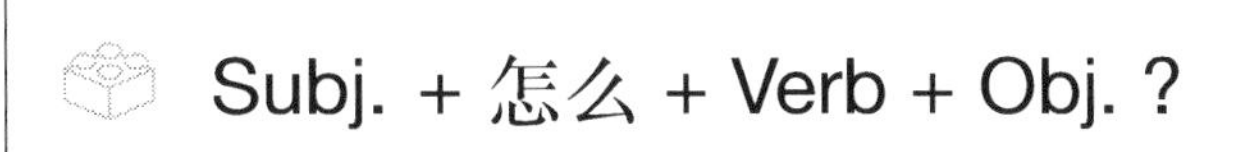

Subj. + 怎么 + Verb + Obj. ?

This has similar connotations to saying "how come" in English. It not only asks why, but expresses some surprise at the situation, and in some cases even disagreement with it.

Examples

- 他 怎么 还没来?
  Tā zěnme hái méi lái?
  How come he's not here yet?
- 你们 怎么 打人?
  Nǐmen zěnme dǎ rén?
  How can you hit people?
- 他帮了你，你 怎么 不说"谢谢"？
  Tā bāng le nǐ, nǐ zěnme bù shuō "xièxie"?
  He helped you. How come you didn't say thank you?
- 你结婚的时候 怎么 不告诉我?
  Nǐ jiéhūn de shíhou zěnme bù gàosu wǒ?
  How come you didn't tell me when you got married?
- 我们还没开始吃，他 怎么 已经吃完了?
  Wǒmen hái méi kāishǐ chī, tā zěnme yǐjīng chī wán le?
  We haven't started eating yet. How come he has already finished eating?

---

1. How to do something with "zenme" (A1), page 79

- 今天是星期一，你 怎么 不去上班？
  Jīntiān shì Xīngqīyī, nǐ zěnme bù qù shàngbān?
  Today is Monday. Why aren't you going to work?

With an Adjective

Structure

In this case, it's most common to negate the adjective after 怎么 (zěnme).

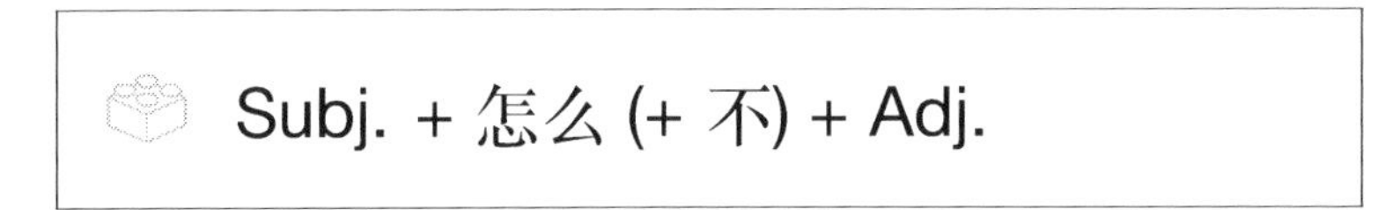

Examples

- 水 怎么 不热？
  Shuǐ zěnme bù rè?
  Why is the water not hot?
- 这里的川菜 怎么 不辣？
  Zhèlǐ de chuāncài zěnme bù là?
  Why is the Sichuan food here not spicy?
- 他亲了你，你 怎么 不高兴？
  Tā qīn le nǐ, nǐ zěnme bù gāoxìng?
  He kissed you. How come you're not happy?
- 她的小猫死了，她 怎么 不难过？
  Tā de xiǎomāo sǐ le, tā zěnme bù nánguò?
  Her kitten died. Why isn't she sad?
- 每天工作十二个小时，你 怎么 不累？
  Měi tiān gōngzuò shí'èr gè xiǎoshí, nǐ zěnme bù lèi?
  Every day you work 12 hours. Why are you not tired?

"Why So…" Usage

Structure

One pattern this use of 怎么 (zěnme) frequently appears in is with 这么 (zhème) or 那么 (nàme). (For more on 这么 (zhème) and 那么 (nàme), see adjectives with "name" and "zheme.")

Subj. + 怎么 + 这么 / 那么 + Adj.

This use of 怎么 (zěnme) could be translated as either "how" or "why"; the actual meaning sort of falls in the fuzzy region between the two. In any case, it's used to express disbelief: *how can (something) be so (adjective)?!*

Examples

- 他 怎么 那么懒?
  Tā zěnme nàme lǎn?
  How can he be this lazy?
- 昨天 怎么 那么冷?
  Zuótiān zěnme nàme lěng?
  How could it be so cold yesterday?
- 这些人 怎么 这么吵?
  Zhèxiē rén zěnme zhème chǎo?
  How can these people so loud?
- 北京的空气 怎么 那么差?
  Běijīng de kōngqì zěnme nàme chà?
  How can the air in Beijing be so bad?
- 你的汉语 怎么 这么好?
  Nǐ de Hànyǔ zěnme zhème hǎo?
  How is your Mandarin so good?

Similar to

- How to do something with "zenme" (A1), page 79
- Expressing "not often" with "bu zenme"

Questions with "le ma" (A2)

Asking questions about completed actions will involve using both 了 (le) and 吗 (ma). These are simply added to the end of a sentence or statement. Just make sure that 了 (le) comes first, followed by 吗 (ma).

Basic Usage

Structure

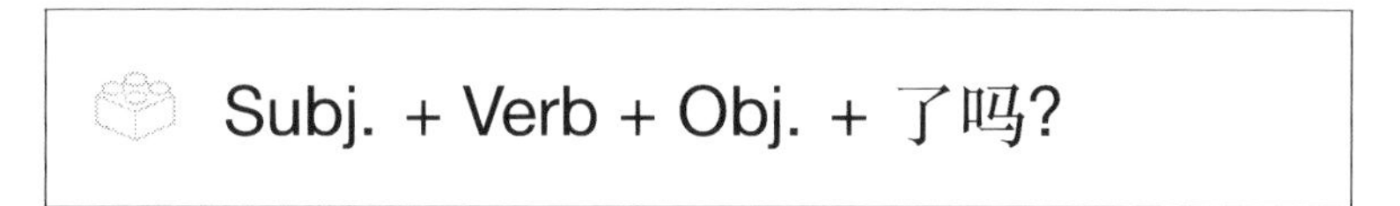

Note the order of 了 (le) and 吗 (ma).

Examples

- 你吃饭了吗？
  Nǐ chīfàn le ma?
  Did you eat?
- 老板走了吗？
  Lǎobǎn zǒu le ma?
  Did the boss leave?
- 你男朋友找到新工作了吗？
  Nǐ nánpéngyou zhǎodào xīn gōngzuò le ma?
  Has your boyfriend found a new job yet?
- 妈妈，你昨天给我打电话了吗？
  Māma, nǐ zuótiān gěi wǒ dǎ diànhuà le ma?
  Mom, did you call me yesterday?
- 你今天去上班了吗？
  Nǐ jīntiān qù shàngbān le ma?
  Did you go to work today?

With a Topic

Structure

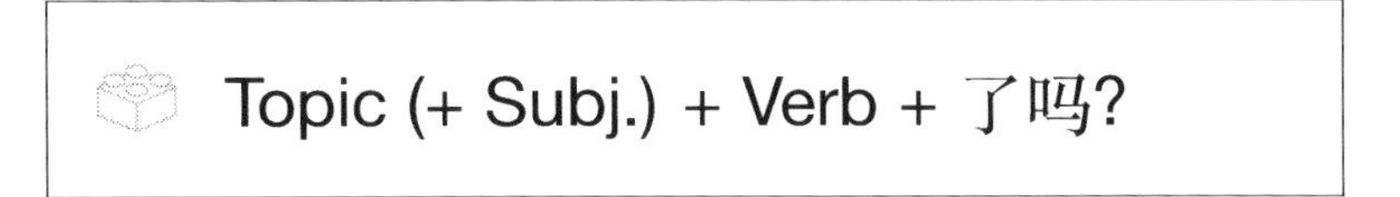

NOTE: in this structure, the topic is also the object for the verb.

Examples

- 晚饭你吃 了吗 ?
  Wǎnfàn nǐ chī le ma ?
  Did you eat dinner?
- 衣服你洗好 了吗 ?
  Yīfu nǐ xǐ hǎo le ma ?
  Have you finished washing the clothes?
- 作业你写完 了吗 ?
  Zuòyè nǐ xiě wán le ma ?
  Have you finishing doing homework?
- 这个电影你看 了吗 ?
  Zhège diànyǐng nǐ kàn le ma ?
  Have you seen this movie?
- 我的邮件你收到 了吗 ?
  Wǒ de yóujiàn nǐ shōudào le ma ?
  Have you received my email?

Finally, please note that this pattern is nothing more than the combination of the expressing completion with "le"[1] pattern and the yes/no questions with "ma"[2] pattern.

Similar to

- Yes-no questions with "ma" (A1), page 120
- Advanced yes-no questions with "ma"

1. Expressing completion with "le" (A2), page 236
2. Yes-no questions with "ma" (A1), page 120

Cause and effect with "yinwei" and "suoyi" (A2)

You will often come across 因为…… 所以…… (yīnwèi... suǒyǐ...) in both written and spoken Chinese. This pattern will give your Chinese a clear logical structure, and can help make you more persuasive.

Using 因为 (yīnwèi) by Itself to Explain Causes

A common way to explain causes in Chinese is with 因为 (yīnwèi). This is equivalent to "because" in English. Usually 因为 (yīnwèi) will begin a new phrase in a sentence.

Structure

In this structure, we first state the result, and then give the reason in the next statement after the 因为 (yīnwèi).

Result, 因为 + Reason

Examples

- 他学得很快，因为 他很聪明。
  Tā xué de hěn kuài, yīnwèi tā hěn cōngming.
  He learns fast because he is smart.
- 我爱吃四川菜，因为 很辣。
  Wǒ ài chī Sìchuān cài, yīnwèi hěn là.
  I love eating Sichuan food because it's very spicy.
- 我在学习中文，因为 我想去中国。
  Wǒ zài xuéxí Zhōngwén, yīnwèi wǒ xiǎng qù Zhōngguó.
  I am studying Chinese because I want to go to China.
- 我不喜欢她，因为 她不友好。
  Wǒ bù xǐhuan tā, yīnwèi tā bù yǒuhǎo.
  I don't like her because she is very unfriendly.
- 今天我们很忙，因为 有很多工作。
  Jīntiān wǒmen hěn máng, yīnwèi yǒu hěn duō gōngzuò.
  We are very busy today because we have lots of work.

Using 所以 (suǒyǐ) by Itself to Explain Results

Just as 因为 (yīnwèi) can be used to explain causes, 所以 (suǒyǐ) can be used to explain results. This is the equivalent of "so···" or "therefore···" in English.

Structure

This pattern is similar to the expression using both 因为 (yīnwèi) and 所以 (suǒyǐ), but it leaves out the beginning 因为 (yīnwèi). This structure is more informal.

Examples

- 汉字太难了，所以我不想学。
  Hànzì tài nán le, suǒyǐ wǒ bù xiǎng xué.
  Chinese characters are too hard, so I don't want to study them.
- 她很漂亮，所以很多男孩喜欢她。
  Tā hěn piàoliang, suǒyǐ hěn duō nánhái xǐhuan tā.
  She is beautiful, so a lot of boys like her.
- 他找到工作了，所以很高兴。
  Tā zhǎodào gōngzuò le, suǒyǐ hěn gāoxìng.
  He found a job so he's happy.
- 我太忙了，所以没有时间给你打电话。
  Wǒ tài máng le, suǒyǐ méiyǒu shíjiān gěi nǐ dǎ diànhuà.
  I was too busy, so I didn't have time to give you a call.
- 我们公司有很多外国人，所以我们要说英文。
  Wǒmen gōngsī yǒu hěn duō wàiguó rén, suǒyǐ wǒmen yào shuō Yīngwén.
  There are a lot of foreigners in our company, so we need to speak English.

Using 因为 (yīnwèi) and 所以 (suǒyǐ) Together

The full pattern 因为······ 所以······ (yīnwèi... suǒyǐ...) is used to clearly indicate cause and effect. They could be thought of as equating to: "Since happened, so happened." It sounds weird to use both "since" and "so" in one sentence in English, but it makes everything crystal clear in Chinese.

Structure

因为 + Cause, 所以 + Effect

This expresses that because of *cause*, therefore there is a *result*.

Examples

- 因为 我有一个中国女朋友，所以 我要学中文。
  Yīnwèi wǒ yǒu yī gè Zhōngguó nǚpéngyou, suǒyǐ wǒ yào xué Zhōngwén.
  Since I have a Chinese girlfriend, I need to study Chinese.
- 因为 他生病了，所以 没去上课。
  Yīnwèi tā shēngbìng le, suǒyǐ méi qù shàngkè.
  Since he was sick, he didn't go to class.
- 因为 我很累，所以 要休息。
  Yīnwèi wǒ hěn lèi, suǒyǐ yào xiūxi.
  I'm very tired, so I want to rest.
- 因为 太远了，所以 我不想去。
  Yīnwèi tài yuǎn le, suǒyǐ wǒ bù xiǎng qù.
  Since it's too far, I don't want to go.
- 因为 太忙，所以 我们没有时间吃中饭。
  Yīnwèi tài máng, suǒyǐ wǒmen méiyǒu shíjiān chī zhōngfàn.
  We were too busy, so none of us had time to eat lunch.

Similar to

- Expressing "then…" with "name"
- Expressing "since" with "jiran"
- Expressing "therefore" with "yinci"
- Stating the effect before the cause
- Using "because" with "er" to indicate effect

Expressing “about to happen” with “le” (A2)

Remember that 了 (le) is not only for the past! When something is *about to happen,* you can also indicate this using 了 (le). Normally it is paired with a 快 (kuài), 快要 (kuàiyào) or a 要 (yào). This is a special form of using 了 to indicate a change of situation[1].

快…… 了 (kuài… le) with Verbs

When using “快…… 了” (kuài… le) with verbs, it takes on a meaning similar to the English “just about to.” Normally you can add 要 (yào) before the verb.

Structure

Examples

- 我们快到了。
  Wǒmen kuài dào le.
  We're almost there.
- 快下雨了，我们走吧。
  Kuài xiàyǔ le, wǒmen zǒu ba.
  It's going to rain soon. Let's go.
- 快要过年了，你什么时候回家?
  Kuài yào guònián le, nǐ shénme shíhou huíjiā?
  It's almost Chinese New Year. When are you going back to your hometown?
- 我女朋友快要过生日了。
  Wǒ nǚpéngyou kuài yào guò shēngrì le.
  My girlfriend is about to have her birthday.

---

1. Change of state with “le” (A2), page 226

- 快 下车 了 ，你再等一会儿。
  Kuài xiàchē le, nǐ zài děng yīhuìr.
  We're about to get off. Just wait a little while.

Notice that for some translations, it's more natural to use the English word "almost" instead of "soon."

快……了 (kuài... le) with Adjectives

In this structure, 快……了 (kuài... le) is closer to the meaning of "almost" in English.

Structure

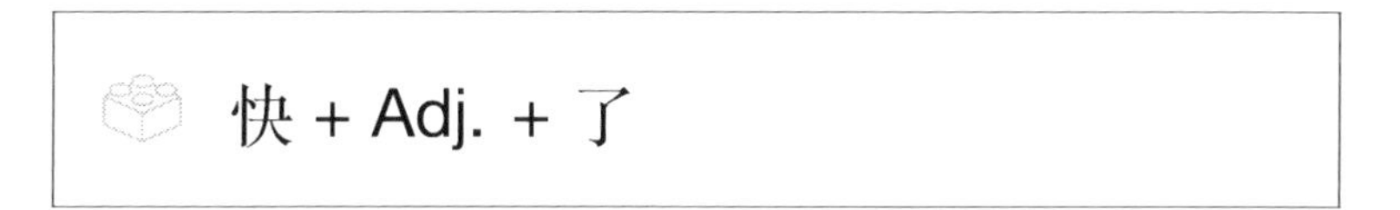

Examples

- 天 快 黑 了 。
  Tiān kuài hēi le.
  It's almost getting dark.
- 我 快 好 了 。
  Wǒ kuài hǎo le.
  I'm almost ready.
- 饭 快 凉 了 。
  Fàn kuài liáng le.
  The food is about to be cold.
- 这些脏衣服 快 臭 了 。
  Zhèxiē zāng yīfu kuài chòu le.
  These dirty clothes are about to smell bad.
- 不能再喝了，我 快 醉 了 。
  Bù néng zài hē le, wǒ kuài zuì le.
  I can't drink another, I am almost drunk.

要……了 (yào... le) with Verbs

Structure

You can also just use 要 (yào) before the verb, without 快 (kuài).

Subj. + 要 + Verb / Verb Phrase / Adj. + 了

Note that occasionally you'll see adjectives (instead of verbs) in this pattern as well.

Examples

- 我要生气了！
  Wǒ yào shēngqì le!
  I'm going to get angry!
- 他们的孩子要出生了。
  Tāmen de háizi yào chūshēng le.
  Their child is about to be born.
- 9 点了，超市要关门了。
  Jiǔ diǎn le, chāoshì yào guānmén le.
  It's 9 o'clock. The supermarket is about to close.
- 我最好的朋友要结婚了！
  Wǒ zuìhǎo de péngyou yào jiéhūn le!
  My best friend is about to get married!
- 圣诞节要到了，你有什么打算?
  Shèngdànjié yào dào le, nǐ yǒu shénme dǎsuàn?
  It's almost Christmas. What plans do you have?

Similar to

- Expressing "be going to" with "yao" (A1), page 67
- Auxiliary verb "yao" and its multiple meanings (A2), page 262

Expressing "everything" with "shenme dou" (A2)

什么⋯⋯都 (shénme... dōu) is a pattern often used to express "all" or "everything." Because it's not just one word, though, it can be a little tricky to get the hang of at first.

Basic Usage

Structure

In this structure, 都 (dōu) is more frequently used than 也 (yě)。

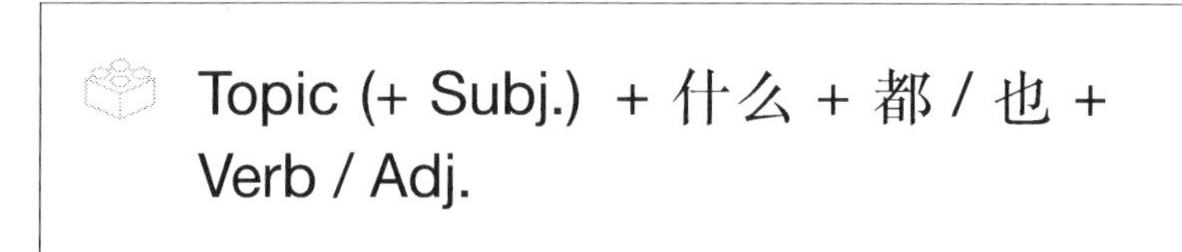

In some sentences, there will be a subject after the topic in the pattern above. See the following sentences for examples.

Examples

When used in the positive sense, it is more natural to follow 什么 (shénme) with 都 (dōu) rather than 也 (yě) to express "everything."

- 我觉得这里的菜 什么 都 好吃。
  Wǒ juéde zhèlǐ de cài shénme dōu hǎochī.
  I think everything is delicious here.
- 中国的历史爸爸 什么 都 知道。
  Zhōngguó de lìshǐ bàba shénme dōu zhīdào.
  My dad knows everything about Chinese history.
- 工作的事情老公 什么 都 跟我说。
  Gōngzuò de shìqing lǎogōng shénme dōu gēn wǒ shuō.
  My husband tells me everything about work stuff.
- 妈妈做的菜我 什么 都 喜欢。
  Māma zuò de cài wǒ shénme dōu xǐhuan.
  I like everything that mom cooks.

- 我女朋友觉得外国的东西 什么 都 好。
  Wǒ nǚpéngyou juéde wàiguó de dōngxi shénme dōu hǎo.
  My girlfriend thinks that all foreign things are good.

Structure with a Noun

Structure

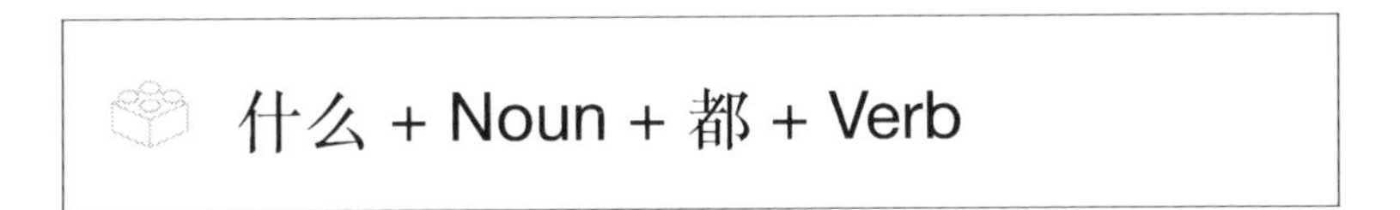

Examples

- 我们 什么 果汁 都 喝。
  Wǒmen shénme guǒzhī dōu hē.
  We drink any kind of fruit juice.
- 她 什么 衣服 都 是黑色的。
  Tā shénme yīfu dōu shì hēisè de.
  All of her clothes are black.
- 妈妈做的 什么 菜 都 好吃。
  Māma zuò de shénme cài dōu hǎochī.
  All of the dishes mom makes are tasty.
- 我男朋友 什么 运动 都 喜欢。
  Wǒ nánpéngyou shénme yùndòng dōu xǐhuan.
  My boyfriend likes all kinds of sports.
- 你不应该 什么 话 都 跟他说。
  Nǐ bù yīnggāi shénme huà dōu gēn tā shuō.
  You shouldn't tell him everything.

Negative Structure

Structures

The negative structure simply adds a 不 (bù) or a 没 (méi) after the 都 (dōu) / 也 (yě). Instead of "all" or "everything," this expresses "none" or "not any."

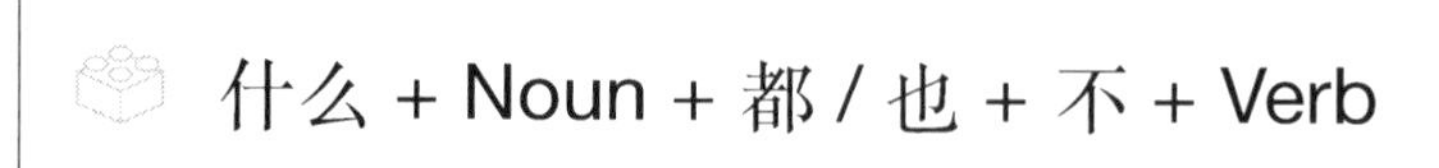

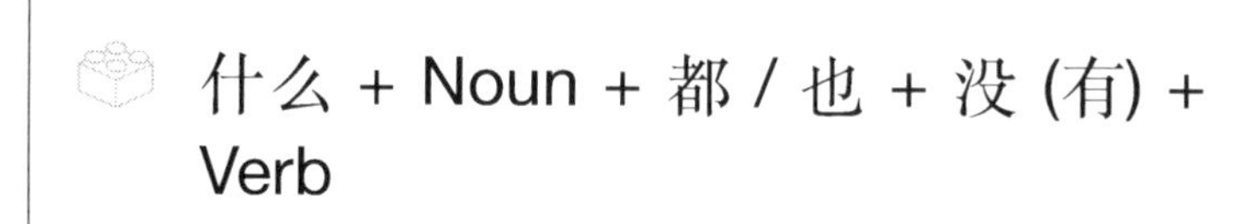

Examples

- 生病以后，爸爸 什么 酒 都 不 能喝了。
  Shēngbìng yǐhòu, bàba shénme jiǔ dōu bù néng hē le.
  After dad got sick, he can't drink any kind of alcohol.
- 老板现在很生气，什么 人 也 不 见。
  Lǎobǎn xiànzài hěn shēngqì, shénme rén yě bù jiàn.
  The boss is very angry. He's doesn't want to see anybody.
- 今天我不舒服，什么 东西 都 没 吃。
  Jīntiān wǒ bù shūfu, shénme dōngxi dōu méi chī.
  Today I don't feel well, so I didn't eat anything.
- 昨天开会的时候，她 什么 话 也 没 说。
  Zuótiān kāihuì de shíhou, tā shénme huà yě méi shuō.
  She didn't say anything at yesterday's meeting.
- 你在家里怎么 什么 事 都 不 做?
  Nǐ zài jiālǐ zěnme shénme shì dōu bù zuò?
  How come you haven't done anything at home?

Similar to

- Expressing “every time” with “mei” and “dou”
- Expressing “every” with question words
- Expressing “not at all” with “yidianr ye bu”
- Indicating the whole with “quan”
- Referring to “all” using “suoyou”

Expressing "stop doing" with "bie... le" (A2)

You may know how to make negative commands with "bie,"[1] but what if someone is already doing it? The pattern 别……了 (bié... le) is all you need to tell someone to *STOP DOING THAT* (which they're already doing).

Structure

别 + Verb / Verb Phrase + 了

Instead of just a verb, it can also be a verb phrase.

Examples

- 别说了，我不想听。
  Bié shuō le, wǒ bù xiǎng tīng.
  Stop talking. I don't want to listen.
- 别问了，我不想说。
  Bié wèn le, wǒ bù xiǎng shuō.
  Stop asking. I don't want to say.
- 别做了，明天再做吧。
  Bié zuò le, míngtiān zài zuò ba.
  Stop doing it. Do it tomorrow.
- 别看了，睡觉！
  Bié kàn le, shuìjiào!
  Stop watching. Go to sleep!
- 别哭了，烦死了。
  Bié kū le, fán sǐ le.
  Stop crying, it's so annoying.
- 别笑了，别人都在看你。
  Bié xiào le, biérén dōu zài kàn nǐ.
  Stop laughing. Other people are looking at you.

1. Negative commands with "bie" (A2), page 156

- 别 吃 了 ，我们要迟到了。
  Bié chī le, wǒmen yào chídào le.
  Stop eating. We're going to be late.
- 别 玩 了 ，去写作业。
  Bié wán le, qù xiě zuòyè.
  Stop playing. Do your homework.
- 别 买 了 ，太贵了！
  Bié mǎi le, tài guì le!
  Don't buy it. It's too expensive!

In this case, the person probably isn't actually paying, but they're about to.

- 别 喝 了 ，你已经喝了五杯了。
  Bié hē le, nǐ yǐjīng hē le wǔ bēi le.
  Stop drinking. You've already drunk five glasses.

Expressing location with "zai... shang / xia / li" (A2)

You can use 在 (zài) to express location[1], but this article will explain how to use 在 (zài) to express location in relation to another object. This way, you can describe if something is "on the table" or "in the room."

在 (zài) with "Big Locations"

If you're talking about a "big place," like a country or city, then all you need is 在 (zài) and the name of the place.

Structure

在 + Place

Examples

For example, these phrases are fine just as they are:

- 在中国
  zài Zhōngguó
  in China
- 在美国
  zài Měiguó
  in the USA
- 在上海
  zài Shànghǎi
  in Shanghai
- 在纽约
  zài Niǔyuē
  in New York

You wouldn't want to add other words to the ends of these place names.

1. Indicating location with "zai" before verbs (A2), page 288

在 (zài) with Specific Locations

To show where an object is in relation to another object, make a "sandwich" starting with 在 (zài), add a place, and then add one of the following words: 上 (shàng), 下 (xià), 里 (lǐ), 旁边 (pángbiān).

Structure

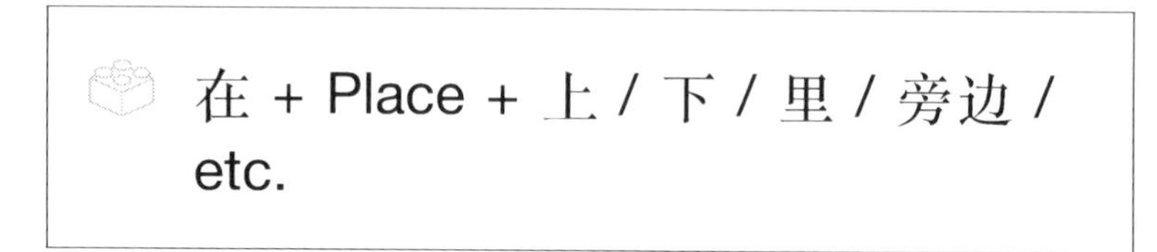

在 + Place + 上 / 下 / 里 / 旁边 / etc.

Notice that the "preposition" comes after the location and object that it modifies. That is, in English we say "on the table," but in Chinese, it is more like "at the table, on." This can be somewhat confusing, but don't worry. Once you start using this construction, it gets easy really quickly.

Examples

- 我 在 火车 上 。
  Wǒ zài huǒchē shàng.
  I am on the train.
- 他 在 楼 下 。
  Tā zài lóu xià.
  He is downstairs.
- Walmart 在 我家 旁边 。
  Walmart zài wǒ jiā pángbiān.
  Walmart is next to my house.
- 你的手机 在 包 里 吗?
  Nǐ de shǒujī zài bāo lǐ ma?
  Is your cell phone in the bag?
- 在 地铁 上 有很多人。
  Zài dìtiě shàng yǒu hěn duō rén.
  On the metro there are a lot of people.

Common Nouns of Locality

The little words that come after the location in the phrases above aren't really "prepositions." They are called "nouns of locality," or 方位词 (fāngwèicí) in Chinese. They actually tend to have several forms, which can be confusing if you're not used to them. The chart below shows their most common forms:

One-Character	Two-Character	English
上 shàng	上面 / 上边 shàngmiàn / shàngbian	top, above
下 xià	下面 / 下边 xiàmiàn / xiàbian	bottom, under
里 lǐ	里面 / 里边 lǐmiàn / lǐbian	inside
外 wài	外面 / 外边 wàimiàn / wàibian	outside
边 biān	旁边 pángbiān	side, beside
前 qián	前面 / 前边 qiánmiàn / qiánbian	front
后 hòu	后面 / 后边 hòumiàn / hòubian	back, behind
左 zuǒ	左边 zuǒbian	left
右 yòu	右边 yòubian	right

Abstract Uses

Some prepositions can be paired with more abstract concepts to form idiomatic phrases. These kinds of phrases can really make your Chinese sound polished. Later on you will learn about these idiomatic phrases with "zai".

Similar to

- Expressing existence in a place with "zai" (A1), page 54
- Indicating location with "zai" before verbs (A2), page 288
- Special cases of "zai" following verbs (A2), page 293

Comparing "bu" and "mei" (A2)

Both 不 (bù) and 没 (méi) can be placed in front of a verb or adjective to negate its meaning. However, 不 (bù) and 没 (méi) are not usually interchangeable, so it's important to learn when you must use 不 (bù) as opposed to 没 (méi), and vice versa.

不 (bù) Negates in the Present and Future

不 (bù) is generally used to negate an action that you *do not want to do* or *do not intend to do* (in the future). So expressing things like "I don't want to go" or "I'm not going" would be uses of 不 (bù).

Structure

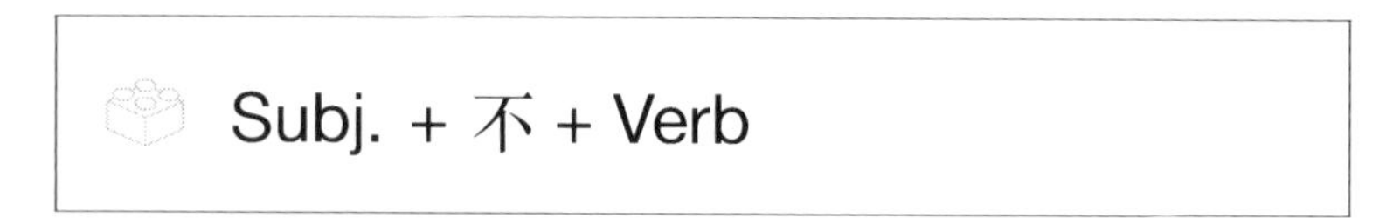

Examples

Whether it's "don't wanna do it" or "not gonna do it," use 不 (bù):

- 我今天晚上不喝酒。
  Wǒ jīntiān wǎnshang bù hējiǔ.
  Tonight I'm not going to drink.
- 爸爸不回来吃晚饭。
  Bàba bù huílái chī wǎnfàn.
  Dad is not coming back to eat dinner.
- 老板明天不来。
  Lǎobǎn míngtiān bù lái.
  The boss won't come tomorrow.
- 我知道这个周末不下雨。
  Wǒ zhīdào zhège zhōumò bù xiàyǔ.
  I know it's not going to rain this weekend.
- 你女朋友不跟你一起去吗?
  Nǐ nǚpéngyou bù gēn nǐ yīqǐ qù ma?
  Is your girlfriend not going with you?

不 (bù) Negates Habitual Actions

不 (bù) can be used to negate habitual actions, to express what you just aren't in the habit of doing, such as eating meat, or watching TV, or drinking alcohol. This is simply done by placing 不 (bù) in front of the verb.

Structure

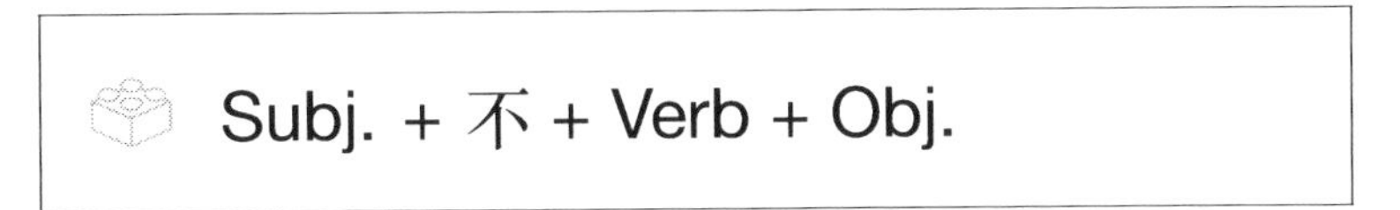

Examples

- 我 不 吃肉。
  Wǒ bù chī ròu.
  I don't eat meat.
- 你们都 不 喝酒吗?
  Nǐmen dōu bù hējiǔ ma?
  Do you all not drink alcohol?
- 他 不 喜欢说话。
  Tā bù xǐhuan shuōhuà.
  He doesn't like to speak.
- 你 不 用手机看书吗?
  Nǐ bù yòng shǒujī kàn shū ma?
  Do you not use your phone to read books?
- 你晚上 不 洗澡吗?
  Nǐ wǎnshang bù xǐzǎo ma?
  Don't you shower at night?

Please note that, while it is grammatically correct to use 没 (méi) in all the sentences above, 没 (méi) does not negate any *habitual* actions. The sentences above, if they contained 没 (méi) instead of 不 (bù), would express that the speaker *didn't do* the named activity (at one particular point *in the past*). So it would not be about *habitual actions*.

不 (bù) is Normally Used with Adjectives

When it comes to a simple negation of an adjective (such as "not cold"), use 不 (bù).

Structure

Examples

- 我们 不 饿。
  Wǒmen bù è.
  We're not hungry.
- 你 不 胖。
  Nǐ bù pàng.
  You are not fat.
- 我家 不 远。
  Wǒ jiā bù yuǎn.
  My home is not far.
- 今天 不 冷。
  Jīntiān bù lěng.
  Today it isn't cold.
- 我觉得 Starbucks 的咖啡 不 好喝。
  Wǒ juéde Starbucks de kāfēi bù hǎohē.
  I think the coffee at Starbucks isn't good.

不 (bù) is for Asking Questions

There are couple ways to use 不 (bù) to ask questions. One such way is through affirmative-negative questions[1]. This is done by stating a verb and then immediately repeating that verb in a negative state (with 不 (bù)).

Structure

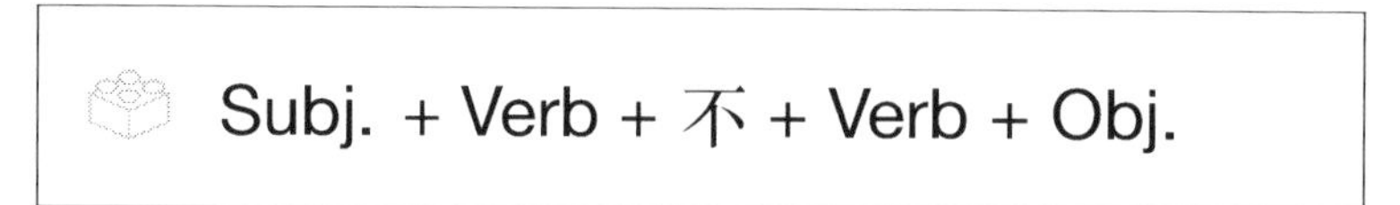

1. Affirmative-negative question (A1), page 99

Examples

- 你是不 是 我的老师？
  Nǐ shì bu shì wǒ de lǎoshī?
  Are you my teacher or not?
- 她想 不 想来？
  Tā xiǎng bu xiǎnglái?
  Does she want to come?
- 你爱 不 爱我？
  Nǐ ài bu ài wǒ?
  Do you love me or not?
- 你们周末上 不 上班？
  Nǐmen zhōumò shàng bu shàngbān?
  Do you all go to work on weekends?
- 你的外国朋友们喜 不 喜欢吃中国菜？
  Nǐ de wàiguó péngyoumen xǐ bu xǐhuan chī Zhōngguó cài?
  Do your foreign friends like to eat Chinese food?

不 (bù) can also be used to form tag questions[1]. Tag questions use the positive-negative question form, but are placed at the end of the sentence. Tag questions are used to seek approval or acceptance for a statement, very similar to the English "OK?" or "right?" You can't use 没 (méi) for this.

✗ 我们去吃饭，好 没 好？
Wǒmen qù chīfàn, hǎo méi hǎo?

✓ 我们去吃饭，好 不 好？
Wǒmen qù chīfàn, hǎo bu hǎo?
Let's go eat, is that OK?

✗ 你们是好朋友，对 没 对？
Nǐmen shì hǎo péngyou, duì méi duì?

✓ 你们是好朋友，对 不 对？
Nǐmen shì hǎo péngyou, duì bu duì?
You are good friends, right?

---

1. Tag questions with "bu" (A1), page 116

没 (méi) Negates Past Actions

没 (méi) and 没有 (méiyǒu) can both be used to negate actions that occurred in the past[1], or to say that something has not happened yet.

Structure

Subj. + 没 (有) + Verb + Obj.

Examples

✔ 他 没有 打电话给我。
Tā méiyǒu dǎ diànhuà gěi wǒ.
He did not give me a call.

✔ 你 没 去上班吗?
Nǐ méi qù shàngbān ma?
You didn't go to work?

✔ 我昨天 没 喝酒。
Wǒ zuótiān méi hējiǔ.
I did not drink alcohol yesterday.

✔ 妈妈 没有 做晚饭。
Māma méiyǒu zuò wǎnfàn.
Mom did not cook dinner.

✔ 他们吃完饭以后 没 付钱。
Tāmen chī wán fàn yǐhòu méi fù qián.
They didn't pay after they finished eating.

✘ 我昨天 不 喝酒。
Wǒ zuótiān bù hējiǔ.
I not drink wine yesterday.

✘ 我上个周末 不 跟他见面。
Wǒ shàng gè zhōumò bù gēn tā jiànmiàn.
I not meet with him last weekend.

---

1. Negation of past actions with “meiyou” (A1), page 81

× 上个月你 不 去北京吗?

Shàng gè yuè nǐ bù qù Běijīng?

You not go to Beijing last month?

There are a few things worth noting in these examples. For one, it is still grammatically correct to leave out the 有 (yǒu) in the sentences using 没有 (méiyǒu). Also, the sentences using 不 (bù) *would be* grammatically correct, if not for the time words telling us that it is definitely the **past** we're talking about.

Only 没 (méi) Negates 有 (yǒu)

没 (méi) can be used to negate the verb 有 (yǒu)[1] ("to have") to mean "do not have." You can only use 没 (méi) to convey this meaning. It is grammatically incorrect to use 不 (bù) to negate 有 (yǒu).

Structure

Subj. + 没有 + Obj.

Examples

× 我 不有 钱。

Wǒ bù yǒu qián.

✓ 我 没有 钱。

Wǒ méiyǒu qián.

I don't have money.

× 他 不有 女朋友。

Tā bù yǒu nǚpéngyou.

✓ 他 没有 女朋友。

Tā méiyǒu nǚpéngyou.

He doesn't have a girlfriend.

There are times when you can leave out 有 (yǒu) entirely while still expressing 没有 (méiyǒu), (meaning "to not have" or "there is no"). One well-known example of this is 没办法 (méi bànfǎ)[2] ("there is no way" [that's gonna happen]). Both 没 (méi) and 没有 (méiyǒu) are correct, however.

1. Negation of past actions with "meiyou" (A1), page 81
2. Inability with "mei banfa" (A2), page 286

- 我 没 办法。
  Wǒ méi bànfǎ.
  I don't have a way.
- 我 没有 办法。
  Wǒ méiyǒu bànfǎ.
  I don't have a way.

(You can also use 没办法 (méi bànfǎ)[1] to express other meanings.)

没 (méi) is for Making Comparisons

没 (méi) or 没有 (méiyǒu) can be used to make simple comparisons[2] meaning "not as… as…":

Structure

 Noun 1 + 没有 + Noun 2 + Adj.

Examples

- ✘ 你 不有 我高。
  Nǐ bù yǒu wǒ gāo.
- ✔ 你 没有 我高。
  Nǐ méiyǒu wǒ gāo.
  You are not as tall as me.
- ✘ 我的手机 不有 他的手机贵。
  Wǒ de shǒujī bù yǒu tā de shǒujī guì.
- ✔ 我的手机 没有 他的手机贵。
  Wǒ de shǒujī méiyǒu tā de shǒujī guì.
  My cell phone isn't as expensive as his.
- ✘ 我们都 不有 老板忙。
  Wǒmen dōu bù yǒu lǎobǎn máng.

---

1. Inability with "mei banfa" (A2), page 286
2. Basic comparisons with "meiyou" (A2), page 258

✔ 我们都 没有 老板忙。

Wǒmen dōu méiyǒu lǎobǎn máng.

We all are not as busy as the boss.

✖ 上海的冬天 不有 北京的冬天冷。

Shànghǎi de dōngtiān bù yǒu Běijīng de dōngtiān lěng.

✔ 上海的冬天 没有 北京的冬天冷。

Shànghǎi de dōngtiān méiyǒu Běijīng de dōngtiān lěng.

Shanghai winters are not as cold Beijing winters.

You can only use 没 (méi) or 没有 (méiyǒu) for this purpose, and **not** 不 (bù).

不 (bù) is Used Almost Exclusively with Certain Verbs

Certain verbs just don't get negated by 没 (méi) or 没有 (méiyǒu) ever. These include the verbs 是 (shì) ("to be") and 在 (zài) ("to be (in a place)"), as well as some psychological verbs such as 知道 (zhīdào) ("to know") and 认识 (rènshi) ("to know (a person)"). For these verbs, it's best to just take them on a case-by-case basis. Being aware of their existence can save you a fair bit of confusion.

✖ 他以前 没 是我的老板。

Tā yǐqián méi shì wǒ de lǎobǎn.

✔ 他以前 不 是我的老板。

Tā yǐqián bù shì wǒ de lǎobǎn.

He was not my boss before.

✖ 我 没 知道他要来。

Wǒ méi zhīdào tā yào lái.

✔ 我 不 知道他要来。

Wǒ bù zhīdào tā yào lái.

I didn't know he was coming.

✖ 他小时候 没 认识她。

Tā xiǎo shíhou méi rènshi tā.

✔ 他小时候 不 认识她。

Tā xiǎo shíhou bù rènshi tā.

He did not know her when he was young.

⚠ 昨天我 没 在家。
Zuótiān wǒ méi zài jiā.

Use of 没 with 在 is technically incorrect, but you sometimes hear it.

✔ 昨天我 不 在家。
Zuótiān wǒ bù zài jiā.
I was not home yesterday.

Note that in non-standard Mandarin you might encounter exceptions to this rule. It's still useful to know the rule!

Similar to

- Affirmative-negative question (A1), page 99
- Negation of "you" with "mei" (A1), page 12
- Negation of past actions with "meiyou" (A1), page 81
- Standard negation with "bu" (A1), page 85
- Tag questions with "bu" (A1), page 116
- Basic comparisons with "meiyou" (A2), page 258

Comparing "yao" and "xiang" (A2)

Both 要 (yào) and 想 (xiǎng) can essentially mean "want," but they can also be used in quite different ways, such as 想 (xiǎng) also meaning "to miss" when followed by a noun, and 要 (yào) also meaning "going to (do something)."

Followed by a Noun

Both 要 (yào) and 想 (xiǎng) may be followed by nouns, but pay attention to how the meaning of 想 (xiǎng) totally changes when used this way.

要 (yào) as "to Want"

Structure

In this pattern, 要 (yào) is directly followed by a thing (a noun), rather than by a verb. It is often used to buy something, or to order food at a restaurant.

It may be helpful to imagine a demanding child using this pattern to get stuff from his parents. This "*I want x!*" pattern can seem slightly impolite, but to the Chinese ear it's not as inherently rude as it may seem when translated directly into English. Tone of voice plays a key role when using this pattern in spoken Chinese.

Examples

- 你也 要 茶吗? *ordering in a restaurant*
  Nǐ yě yào chá ma?
  Do you also want tea?
- 我们都 要 咖啡。 *ordering in a cafe*
  Wǒmen dōu yào kāfēi.
  We all want coffee.
- 大家 要 不 要 米饭? *ordering in a restaurant*
  Dàjiā yào bù yào mǐfàn?
  Does everyone want rice?
- 你们 要 冰水还是热水? *ordering in a restaurant*
  Nǐmen yào bīng shuǐ háishì rè shuǐ?
  Do you want ice water or hot water?

- 谢谢，我什么都不 要 。 *ordering in a restaurant*

  Xièxiè, wǒ shénme dōu bù yào.

  Thank you. I don't need anything.

想 (xiǎng) as "to Miss"

Pay attention here: unlike "想 (xiǎng) + Verb," the meaning of 想 (xiǎng) in the "想 (xiǎng) + Noun" pattern becomes "to miss."

Structure

Examples

- 我 想 你。

  Wǒ xiǎng nǐ.

  I miss you.

- 我有点 想 我的家人。

  Wǒ yǒudiǎn xiǎng wǒ de jiārén.

  I sort of miss my family.

- 你们回美国以后，会 想 中国菜吗？

  Nǐmen huí Měiguó yǐhòu, huì xiǎng Zhōngguó cài ma?

  Will you all miss Chinese food after you go back to the U.S.?

- 你女朋友不在的时候，你会 想 她吗？

  Nǐ nǚpéngyou bù zài de shíhou, nǐ huì xiǎng tā ma?

  Do you miss your girlfriend when she is not around?

- 妈妈打电话的时候跟我说，她很 想 我。

  Māma dǎ diànhuà de shíhou gēn wǒ shuō, tā hěn xiǎng wǒ.

  Mom called me and said she misses me a lot.

Followed by a Verb

要 (yào) and 想 (xiǎng) have similar meanings when followed by verbs. The difference is rather subtle, but 要 (yào) can sound more urgent or demanding (sometimes even childish), while 想 (xiǎng) is usually a bit more mature and polite. Tone of voice plays a big role here as well, though, so don't be afraid of offending people by using 要 (yào); the word itself isn't rude.

要 (yào) as "Want to"

Structure

It might help to think of 要 (yào) in this sense as meaning "want to" and 想 (xiǎng) as meaning "would like to."

Examples

- 我要休息。
  Wǒ yào xiūxi.
  I want to rest.
- 你也要回家吗?
  Nǐ yě yào huíjiā ma?
  Do you also want to go home?
- 你们要喝什么?
  Nǐmen yào hē shénme?
  What do you want to drink?
- 我要帮老板做完这些工作。
  Wǒ yào bāng lǎobǎn zuò wán zhèxiē gōngzuò.
  I want to help the boss finish this work.
- 大家晚上要不要出去吃?
  Dàjiā wǎnshang yào bu yào chūqù chī?
  Does everyone want to go out to eat tonight?

想 (xiǎng) as "Would Like to"

Structure

It might help to think of 想 (xiǎng) as meaning "would like to" instead of "want to." In English, as well, "would like to" feels more indirect, and thus less demanding and more more polite.

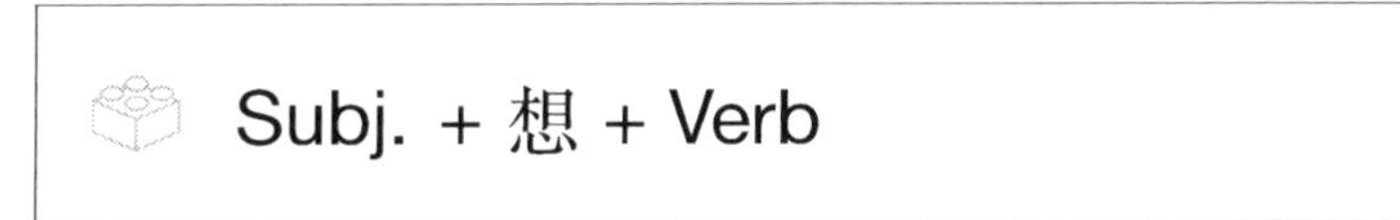

Examples

- 你 想 去吗?
  Nǐ xiǎng qù ma?
  Would you like to go?
- 我不 想 见她。
  Wǒ bù xiǎng jiàn tā.
  I wouldn't like to see her.
- 周末你们 想 看电影吗?
  Zhōumò nǐmen xiǎng kàn diànyǐng ma?
  Would you like to see a movie this weekend?
- 我 想 请你吃饭。
  Wǒ xiǎng qǐng nǐ chīfàn.
  I'd like to treat you to dinner.
- 他们春节不 想 回家吗?
  Tāmen Chūnjié bù xiǎng huíjiā ma?
  Don't they want to go back home for Spring Festival?

要 (yào) as "Going to"

要 is used to indicate plans for the near future, much like "going to" in English. 想 (xiǎng) is not used in this way.

Structure

Subj. + 要 + Verb

Examples

- 星期六我 要 去北京。
  Xīngqīliù wǒ yào qù Běijīng.
  I'm going to Beijing on Saturday.
- 下个月她 要 找新工作。
  Xià gè yuè tā yào zhǎo xīn gōngzuò.
  She is going to look for a new job next month.

- 这个周末你们 要 出去玩吗?
  Zhège zhōumò nǐmen yào chūqù wán ma?
  Are you going out partying this weekend?
- 结婚以后，你 要 跟父母住在一起吗?
  Jiéhūn yǐhòu, nǐ yào gēn nǐ fùmǔ zhù zài yīqǐ ma?
  Are you going to live together with your parents after you get married?
- 生完孩子以后，你太太 要 回去工作吗?
  Shēng wán háizi yǐhòu, nǐ tàitai yào huíqù gōngzuò ma?
  Is your wife going back to work after she finishes giving birth to the baby?

想要 (xiǎngyào) as "Want"

Structure

You can put 要 (yào) and 想 (xiǎng) together to make the word 想要 (xiǎngyào), which means "to want." You can put either nouns or verbs after it.

 Subj. + 想要 + Noun / Verb

Examples

- 你 想要 几个孩子?
  Nǐ xiǎngyào jǐ gè háizi?
  How many kids do you want to have?
- 我老婆总是 想要 最贵的包。
  Wǒ lǎopo zǒngshì xiǎngyào zuì guì de bāo.
  My wife always wants the most expensive bags.
- 她 想要 找一个有钱的男朋友。
  Tā xiǎngyào zhǎo yī gè yǒuqián de nánpéngyou.
  She wants to find a rich boyfriend.

- 你们为什么 想要 离开北京?
  Nǐmen wèishénme xiǎngyào líkāi Běijīng?
  Why do you all want to leave Beijing?
- 他 想要 帮你找一个更好的工作。
  Tā xiǎngyào bāng nǐ zhǎo yī gè gèng hǎo de gōngzuò.
  He wants to help you find a better job.

Glossary

We strive to avoid unnecessarily technical terms on the Chinese Grammar Wiki, but occasionally it's sort of necessary, and sometimes even useful (yes, really!). So to help you out, we've placed all of the grammatical terms related to Mandarin Chinese in one place. Each term has a page on the wiki with a more complete description, and many pages also have lists of grammar points related to the term.

List of Mandarin Grammar Terms

Action verb — *Also known as: 动作动词 (dòngzuò dòngcí) and 行为动词 (xíngwéi dòngcí).* Action verbs describe what a subject did, is doing, or will do, physically.

Action-measure complement — *Also known as: 动量补语 (dòng-liàng bǔyǔ).* Action-measure complements are words placed after a verb to show the frequency of action.

Adjective — *Also known as: 形容词 (xíngróngcí).* Adjectives are the "describing" words of a language. In Chinese, they have some characteristics that they don't have in English.

Adjectival predicate sentence — *Also known as: 形容词谓语句 (xíngróngcí wèiyǔ jù) and 形容词性谓语句 (xíngróngcí-xìng wèiyǔ jù).* A fancy name for a sentence where the predicate consists of an adjective.

Adverb — *Also known as: 副词 (fùcí).* Adverbs are words that modify verbs and adjectives. In Chinese, word order of adverbs is much stricter than in English. Chinese adverbs normally come before the main verb of a sentence, but in some cases come right at the beginning of a sentence.

Adverbial — *Also known as: 状语 (zhuàngyǔ).* An adverbial is a sentence element that functions like an adverb, modifying a verb or adjective.

Adverbial phrase — *Also known as: 副词短语 (fùcí duǎnyǔ).* An adverbial phrase is a phrase with two or more words that act like an adverb, modifying a verb or adjective.

Affirmative-negative question — *Also known as: 正反问句 (zhèng-fǎn wènjù) and alternative questions.* A common way to form questions in Chinese is to first use a verb in the positive, then repeat the same verb in its negative form, similar to how in English we can say, "Do you have money or not?" or "Have you or have you not been to the park?" This sentence pattern feels a lot more natural in Chinese than those admittedly awkward English equivalents, however.

Affix — *Also known as: 词缀 (cízhuì).* An affix is a linguistic unit added to the beginning, middle or end of a word to change its meaning (e.g. prefix, infix, suffix).

Aspect — *Also known as: 动作状态 (dòngzuò zhuàngtài) and 语态 (yǔtài).* Chinese does not use the concept of formal tenses. Instead, it employs what is called "grammatical aspect." Rather than conjugating its verbs, Chinese uses particles to indicate how a verb works within a particular timeframe, or how the verb relates to the flow of time. The particles most often used to indicate aspect in Chinese are 了 (le), 过 (guo), and 着 (zhe).

Aspectual particle — *Also known as: 时态助词 (shítài zhùcí) and 动态助词 (dòngtài zhùcí).* These words are added to verbs to indicate aspect (not the same as tense). The particles most often used to indicate aspect in Chinese are 了 (le), 过 (guo), and 着 (zhe).

Attributive — *Also known as: 定语 (dìngyǔ).* An attributive is the word or phrase that directly precedes the noun it describes. Frequently it is linked to the noun with the structural particle 的 (de).

Auxiliary verb — *Also known as: modal verb, 助动词 (zhùdòngcí), 情态动词 (qíngtài dòngcí) and 能愿动词 (néngyuàn dòngcí).* Auxiliary verbs are "helping" verbs that come before main verbs and help express a tone or mood. (The word "modal" comes from "mood.") In English, auxiliary verbs include words like "should," "will," and "can," which all change something about the situation and the speaker's attitude. Auxiliary verbs express capability, possibility, necessity, obligation or willingness.

Cardinal number — *Also known as: 基数词 (jīshùcí).* Cardinal numbers are numbers such as 1, 2, or 3 used to indicate quantity. They contrast with ordinal numbers.

Causative verb — *Also known as: 使令动词 (shǐlìng dòngcí) and 使役动词 (shǐyì dòngcí).* A causative verb is a kind of verb that is used to indicate that someone or something causes something else to do or be something. In Chinese, 让 (ràng) is a major player in this space.

Complement — *Also known as: 补语 (bǔyǔ) and objective complement.* A complement is a word or phrase following a verb (or sometimes an adjective) that provides additional meaning to the verb phrase. Complements are not the same as objects, and can be as short as one character, or practically as long as a sentence. According to A Practical Chinese Grammar for Foreigners, complements "show the duration, quantity, degree, result, direction or possibility of an action; or to illustrate the state, number, degree of a thing." Complements are not a form of flattery (those are compliments); they're much more versatile than that!

Complex sentence — *Also known as: 复句 (fùjù).* A complex sentence is a sentence with one main clause and one or more subordinate clauses.

Conjunction — *Also known as: 连词 (liáncí).* Conjunctions in Chinese do exactly what they do in English: connect things. They help make the transition between ideas smoother and also show the relationships between those ideas.

Content word — *Also known as: 实词 (shící).* Content words refer to real objects in the real world, whether solid and palpable, or observable in some other way. These words refer to objects, actions, concepts, and even emotions, which exist in some real way as more than just grammatical tools. Words that serve purely grammatical roles are called function words.

Coverb — *Also known as: 副动词 (fùdòngcí) and 伴动词 (bàndòngcí).* A coverb is a verb that modifies the main verb of a sentence when used with its own object.

Degree adverb — *Also known as: 程度副词 (chéngdù fùcí).* Degree adverbs intensify or in some other way modify the degree of expression of the adjective (or verb).

Degree complement — *Also known as: 程度补语 (chéngdù bǔyǔ) and complement of degree.* While most complements follow verbs, degree complements very often follow adjectives. They intensify or in some other way modify the degree of expression of the adjective (or verb).

Demonstrative pronoun — *Also known as: 指示代词 (zhǐshì dàicí).* A demonstrative pronoun is a pronoun used in the place of a noun and specifies what is being referred to.

Dependent clause — *Also known as: 从句 (cóngjù).* A dependent clause is a clause that is dependent on and modifies or supplies with additional information the independent clause. There is a subordinate conjunction at the beginning of dependent clauses causing it to become dependent on independent clauses, even though they have a subject and verb.

Direct object — *Also known as: 直接宾语 (zhíjiē bīnyǔ).* A direct object is what is being acted upon, thus receiving the action of a verb. In Chinese grammar, direct objects are often simply referred to as "objects."

Direction complement — *Also known as: 趋向补语 (qūxiàng bǔyǔ), directional complement and complement of direction.* A *direction complement* is a complement that's used, you guessed it, to describe the direction of the action of a verb.

Directional verb — *Also known as: 趋向动词 (qūxiàng dòngcí).* Directional verbs can be added to other verbs in a direction complement, illustrating which direction the verb is going.

Directional complement — See **direction complement**

Distinguishing word — *Also known as: 区别词, distinguishing words and attributive adjectives.* "Distinguishing words" are rather foreign to the English speaker. On the surface they may seem like regular adjectives, but distinguishing words do not have degree, so they are not modified by adverbs. Unlike normal adjectives, sentences involving distinguishing words use 是 (shì), and usually 的 (de) as well. Common words include the Chinese words for "male," "female," "real," "fake," and colors.

Existential verb — *Also known as: 存现动词 (cúnxiàn dòngcí).* Existential verbs declare the existence or nonexistence of things.

Function word — *Also known as: 虚词 (xūcí).* Function words do not refer to real objects in the real world; rather they serve purely grammatical roles in sentences, drawing relationships and logical connections between the content words in a sentence. Words that refer to real objects in the real world are called content words.

Judgement verb — *Also known as: 关系动词 (guānxì dòngcí) and 判断动词 (pànduàn dòngcí).* Judgment verbs are verbs used to express the speaker's judgment. This can be as simple as the verb "to be," but also covers a wide range of other verbs.

Indirect object — *Also known as: 间接宾语 (jiànjiē bīnyǔ).* Indirect objects occur when there are two objects in a sentence. The indirect object is for/to whom/what the action of the verb is done and who/what is receiving the direct object. In Chinese grammar, indirect objects are often referred to as second objects.

Independent clause — *Also known as: 主句 (zhǔjù).* An independent clause is a clause that has a subject and a predicate that modifies the subject, allowing it to stand alone as a sentence.

Independent phrase — *Also known as: 独立语 (dúlì yǔ).* An independent phrase has no subject acting out the verb in the sentence.

Interjection — *Also known as: 叹词 (tàncí) and 感叹词 (gǎntàncí).* Express exclamation or various kinds of emotional response.

Interrogative pronoun — See **question word**

Intransitive verb — *Also known as: 不及物动词 (bùjíwù dòngcí).* Intransitive verbs are verbs which take no direct object.

Location word — *Also known as: 方位名词 (fāngwèi míngcí), 方位词 (fāngwèi cí) and noun of locality.* Location nouns are nouns showing direction and location.

Main clause — See **independent clause**

Measure word — *Also known as: 量词 (liàngcí) and classifier.* Measure words are used together with numerals to indicate the quantity of a noun, and sometimes even of an action. The general term for "measure word" in linguistics is "classifier," because measure words involve some kind of classification of the noun (or action) being counted.

Mimetic word — See **onomatopoeia**

Modal adverb — *Also known as: 语气副词 (yǔqì fùcí) and tone adverb.* Modal adverbs express likelihood with adverbs such as probably, possibly, evidently, certainly, etc.

Modal particle — *Also known as: 语气助词 (yǔqì zhùcí), 语气词 (yǔqì cí), Sentence-final particle and Sentential particle.* Modal particles are words used at the end of sentences to indicate mood, or attitude. They tend to be neutral tone and hard to translate, but they add a bit of "flavor" to a sentence. See also particles.

Modal verb — See **auxiliary verb**

Negative adverb — *Also known as: 否定副词 (fǒudìng fùcí).* Negative adverbs negate verbs and adjectives to make a negative statement. The main ones in Chinese are 不 (bù) and 没 (méi).

Noun — *Also known as: 名词 (míngcí).* You may have learned these as "person, place, or thing." Nouns often act as subjects, are modified by adjectives, and can be counted with measure words in Chinese.

Noun measure word — *Also known as: 名量词 (míngliàngcí).* As the name suggests, these are measure words that are only used for nouns.

Noun phrase — *Also known as: 名词短语 (míngcí duǎnyǔ).* A noun phrase is a phrase with a noun or pronoun as a head word that has any sort of modifier.

Numeral — *Also known as: 数词 (shùcí).* A numeral is a symbol that represents a number.

Nominal predicate sentence — *Also known as: 名词谓语句 (míngcí wèiyǔjù).* Nominal predicate sentences are sentences with a noun phrase that functions as the main predicate of the sentence.

Object — *Also known as: 宾语 (bīnyǔ).* The object is the receiver of the action of the verb.

Onomatopoeia — *Also known as: 象声词 (xiàngshēngcí) and 拟声词 (nǐshēngcí).* Onomatopoeia are words which represent sounds and noises.

Ordinal number — *Also known as: 序数词 (xùshù cí).* Ordinal numbers are numbers used to express rank or sequence. Think "1st," "2nd," etc. Ordinal numbers contrast with cardinal numbers.

Particle — *Also known as: 助词 (zhùcí).* Particles are function words that depend on other words or phrases to impart meaning. They're kind of like prepositions, but more abstract. In Chinese, the key ones are aspectual particles (for indicating aspect), structural particles (for indicating relationships between words), and modal particles (for indicating mood). Chinese particles are also special words because they tend to always take the neutral tone.

Passive voice — *Also known as: Passive structure, 被动结构 (bèidòng jiégòu), 被动句式 (bèidòng jùshì) and 被动语态 (bèidòng yǔtài).* "Passive voice" is a grammatical term used to refer to sentences in which the "recipient" of an action (often referred to as the "direct object" or simply "object") becomes the subject of the sentence, and the "doer" of the action is demoted to secondary importance or omitted altogether.

Passive structure — See **passive voice**

Personal pronoun — *Also known as: 人称代词 (rénchēng dàicí).* Personal pronouns include 我 (wǒ), 你 (nǐ), 他 (tā), and 她 (tā). To make them plural, all you need to do is add the suffix -们 (-men) to it. Additionally, there is a polite second person form 您 (nín), which cannot normally take the -们 (-men) suffix.

Place noun — *Also known as: 处所名词 (chùsuǒ míngcí).* Place nouns are nouns describing the position or place of something.

Place adverb — *Also known as: 处所副词 (chùsuǒ fùcí), location adverb, adverb of place and adverb of location.* Place adverbs modify the location of a verbs or adjective.

Placement verb — See **existential verb**

Phrase — *Also known as: 短语 (duǎnyǔ) and 词组 (cízǔ).* A phrase is a group of words that expresses a concept. It can be focused on fleshing out a particular word, as in a noun phrase or verb phrase. See also clause, which expresses a more complete thought.

Possessive pronoun — *Also known as: 物主代词 (wùzhǔ dàicí).* Possessive pronouns take the place of a noun and show ownership.

Potential complement — *Also known as: 可能补语 (kěnéngbǔyǔ) and complement of potentiality.* Potential complements are a type of complement used to express the possibility (potential) of achieving an expected result. Potential forms most commonly occur in negative statements. Affirmative statements using the potential form, when they do occur, usually give answers to questions or serve as rebuttals.

Predicate — *Also known as: 谓语 (wèiyǔ).* Predicates are the main verb/verb phrase of a sentence that state something about the subject.

Preposition — *Also known as: 介词 (jiècí).* Prepositions are words that indicate location or direction. They are called **pre**positions because they come before the words that they modify.

Prepositional phrase — *Also known as: 介词短语 (jiècí duǎnyǔ).* A prepositional phrase is a phrase beginning with a preposition that precedes the word it modifies and clarifies that word's relationship with another word in the sentence.

Pronoun — *Also known as: 代词 (dàicí).* Pronouns substitute in for regular nouns and proper nouns to avoid unnecessary repetition of the same words over and over again.

Proper noun — *Also known as: 专有名词 (zhuānyǒu míngcí).* A proper noun is specific person, place or thing. Proper nouns are generally capitalized (e.g. John, China, AllSet Learning), both in English and in pinyin.

Psychological verb — *Also known as: 心理动词 (xīnlǐ dòngcí) and psych verb.* A psychological verb is a verb that conveys the speaker's mental state or attitude.

Qualitative adjective — *Also known as: 性质形容词 (xìngzhì xíngróngcí).* Qualitative adjectives describe the quality or nature of something.

Quantitative phrase — *Also known as: 数量短语 (shùliàng duǎnyǔ).* Quantitative phrases express a measurement of amount.

Quantity complement — *Also known as: 数量补语 (shùliàng bǔyǔ), quantitative complement and complement of quantity.* A quantity complement follows a verb and completes the expression of measurement of amount.

Question pronoun — See **question word**

Question word — *Also known as: 疑问代词 (yíwèn dàicí), question pronoun, interrogative pronoun.* A **question word** refers to a special kind of pronoun used to ask questions. These would include 什么 (shénme), 什么时候 (shénme shíhou), 谁 (shéi), 哪儿 (nǎr) / 哪里 (nǎlǐ), 哪个 (nǎge), 为什么 (wèishénme), 怎么 (zěnme). Beginners should pay attention to the placement of question words.

Reduplication — It is one of the great ironies of linguistics that the term for repeating a word is overly repetitive itself. You'd think that the word "duplication" would work just fine, but the linguistic term really is reduplication. In Chinese, verbs and adjectives are often reduplicated.

Relational verb — See **judgement verb**

Result complement — *Also known as: 结果补语 (jiéguǒ bǔyǔ), complement of result, resultative complement and result compound.* Result complements are a kind of verbal complement that appears very frequently in Chinese. Surprisingly enough, they're used to describe the result of a verb.

Scope adverb — *Also known as: 范围副词 (fànwéi fùcí).* Scope adverbs modify and expand a verb or adjective.

Sentence with a nominal predicate — See **nominal predicate sentence**

Sentence with a verbal predicate — *Also known as: 动词谓语句 (dòngcí wèiyǔ jù).* A sentence with a verb as the main element of its predicate is called a sentence with a verbal predicate. This type of sentence is extremely common.

Sentence with an adjectival predicate — See **adjectival predicate sentence**

Sentence with a subject-predicate structure as predicate — *Also known as: 主谓谓语句 (zhǔ-wèi wèiyǔ jù).*

Sentence-final particle — See **modal particle**

Sentential particle — See **modal particle**

Separable verb — *Also known as: 离合词 (líhécí) and verb-object phrase.* "Separable verbs" get their name from their ability to "separate" into two parts (a verb part and an object part), with other words in between. In fact, you could also simply call separable verbs "verb-object phrases."

Subject — *Also known as: 主语 (zhǔyǔ).* A subject is a noun or pronoun that the sentence centers around. It is the actor of the verb and is what something is said about.

Subject-predicate construction — *Also known as: 主谓结构 (zhǔ-wèi jiégòu).* The subject-predicate construction consists of a subject and a predicate, and may be part of a larger sentence, or may serve as a sentence on its own.

Subject-predicate sentence — *Also known as: 主谓句 (zhǔ-wèi jù).* A sentence composed of a subject and a predicate. The vast majority of sentences fit this description.

Subordinate clause — See **dependent clause**

State complement — *Also known as: 状态补语 (zhuàngtài bǔyǔ), 情态补语 (qíngtài bǔyǔ) and complement of state.* State complements describe an achieved state of an action. State complements are usually adjective phrases (adverb + adjective) but can take the form of verbal phrases, subject-predicate phrase or other complements. State complements that are adjective phrases often look the same as degree complements and thus often lumped together with degree complements in textbooks.

Stative adjective — *Also known as: 状态形容词 (zhuàngtài xíngróngcí).* A stative adjective is an adjective describing a relatively unchanging or permanent condition/state.

Stative verb — *Also known as: 状态动词 (zhuàngtài dòngcí), 静态动词 (jìngtài dòngcí), state verb and static verb.* A stative verb is a verb describing a relatively unchanging or permanent condition/state. Stative verbs in Mandarin are usually translated as adjectives in English.

Structural particle — *Also known as: 结构助词 (jiégòu zhùcí).* A structural particle is a function word that denotes the structural/grammatical relationship between elements of a sentence.

Time adverb — *Also known as: 时间副词 (shíjiān fùcí).* Adverbs of time express the when, how long, or how often of a verb.

Time phrase — *Also known as: 时间短语 (shíjiān duǎnyǔ).* A time phrase occurs before the verb phrase and indicates the when, how long, or how often of a situation.

Time noun — *Also known as: 时间名词 (shíjiān míngcí), 时间词 (shíjiāncí), time nominal and temporal noun.* Time nouns are nouns that indicate a point in time.

Time-measure complement — *Also known as: 时量补语 (shí-liàng bǔyǔ).* Time-measure complements show the state or duration of an action.

Tone adverb — See **modal adverb**

Topic-comment structure — *Also known as: 主题句 (zhǔtí-jù), 主题结构 (zhǔtí jiégòu), 主题评论结构 (zhǔtí-pínglùn jiégòu), 主题述题结构 (zhǔtí-shùtí jiégòu) and 主题评述结构 (zhǔtí-píngshù jiégòu).* A topic-comment structure is an alternative to the typical subject-predicate sentence structure, whereby a topic (or theme) is followed by the speaker's comment on that topic. The topic is not the "doer" (subject) of the sentence, but rather sets the scope of the comments (some thoughts related to the topic).

Transitive verb — *Also known as: 及物动词 (jíwù dòngcí).* A transitive verb is an verb which takes a direct object.

Verb — *Also known as: 动词 (dòngcí).* Verbs are the "action" words which make up the predicates of most sentences, but may also simply indicate relationships, changes, or mental activity rather than physical actions. Verbs may take objects, and can also be reduplicated in Chinese. They can be negated, as well as modified by particles.

Verb measure word — *Also known as: 动量词 (dòng liàngcí), verbal measure word and verbal classifier.* A verb measure word accompanies the number of times a verb occurred to count the frequency or re-occurrence of an action.

Verb phrase — *Also known as: 动词短语 (dòngcí duǎnyǔ).* A verb phrase is a phrase with a verb as a head word that has any sort of modifier. It commonly includes modal verbs before it and objects after it.

Verbal predicate sentence — See **sentence with a verbal predicate**

Acknowledgments

The Chinese Grammar Wiki may have been pioneered by AllSet Learning, but it would not be possible without the hard work of many selfless individuals, including AllSet Learning interns, students, teachers, and regular users. Thank you!

AllSet Interns

· Donna Yee · Lucas Simons · Hugh Grigg · Greg McAndrews · Jonathan Pope · Pavel Dvorak · Parry Cadwallader · Jack Overstreet · Dan Emery · Erick Garcia · Mei Tong · Ben Slye · Brandon Sanchez · Logan Pauley · Ashlyn Weber · Michelle Birkenfeldt · Zach Herzog · Jazlyn Akaka · Salomé Vergne · Natalie Kuan · Jack Du · Erick Garcia · Cai Qingyang · Michael Moore · Liza Fowler · Mike Blood · Jacob Rodgers · Dominic Pote · Amani Core · Michelle Guerra · Amanda Gilbride · Callan Mossman · Jenna Salisbury ·

Special thanks to interns Michelle Guerra, Amanda Gilbride, and Callan Mossman for all the excruciating pinyin and typo checking they did.

Volunteer Editors

Some of these editors did tons of work on their own, while others emailed in issues they found. We thank them all for the hard work and valuable contributions!

· Nicholas Fiorentini · Noémi Németh · Betsy · HuaWei · Kryby · Jay · Luolimao · Trackpick · Morris · Philip Harding · Gintaras Valentukonis ·

AllSet Teachers and Staff

· 陈世霜 (Chén Shìshuāng) · 刘倖倖 (Liú Xìngxìng) · 赵以华 (Zhào Yǐhuá) · 于翠 (Yú Cuì) · 杨仁君 (Yáng Rénjùn) · 毛思平 (Máo Sīpíng) · 吴蒙蒙 (Wú Méngméng) · 贾贝茜 (Jiǎ Bèixī) · Parry Cadwallader · Michael Moore · John Pasden ·

Although many AllSet Learning employees have worked on the wiki over the years, both part-time and full-time staff, a special shout-out goes to 陈世霜 (Chén Shìshuāng), who has toiled tirelessly on the wiki behind the scenes for years without complaining. This print book is your victory as well!

Sincere thanks to Parry Cadwallader for making both the original wiki itself as well as the ebook version of the Chinese Grammar Wiki possible technically, with very little extra production work needed from the academic team. A big thank you also to Adam Zydney for all the layout work that went into creating the print version.

Other Credits

The Chinese Grammar Wiki website and ebook both make use of the **Silk** icon set **FamFamFam.com**. The Chinese Grammar Wiki BOOK (print edition) uses a "structure" icon from **Pixeden.com**, as well as several icons from **Icomoon.io**.

References

This page is a bibilography for the Chinese Grammar Wiki. It lists all sources referenced extensively when researching the content of the Chinese Grammar Wiki grammar points.

- Chen, Ru 陈如, and Xiaoya Zhu 朱晓亚. *Hanyu Changyong Geshi 330 Li 汉语常用格式 330 例 [Common Chinese Patterns 330]*. Beijing: Beijing Foreign Languages Printing House, 2010. Print.
- Fang, Yuqing 房玉清. *Shiyong Hanyu Yufa 实用汉语语法 [A Practical Chinese Grammar]*. Beijing: Beijing Yuyan Daxue Chubanshe, 2008. Print.
- Herzberg, Qin Xue, and Larry Herzberg. *Basic Patterns of Chinese Grammar: A Student's Guide to Correct Structures and Common Errors*. Berkeley, CA: Stone Bridge, 2011. Print.
- Ho, Yong. *Intermediate Chinese*. New York: Hippocrene, 2004. Print.
- Li, Charles N., and Sandra A. Thompson. *Mandarin Chinese: A Functional Reference Grammar*. Berkeley: U of California, 1981. Print.
- Li, Dejin 李德津, and Meizhen Cheng 程美珍, eds. *Waiguoren Shiyong Hanyu Yufa 外国人实用汉语语法 [A Practical Chinese Grammar for Foreigners]*. Beijing: Beijing Yuyan Daxue Chubanshe, 1998. Print.
- Li, Luxing 李禄兴, Ling Zhang 张玲, and Juan Zhang 张娟. *Hanyu Yufa Baixiang Jianglian: Chuzhongji 汉语语法百项讲练：初中级 [Chinese Grammar–Broken Down Into 100 Items]*. Beijing: Beijing Language and Culture UP, 2011. Print.
- Li, Xiaoqi 李晓琪, ed. *Xiandai Hanyu Xuci Shouce 现代汉语虚词手册 [Modern Chinese Function Words Handbook]: A Guide to Function Words in Modern Chinese*. Beijing: Beijing Daxue Chubanshe, 2003. Print.
- Liu, Delian 刘德联, and Xiaoyu Liu 刘晓雨. *Hanyu Kouyu Changyong Jushi Lijie 汉语口语常用句式例解 [Exemplification of Common Sentence Patterns in Spoken Chinese]*. Ed. Liwen Song 宋立文. Beijing: Beijing Daxue Chubanshe, 2005. Print.
- Liu, Xun 刘珣, ed. *Xin Shiyong Hanyu Keben 新实用汉语课本 [New Practical Chinese Reader Textbook 1]*. Beijing: Beijing Language and Culture UP, 2002. Print.
- Liu, Xun 刘珣. *Xin Shiyong Hanyu Keben 新实用汉语课本 [New Practical Chinese Reader Textbook 2]*. Beijing: Beijing Language and Culture UP, 2002. Print.
- Liu, Xun 刘珣. *Xin Shiyong Hanyu Keben 新实用汉语课本 [New Practical Chinese Reader Textbook 3]*. Beijing: Beijing Language and Culture UP, 2003. Print.

- Liu, Yuehua 刘月华, Wenyu Pan 潘文娱, and Wei Gu 故桦. *Shiyong Xiandai Hanyu Yufa 实用现代汉语语法 [Practical Modern Chinese Grammar]*. Beijing: Shangwu Yinshuguan Chuban, 2001. Print.
- Liu, Yuehua, and Tao-chung Yao. *Zhongwen Tingshuo Duxie 中文听说读写 [Integrated Chinese Textbook Simplified Characters Level 1 Part 2]*. 3rd ed. Boston: Cheng & Tsui, 2009. Print.
- Liu, Yuehua, and Tao-chung Yao. *Zhongwen Tingshuo Duxie 中文听说读写 [Integrated Chinese Textbook Simplified Characters Level 2 Part 2]*. 3rd ed. Boston: Cheng & Tsui, 2009. Print.
- Liu, Yuehua, and Tao-chung Yao. *Zhongwen Tingshuo Duxie 中文听说读写 [Integrated Chinese Textbook Simplified Characters Level 1 Part 1]*. 3rd ed. Boston: Cheng & Tsui, 2009. Print.
- Liu, Yuehua, and Tao-chung Yao. *Zhongwen Tingshuo Duxie 中文听说读写 [Integrated Chinese Textbook Simplified Characters Level 2 Part 1]*. 3rd ed. Boston: Cheng & Tsui, 2009. Print.
- Lü, Shuxiang 吕叔湘, comp. *Xiandai Hanyu Babai Ci 现代汉语八百词 [800 Modern Chinese Words]*. Beijing: Shangwu Yinshuguan, 1980. Print.
- Ma, Jing-heng Sheng, and Claudia Ross. *Modern Mandarin Chinese Grammar: A Practical Guide*. London: Routledge, 2006. Print.
- Mu, Ling, Rongzhen Li, and Peisong Xu. *Chinese Usage Dictionary*. Center for Language Study, Yale University, 2004. Web.
- "Qingwen." Podcast audio content. *ChinesePod*. Web.
- Ross, Claudia. *Schaum's Outline of Chinese Grammar*. New York: McGraw-Hill, 2004. Print.
- Teng, Wen-Hua. *Yufa!: A Practical Guide to Mandarin Chinese Grammar*. London: Hodder Education, 2011. Print.
- *Xiandai Hanyu Xuci Lishi 现代汉语虚词例释 [Modern Chinese Function Words Examples and Explanations]*. Beijing: Shangwu Yinshuguan, 1957. Print.
- Yip, Po-ching, and Don Rimmington. *Chinese: An Essential Grammar*. London: Routledge, 1997. Print.
- Yip, Po-ching, Don Rimmington, Xiaoming Zhang, and Rachel Henson. *Basic Chinese: A Grammar and Workbook*. London: Routledge, 1998. Print.
- Zhang, Jing 张婧, ed. *Yufa Jingjiang Jinglian 语法精讲精练 [Practicing HSK Grammar]*. 1st ed. Beijing: Sinolingua, 2008. Print.
- Zhu, Xiaoxing 朱晓星, ed. *Jianming Hanyu Yufa Xuexi Shouce 简明汉语语法学习手册 [Simple Chinese Grammar Study Handbook]: Chinese Grammar without Tears*. Beijing: Beijing Daxue Chubanshe, 2002. Print.

Made in the USA
Lexington, KY
29 April 2019